Conceptions of Professionalism

Conceptions of Professionalism

Meaningful Standards in Financial Planning

KEN BRUCE
and
ABDULLAHI D. AHMED

Routledge
Taylor & Francis Group

LONDON AND NEW YORK

First published in paperback 2024

First published 2014 by Gowar Publishing

Published 2016 by Routledge
4 Park Square, Milton Park, Abingdon, Oxon OX14 4RN

and by Routledge
605 Third Avenue, New York, NY 10158

Routledge is an imprint of the Taylor & Francis Group, an informa business

Publisher's Note
The publisher has gone to great lengths to ensure the quality of this reprint but points out that some imperfections in the original copies may be apparent.

Gower Applied Business Research
Our programme provides leaders, practitioners, scholars and researchers with thought provoking, cutting edge books that combine conceptual insights, interdisciplinary rigour and practical relevance in key areas of business and management.

British Library Cataloguing in Publication Data
A catalogue record for this book is available from the British Library.

The Library of Congress has cataloged the printed edition as follows:
Bruce, Ken.
  Conceptions of professionalism : meaningful standards in financial planning / by Ken Bruce and Abdullahi D. Ahmed.
     pages cm
  Includes bibliographical references and index.
  ISBN 978-1-4724-1250-8 (hbk) -- ISBN 978-1-4724-1251-5 (ebk) -- ISBN 978-1-4724-1252-2 (epub) 1. Financial planners--Practice. 2. Financial planners--Professional ethics. 3. Financial services industry--Standards. I. Ahmed, Abdullahi Dahir. II. Title.
  HG179.5.B77 2014
  332.024--dc23

                                                                        2013042256

ISBN: 978-1-4724-1250-8 (hbk)
ISBN: 978-1-03-283699-7 (pbk)
ISBN: 978-1-315-57328-1 (ebk)

DOI: 10.4324/9781315573281

Contents

List of Figures

List of Tables

Foreword

This book examines professionalism in the context of the emerging profession of financial planning and, as such, makes an important contribution to this profession. Although much has been written about professionalism and the professions, very little has been written about the profession of financial planning. This is partly explained by the relatively short time financial planning has existed, especially when compared to the more established professions such as accountancy. The book chronicles the history of financial planning as referenced by the CFP® certification process stemming from a meeting in Chicago in 1969 to today with over 147,000 CFP® professionals across 24 countries.

The demand for personal finance advice is growing globally, fuelled by ageing populations and a rapidly expanding middle class. However, this is against a backdrop of the financial services sector struggling with reputation and image, particularly as a result of the 2007–10 global financial crisis and the collapses of many high-profile financial corporations. This has eroded consumer and government confidence in financial product and service providers resulting in increased government regulation. The need for professionalism has never been higher.

The contribution this book makes to the global financial planning community is to see how CFP® professionals in three distinct cultural regions of the world think about professionalism. The richness of this book is captured in the words of CFP® professionals themselves. This makes for engaging reading. The content of the book reflects a dual focus of the application of a relatively new qualitative research methodology and the experience of a relatively new professional group. The authors have attempted to satisfy two different audiences. Researchers utilising a phenomenographic approach will take a critical view of how phenomenography has been applied in this book. Financial planners will be keen to benchmark their own experience of the phenomenon of professionalism to see if they can identify themselves within the conceptions uncovered by the research.

The pleasing thing is that professionalism means more or less the same to CFP® professionals in Australia, Hong Kong and the United States. Differences in how professionalism is experienced can largely be explained by culture and, to a lesser extent, regulation. The outcomes of the research are summarised before the presentation of a reflection on the potential contributions this research project has made to CFP® professionals, professional bodies entrusted with the responsibility of developing the profession of financial planning, and regulators, including any policy implications around professionalism. Several recommendations are also proposed for financial planners, professional bodies and regulators.

Professor Dr Anona Armstrong AM
Director Research & Research Training
Chair Editorial Board – *Journal of Business Systems Governance and Ethics*
College of Law & Justice
Victoria University, Melbourne, Australia

Preface

Financial planning may not meet all the accepted criteria of traditional professions such as divinity and law, it does however, fit the post-modernist view of professions characterised by the role played by professional associations. The hallmark of a profession is the presence of a common body of knowledge and it can be claimed that a theoretical body of knowledge for the "financial planning profession" has always existed, although it has only been in recent times that agreement has been reached on a common understanding of the theoretical basis of the financial planning profession. This common body of knowledge is the basis upon which the international standard setting body for the CERTIFIED FINANCIAL PLANNER/CFP professional designation. Financial Planning Standards Board (FPSB) is attempting to develop global standards among its affiliate organisations from 24 countries. Financial planning is in this context a new and emerging profession.

This book examines how financial planners who hold the professional designation CERTIFIED FINANCIAL PLANNER think about being professional. The underlying research seeks to understand what professionalism means to this cohort and how they think about acting professionally. CFP professionals are represented in 24 countries including those in the United States certified by the CFP Board of Standards and 23 countries outside the United States certified by FPSB against the same standards. An ancillary question examined by this book is whether CFP professionals from different countries have the same experience of professionalism.

CFP professionals from Australia, Hong Kong and the United States were interviewed to gather data on *what* professionalism means to them and *how* they think about acting professionally. What makes this book unique is, first, that it is the first transnational study undertaken independently of the financial planning standard setting bodies which seeks to understand how financial planners experience professionalism, and, second, the book takes a second order perspective with the research attempting to see the world through the eyes of CFP professionals themselves. In order to do this, the qualitative research methodology of phenomenography was applied. Phenomenographic studies typically involve small groups of participants and use open, explorative data collection to investigate the qualitatively different ways in which a phenomenon can be experienced. Phenomenography only requires a relatively small number of representatives of a group to be interviewed in order to discover the limited number of ways this group experience a phenomenon.

The utterances of 15 CFPs from Australia, 16 from Hong Kong and 17 from the United States have been analysed into categories of description comprising *what* aspects and *how* aspects. The *what* aspect is comprised of participant understandings of what professionalism means to them, and the *how* aspect comprises conceptualised acts that explain how participants think about acting professionally. The relationship between these *what* and *how* categories form a conceptual map as an outcome space. Interview participants from the three countries were interviewed *in situ* and the interviews were digitally recorded and transcribed verbatim. The interview transcripts were analysed using iterative content analysis, where the utterances of the research participants are taken at face value and the researcher carries out a phenomenological reduction by delimiting his or her own understanding of the phenomenon.

The research findings have produced a high degree of similarity and correlation between how CFP professionals in each of the three countries experience professionalism. The different labels and descriptions given to the conceptions reflect differences which can be largely explained by cultural, regulatory and practice differences. A common conception among CFP professionals from the three countries was putting client's interests first. In Australia, CFP professionals' awareness of professionalism is affected as much by government regulation as it is by CFP certification requirements. In Hong Kong, CFP professionals have to reconcile and manage employers' expectation of selling products with the professional standards of being a CFP. In the United States, CFP professionals have a more holistic and altruistic experience of professionalism. Member checking and presentation of the research findings in peer-reviewed conference proceedings were used as methods to validate and test the reliability of the results.

This book should be useful to CFP professionals, the CFP Board of Standards in the United States, the Institute of Financial Planners of Hong Kong, the Financial Planning Association of Australia, FPSB and regulators in each country as well as students, academics and researchers utilising a phenomenographic approach.

Dr Kenneth J. Bruce
Higher Education Project Coordinator
Ozford College of Business
Melbourne, Australia

Dr Abdullahi D. Ahmed
Senior Lecturer in Finance,
Flinders Business School,
Flinders University
Adelaide, Australia

List of Abbreviations

AFSL	Australian Financial Services Licensee
ANZSIC	The Australian and New Zealand Standard Industrial Classification
ASIC	Australian Securities & Investments Commission
CA	Chartered Accountant
CBOK	Common Body of Knowledge
CFP Board	CFP Board of Standards
CHFC	Chartered Financial Consultant
CPA	Certified Practicing Accountant (Australia)
	Certified Public Accountant (USA)
FPA	Financial Planning Association (Australia, United States)
FPAM	Financial Planning Association of Malaysia
FPEC	Financial Planning Education Council
FPSB	Financial Planning Standards Board
FSRHK	Financial Services Regulator of Hong Kong
GAO	The Government Accountability Office
HKMA	Hong Kong Monetary Authority
IBCFP	International Board of Standards and Practices for Certified Financial Planners, Inc.
IFP	Institute of Financial Planning
IFPHK	Institute of Financial Planners of Hong Kong
IIA	Institute of Internal Auditors
ISO	International Organization for Standardization
MPFA	Mandatory Provident Funds Schemes Authority
OCI	Office of the Commissioner of Insurance
SEC	Securities Exchange Commission
SFC	Securities and Futures Commission

1 *Professions and Professionalism*

1.1 What this Chapter is About

The aim of this chapter is to provide background to the investigation of the conceptions of the professionalism of financial planners. The background covers a broad range of literature to provide context to understanding how CFP® professionals experience *professionalism*. The CFP®, CERTIFIED FINANCIAL PLANNER™ and ᴄꜰᴘ marks are owned in the United States by the CFP Board of Standards. The Financial Planning Standards Board (FPSB) owns the CFP® marks outside the United States.

The chapter will position the terms *profession* and *professionalism* within the research literature and provide an analysis on traditional notions of profession, professionalism and post-professionalism, as well as the role played by professional associations. One of the hallmarks of a profession is the existence of a *body of knowledge* (Lander and Reinstein 1987). The chapter will discuss the importance of a body of knowledge with particular reference to the accounting and auditing professions followed by a discussion of the issues surrounding the emerging body of knowledge for financial planning. This will be followed by a review of the relatively short history of financial planning as we know it today. The role played by the International Organization for Standardization (ISO) in developing a personal financial planning standard will also be discussed. Given its relatively short history and a dearth of literature on the history of financial planning, a review of the closely allied profession of accounting will be provided as a benchmark for signposts of professionalism. The chapter will conclude with an analysis of the current CERTIFIED FINANCIAL PLANNER™ certification requirements prescribed by the standard setting and professional associations in the study.

1.2 Profession and Professionalism

The concepts of *profession* and *professionalism* are widely used among many contemporary occupation groups. These concepts are central to the thesis espoused in this book in that they form a reference point by which CFP® professionals experience the professionalism of financial planners. There is a substantial body of work on the professions and professionalism. Much of what is written about professions is from a sociological point of view, as studies of professions indicate clearly the interplay between the professions and society generally (Brante 1988). It is not the intent of this book to extensively explore the literature on the sociology of the professions and professionalism, but rather provide context to identifying how CFP® professionals experience professionalism. We are in a period where the traditional sociology of professions has been questioned and have moved into a period of post-professionalism and this is relevant to understanding the conceptions of professionalism. Traditional theories supporting the sociology of professions and developing theories will be considered in forming a construct of *profession* and *professionalism* which will help frame the central research question of this thesis.

1.2.1 PROBLEMS OF DEFINITION

The word profession itself is derived from a combination of the Latin words of *pro* and *fateri* meaning *forth* and *confess*, respectively, which translates literally as "to announce a belief", as in making public vows of faith (Roddenberry 1953). Hence the occupations of medicine, law and theology which required public vows of faith became known as professions (Roddenberry 1953). Others have argued that the origins of the professions stemmed from divinity, the armed service, medicine, law and education (Carr-Saunders and Wilson 1933) and others have extended this to include architecture and teaching (Cheetham and Chivers 2005).

VanZandt (1990) defines a *profession* as an occupation that has gained its status by meeting certain criteria and that *professionalism* is an attitude that individuals assume to portray and protect the image of the profession. This is supported by Kritzer (1999) who argues that the lay definition of *profession* is almost synonymous with *occupation*. This lay definition can include occupations such as fire fighter, social worker, salesperson and other occupations comprised of individuals who pride themselves on being professional. In this sense, *professionalism* to a lay person can apply to people who occupy an occupation labelled a *profession* without any due regard to an ideological view of professionalism (Kritzer 1999).

Professions Australia, which is a national organisation of professional associations and promotes professionalism, defines a profession as:

> *A profession is a disciplined group of individuals who adhere to ethical standards and who hold themselves out as, and are accepted by the public as possessing special knowledge and skills in a widely recognised body of learning derived from research, education and training at a high level, and who are prepared to apply this knowledge and exercise these skills in the interest of others. It is inherent in the definition of a profession that a code of ethics governs the activities of each profession. Such codes require behaviour and practice beyond the personal moral obligations of an individual. They define and demand high standards of behaviour in respect to the services provided to the public and in dealing with professional colleagues. Further, these codes are enforced by the profession and are acknowledged and accepted by the community (Professions Australia 2010, p. 2 of 11).*

The main characteristics of a profession that can be derived from Professions Australia's definition are ethical standards, enforcement of those standards, acceptance by the public, specialised knowledge based on a body of knowledge derived from research education and training at a high level. This present research study is aimed at discovering how CFP® professionals understand or experience *professionalism*.

Evetts (2003) provides a theoretical background for looking at *professionalism* by seeing professionalism as a value system and as an ideology. A closer examination of the historical or traditional definition of *professionalism* would suggest membership of selection is based on merit associated with some form of education qualifications which have been set by similarly credentialed peers (Bell 1973; Perkin 1989) who prevent others from performing this work if not suitably qualified (Freidson 2001). A sociological definition of *professionalism* brings in notions of exclusivity and altruism (Marshall 1950; Kritzer 1999; Cheetham and Chivers 2005). *Professionalism* can be viewed therefore as a normative value system (Parsons 1951; Evetts 2003) where a group of individuals share common values and beliefs about a particular occupation. This extends to the socialisation of new workers in the preservation and maintenance of a fragile normative order which also recognises the power and self-interests of some professional groups who promote this ideal (Evetts 2003). Max Weber, the renowned scholar and founder of modern sociology, posited many theories on sociology including *professionalism*. He linked the notion of bureaucratisation to professionalisation as part of the rationalisation of society (Ritzer 1975). Weber does not directly define *profession*, but characteristics of a profession can be seen in how he describes various occupations (Ritzer 1975). Ritzer (1975) analyses the seminal writings of Max Weber on professionalisation in the context of bureaucratisation and rationalisation. He argues that both professionalisation and bureaucratisation are part of the rationalisation of society.

Weber (1968) identifies 11 characteristics that distinguish a priest from a sorcerer. As pointed out by Ritzer (1975) these are remarkably consistent with contemporary efforts to define the distinguishing characteristics of a *profession*. The 11 characteristics as outlined in Ritzer (1975) include the notions of *power*, a *doctrine, rational training, vocational qualifications, specialisation, full-time occupation*, having *clients, salaries, promotion* and *professional duties*. Professions have been seen as rendering a service to the public (Rueschemeyer 1964; Schaefer 1984; Downie 1990) for which remuneration is not a requirement for a professional to provide this service (Schaefer 1984). A professional is someone who finds intrinsic enjoyment in the act of providing service (Schaefer 1984).

Further support of these defining characteristics of a profession can be seen by other writers such as Millerson (1964) where he lists:

1. the use of skills based on theoretical knowledge;
2. education and training in these skills;
3. examinations ensure the competence of professionals;
4. a code of conduct to ensure professional integrity;
5. performance of a service which is for the common good (serving the public); and
6. a professional activity which organises its members.

Roddenberry (1953) enumerates the characteristics of an occupational group which can be described as a profession by a series of duties covering:

1. A duty to serve mankind rather than self-serving.
2. A duty to prepare as fully as possible before practising.
3. A duty to continually improve skills and to freely communicate the knowledge gained from these skills.
4. A duty to apply full skills irrespective of personal gain or safety.
5. A duty to set high standards of entry to the profession and to upgrade peers solely on merit and to protect society from substandard or unethical practice.
6. A duty to uphold the honour of the profession by exemplary public and private living.

7. A duty to constantly improve self-discipline as an individual must be a master of himself to be a servant to others.

Implicit in the common defining characteristics of a profession is the notion of *professional trust* which has been an essential component of what it means to be "professional" (Frowe 2005). This concept of professional trust as espoused by Frowe (2005) is based on an understanding that knowledge is of two types – information and judgment as proposed by Oakeshott (1989). Knowledge in this sense is the outcome of the relationship between information which may or not be factually based and how that information is used. This is explained by Frowe (2005, p. 34):

> The central argument is that the exercise of judgement through the possession of 'discretionary powers' is central to being a professional, but that judgement itself resists reduction to propositional formulation because it is essentially tacit and individual.

The medical profession provides a useful insight into how those involved with it view *professionalism*. Some of the notions expressed by Wagner et al. (2007), for example that medical education is not just about acquiring knowledge and skills, but it is about acquiring an identity as a medical professional, are consistent with the traditional notions of professionalism. However the authors also acknowledge that acquiring the traits and behaviours associated with professionalism is one of the difficult areas with medical education. One of the telling observations by Wagner et al. (2007) is that despite numerous attempts there has not been any notable success in identifying the faculty and curriculum to effectively teach professionalism. The CFP® curriculum covers ethical considerations including the code of ethics of the relevant professional association, but *professionalism* per se is not specifically covered in the curriculum. According to Wagner et al. (2007) in respect of the medical profession there is general consensus that medical professionalism should be taught, but educators are not so convinced that professionalism can be taught. Richard Wagner (2004), writing in the *Journal of Financial Planning*, argues that for financial planning in general, and CERTIFIED FINANCIAL PLANNER/CFP® recipients in particular, to become accepted and respected as a real profession and as real professionals, CFP® practitioners must think as professionals. This means developing a professional identity, a tradition, a common way planners look at themselves and at their relationships with their clients. Instead of being viewed as a service delivery system that provides a unique and powerful role in today's society, financial planning has been defined by those who are not true planners.

1.2.2   PROFESSIONAL ASSOCIATIONS

An important theme to be investigated is the role played by professional associations and how these organisations build legitimacy through this role. Various authors provide useful and different perspectives on this.

The traditional model of the professions is a manifestation of the state legitimising the monopolistic claim of an association to the ownership, means and distribution of a set of knowledge (Gaskell and Ashton 2008). Gaskell and Ashton (2008) contend that the authority of professional bodies in the UK is enshrined from within a system of royal charter, whereby legitimising power to the professions is granted by the Privy Council.

The authors provide the examples of how the Law Society acquired its first royal charter in 1831, the Institute of Chartered Accountants in England and Wales was incorporated by royal charter in May 1880, and the Chartered Institute of Secretaries for Stock Companies and other Public Bodies followed shortly afterwards in 1902. There are now 750 chartered bodies in the UK, but new grants of royal charters are nowadays reserved for eminent bodies or charities, which have a solid record of achievement in a field that is unique and perceived to be in the public interest (Gaskell and Ashton 2008). Internalised self-regulation is also intrinsic to the traditional liberal professional ideal.

The profession itself may be perceived as the most efficient mechanism for securing acceptable levels of professional competence, and protecting the consumer from the abuse of power and privilege. This is supposed to exist through the "gentlemanly ideal" (McMillan 2004) and revolves around the notions of competence, integrity and satisfactory relationships between advisor and client. Further, discussion of personal finance issues has long been considered a very private act. Consequently, discussion of personal finance is often limited to either family or persons with a professional standing which provides the assurance of confidentiality (Aldrige 1998).

Professional associations are commonly understood as agents of reproduction rather than of change, which is achieved through the routines of licensing, training and professional development, and the monitoring and disciplining of behaviour, and, in this way, associations supposedly act to underpin existing conventions and values (Greenwood et al. 2002). In a study carried out in 2002, Greenwood et al. noted that little change occurred in the CICA's and ICAA's routines with entry to the chartered accounting profession still requiring completion of examinations that emphasised accounting, with particular emphasis upon audit for third-party purposes. The authors also observed that practice reviews focused solely upon enforcement of standards relating to the audit and programmes of professional development changed only to reflect demands from members for courses on information technology. Greenwood et al. (2002) contend that professional communities such as law and accounting are highly *organised* as communities where association membership may be mandatory, association participation is extensive, and formal interaction and communication are highly developed. Further the authors argue that associations use committees and task forces that host intra-professional discourses, and transmit official publications, ideas, developmental programmes and thus gather professionals and provide for interaction and discussion.

Professional associations play a role in socialising their members to the skills, competencies and roles needed to perform effectively in bureaucratic organisations (Rusaw 1995). Professional associations play three primary learning roles: (1) as providers of formal and informal learning opportunities; (2) as constructors of frames of reference in which professional and bureaucratic norms can be blended; and (3) as catalysts for changing conditions and relationships in external environments (Rusaw 1995). Professionalism is also related to autonomy. Horsley and Thomas (2003) carried out a study to look at the exploration of unprofessional conduct procedures across the professions. A study was conducted to analyse (1) comparative information on how different professions structure, manage and organise procedures for accountability and professional misconduct; (2) the role of professional associations in the accountability process; (3) the role of government bodies' accreditation, registration and licensing as they relate to accountability. The researchers found that peer review played a pivotal role in the professional autonomy.

Given the strong link between autonomy and professionalism and the limited relative autonomy apparent in most teacher-standards developments, peer review processes may offer a way forward in developing accountability processes which strengthen the autonomy and professionalism of teachers (Horsley and Thomas 2003, p. 7).

Other writers such as Karseth and Nerland (2007) have argued that discourses of knowledge are employed by modern-day professional associations as a means of promoting professionalism. By analysing policy documents from the Norwegian associations for teachers, nurses, engineers and accountants, the authors revealed dominant knowledge discourses and argued how that these discourses serve to position the associations in distinct ways towards practitioners, working fields and the public community.

Professional associations can also potentially play a role of a Global Public Policy Network (GPPN). Stone (2004) looked at international organisations such as the Organisation for Economic Co-operation and Development (OECD), the United Nations (UN) and their role in developing common policy responses in some fields and found how networks are increasingly being cultivated by governments and international organisations for the delivery of public goods and services. Stone (2004) argues this is because, for many issue areas, governments and international organisations no longer have the ability to design and/or implement effective public policies where treaties and conventions are often too slow for immediate issues. Stone (2004) says that GPPNs are helpful in some issue areas in coming to terms with these challenges, for example with the ISO 14000 process. The Financial Planning Standards Board has effectively positioned itself as a global standard setter in financial planning; and governments of its 24 affiliate organisations might rely on its standards as a more effective way of implementing government policy in this area. There is some evidence of this with the recognition of CERTIFIED FINANCIAL PLANNER certification for licensing in Malaysia.

1.2.3   BODY OF KNOWLEDGE

The hallmark of any profession is the presence of a common body of knowledge (CBOK) whose parts can be defined and defended (Lander and Reinstein 1987). The following section will provide a review of the literature on bodies of knowledge, in relation to the accounting and internal auditing professions as being closely allied to financial planning. Analysis of the accounting and internal auditing professions provides some clues for an approach for identifying the global and regional bodies of knowledge for financial planning. This will be followed by a review of the financial planning body of knowledge which has a history of less than 40 years and arguably is still in its infancy. Universities traditionally have had a role in developing the body of knowledge for a profession through research and teaching activities and the role of universities in contributing to the financial planning body of knowledge will also be discussed.

Much has been written about a CBOK in the accounting profession dating back to before the early beginnings of financial planning. Given the realtively short history of financial planning, there is a dearth of literature about the financial planning CBOK. Ioannides (2005) asserted that as the common body of knowledge grows and planners continue to accept responsibility for their advice, financial planning will be recognised as a true profession. Clients will need planners because they will realise that experts are required to integrate financial aspects of life to achieve broader life goals, often using complex products, techniques and practices. Peck (2004) explains that part of the mission of the *Journal of Financial Planning* is to expand the body of knowledge of the financial planning profession. This body of knowledge lays the foundation for the profession's expertise and ability to provide invaluable service. Overton (2008) claims that a theoretical body of knowledge for the financial planning profession has always existed. Until recently theory was not often explored as such, and there was no written common understanding or agreement on the theoretical basis of the financial planning profession.

A survey of the financial planning literature over the past 50 years was performed, and certain basic theories from many existing disciplines were identified, although their application in personal financial planning has sometimes resulted in modifications. The theories identified from the literature were compared with the financial planning educational topics list of the CFP Board of Standards and the core financial planning process was explored in detail. A definition of financial planning as values and goals-driven strategic management of the client's financial resources was fashioned and the financial planning process as the strategic planning process applied to the financial and economic resources of the person or family was also defined.

The first CBOK for accountants in the United States was produced in 1967 by Roy and MacNeil (Palmer et al. 2004). Accounting as a field of study has developed over a much longer time horizon than financial planning. The evolutionary process of accounting as a field of study has created a global body of knowledge which has centered primarily on principles and standards, such a generally accepted accounting principles (GAAP). The accounting profession has largely collaborated globally on international accounting standards. However these standards are not so much about identifying a body of knowledge, but more designed to present common standards for financial reporting. International accounting standards have helped address the issue of multinational companies complying with multiple sets of standards converting financial statements to the local GAAP (Fajardo 2007). While many countries have adopted or are moving towards adopting International Financial Reporting Standards, there have been significant problems identified including the complicated nature of certain standards and the tax-driven nature of national standards (Fajardo 2007). This may provide some lessons for FPSB in identifying the global and regional bodies of knowledge for financial planning.

In 2006, the Institute of Internal Auditors (IIA) undertook a CBOK study to provide information about the practice of the internal audit profession worldwide (Institute of Internal Auditors 2010a). The study was conducted in the form of surveys to internal auditing and comprised a team of 15 researchers from North America, Europe, Africa and Australia. The outcome was an exhaustive literature review and survey questionnaires, captured in the report *A Summary of the Common Body of Knowledge 2006* (Institute of Internal Auditors 2010b). Over 12,000 responses were received to the surveys. Responses were received from 89 IIA affiliates and internal auditors in 91 countries. Salierno (2007) discusses the common body of knowledge (CBOK), a study conducted by the Institute of Internal Auditors (IIA) Research Foundation to assess the current state of internal auditors. The CBOK assesses internal auditors across different areas of practice, such as governance, compliance, finance, information security and operational efficiency. It is noted that the findings point to a vibrant, dynamic profession that is responding well to organisational challenges and is valued by its clients. Auditors' global consistency of practices may be explained by the geographic scope of their organisations and by their working from a common set of standards. Burnaby et al. (2006) undertook a survey to validate the scope of topics to be included in the IIA's Global Common Body of Knowledge Study of 2006. This survey not only validated the planned scope but also added additional topic areas for inclusion in the CBOK 2006. Given the common nature of the practice of auditing globally, there was no need to identify territory-specific common characteristics of the CBOK.

A CBOK can influence the training provided to those who are to become professionals in a chosen field (Roy and MacNeill 1966). Roy and MacNeill (1966) analysed the common body of knowledge required by those about to begin their professional careers as certified public accountants (CPAs) and found that emphasis should be on conceptual understanding rather than procedural skill. Around the same period, Zald (1968) described comments of the community leaders on the study report "The common body of knowledge for CPAs: Some problems in analysis". He takes a critical perspective of the report with particular reference to the recommendation for mathematics training for the beginning CPA. The author states that the sociology of the study report would not question whether a given set of recommendations was right or wrong but would examine the social process of the report. For example, he argues that although the report states that better accountants must be recruited, he says no attention is actually given to who is recruited into accounting, to the social background, intellectual attitudes, values and life commitments of CPAs. Also during this period, Trump and Ball (1968) discussed the impact of the 1967 Study of the Common Body of Knowledge for Certified Public Accountants (CPA) on the accounting profession in the United States. The authors analysed the usefulness of the report with respect to the establishment of minimum standards of formal education and experience for licensing, the academic curriculum development, the CPA examinations and the study as a foundation for future research and discussion.

Competency studies have also been used in the fields of accounting and auditing in the United States to design accounting curricula (Palmer et al. 2004). In Australia, the late Professor Bill Birkett developed a comprehensive competency framework for the major accounting bodies in the early 1990s. Professor Birkett also developed competency standards for the Financial Planning Association of Australia for financial planners in Australia and New Zealand published in 1996. The ISO standard on personal financial planning identifies general and specific requirements of competence for personal financial planners (International Organization for Standardization 2005). Competency Studies are considered more extensive than CBOK studies because they are outcome-based and focus on an individual's ability to perform professional responsibilities including knowledge and skills (Palmer et al. 2004). A CBOK considers only knowledge requirements.

1.2.4   POST-PROFESSIONALISM

Some writers have proposed post-professionalism as an alternative approach to study of the sociology of professions (Kritzer 1999; Burns 2007). Post-professionalism comes about because of the loss of exclusivity of the professions, increased specialisation resulting in the segmentation of abstract knowledge and the power of technology in accessing information (Kritzer 1999). Kritzer (1999) contends that post-professionalism provides a fresh perspective for looking at the sociology of the professions and it challenges some of the traditional traits of profession such as that of exclusivity and their monopoly over a particular discipline as explained by closure theory.[1] Burns (2007) explains that post-professionalism is *post* not in a chronological sense, but in the sense that it provides a contrast to the prevailing orthodoxies and hegemonies of how professions have been viewed. Although, from a chronological perspective, Burns (2007) argues that post-professionalism began from about 1970 when professionals and society started to question the certitude of the professions.

Burns (2007) argues that there are new social realities such as the less sharply defined boundaries between professions and organisations, and the increased use of technology which weakens the relativities of power and control between occupation groups. Similarly Burns (2007) contends that post-professionalism challenges the periodisation of theory in the field, and this challenge relates to how the "power" approach is positioned in relation to the "trait" approach and alternative approaches. Finally, he argues that post-professionalism is multidisciplinary in terms of subject matter and intellectual attribution and as such represents an inclusive sociology rather than a narrow specialised project.

Kritzer (1999) see post-professionalism as a combination of three factors: the loss of exclusivity, increased segmentation of knowledge and the growth of technology in accessing information. He argues that professions are losing control through the changing nature of work and technology where services previously provided only by members of formal professions can now be provided by specialised general professionals, paraprofessionals or non-professionals. Kritzer (1999) provides examples such as the transfer of land where it is common for conveyancing specialists rather than lawyers to provide the service; and where nurses carry out many of the functions and duties previously carried out by medical doctors and, as a consequence, the occupation of nursing is now accepted by the public as a profession. Kritzer (1999) argues therefore that formal professions are being eclipsed by a much more general notion of profession and thus are losing their uniqueness and control over a particular field. Kritzer (1999) also provides the example of large accounting firms who now employ information professionals and non-CPA tax specialists. This present study involves CFP® professionals being asked to express their thoughts on how they experience professionalism in a period of post-professionalism. CFP® professionals from Australia, Hong Kong and the United States will each as three distinct groups experience professionalism in a way that will illustrate the characteristics of post-professionalism.

More evidence of the shift in the notion of professions during this current period of post-professionalism can be seen when we look at professions moving into for-profit spin-offs. Shafer and Owsen (2003) provide an example of this shift from traditional notions of professions by evaluating a for-profit company spin-off from the American Institute of Certified Public Accountants (AICPA), a non-profit professional association in the creation of CPA2Biz.[2] The authors point to the hostile reactions of many of the organisation's members to CPA2Biz, and the ensuing allegations of self-dealing and conflicts of interest. Much criticism of this for-profit spin-off was voiced by professional leaders and accounting regulators and they argue that these criticisms are grounded in widely recognised policy principles relating to non-profit conversions.

---

1   Closure theory explains how self-interested groups such as nations, states, industries, professions and occupations strive to monopolise their market segment. In this sense they bring closure as there is no other (external) forum for further discussion, knowledge generation, progress or innovation outside of the particular interest group.

2   CPA2Biz has survived these member criticisms and is alive and well and can be accessed at: http://www.cpa2biz.com/ [accessed 8 June 2011].

1.2.5   THE ROLE UNIVERSITIES PLAY IN PROFESSIONS AND PROFESSIONALISM

Universities clearly have a role as the custodians of the bodies of knowledge of professions. In their submission to the Australian Government Department of Education, Science and Technology (DEST), Professions Australia (2010) acknowledges the role of the university as the principal guardian and repository for knowledge in present-day society. Warschauer (2002) emphasises the importance universities play in the emergence of personal financial planning as a legitimate profession. Most professions are supported and in many cases defined by the university programmes that educate and train new entrants. Universities play an important research role which can be used to inform or predict practice. Research therefore has an important role in adding to the body of knowledge of a profession.

Cowen et al. (2006) pose the question of why the oldest standing Australian universities known as the "Group of Eight" have not been active in the provision of financial planning education. Cowen et al. (2006) suggest that lack of academic expertise, funding and resource issues, and accreditation needs of professional bodies may be the reason. In 2007, one of Australia's first financial planning programmes, the Master of Financial Planning, offered by RMIT University in Melbourne, was discontinued. While there remains speculation as to the reasons for its demise, it seems clear that falling numbers were a major contributor. A probable additional contributing factor has been the dearth of qualified financial planning practitioners prepared to take on an academic career. Prior to the global financial crisis of 2007 to 2009, the practice of financial planning was experiencing an unprecedented boom mainly as a result of government superannuation and taxation policy, resulting in financial planners earning significantly higher remuneration and having better career prospects than they would as academics (Bruce 2007a).

Eyssell (1999) emphasises the importance of maintaining long-term relationships with clients who represent all levels of the socioeconomic spectrum. Some FPSB affiliates have recognised the importance of the soft skills and have incorporated this into their CFP® certification assessment requirements such as the oral presentation requirement as part of the Australian CFP® certification assessment (FPA Australia 2010a). Regulators such as the Australian Securities and Investment Commission have also recognised the importance of skills as a requirement for licensing (ASIC 2008). Eyssell (1999) also emphasises the benefits of a practicum for financial planning students as "an immensely rewarding and eye-opening experience".

Bruce (2008) argues that for the profession of financial planning to continue to grow, it is vitally important that universities embrace it as a research discipline. In Australia in particular, the education of financial planners in recent years has been dominated by vocational education institutions offering competency-based programmes addressing the regulator's minimum licensing requirements at Diploma and Advanced Diploma levels. Given the nature of these types of programmes, it would seem that much of the teaching is being delivered by individuals who may not have actually practised as personal financial planners. This seems to have also been the experience in the United States to some extent. Chieffe and Rakes (1999) contend that many professors begin teaching financial planning without having first practised it. Teachers who haven't practised at all or who haven't practised for some time will soon see their knowledge of the profession, especially product knowledge, deteriorating and becoming obsolete (Chieffe and Rakes 1999). Bruce (2007a) raises the issue of whether it is appropriate to have competent financial planning practitioners teaching and instructing as financial planning educators. The issue being that from a practical perspective it is useful to have financial planning practitioners teaching financial planning courses, but they will have a tendency to reinforce existing practice and would not contribute to the overall development of the body of knowledge. An ideal situation would be the collaboration of financial planning practitioners with researchers to inform teaching and curricula. Teaching should be both descriptive with the help of practitioners and prescriptive with the aim of achieving a higher level of practice and guidance.

It is clear that the profession and universities must work much more closely together. Warschauer (2002) says that practitioners are not using research to better inform their practice and that simplistic models are being sustained when research suggests better models. Bruce (2007b) argues that professional bodies such as FPA Australia have a key role in working with universities in preparing new entrants to the profession. This is supported by Warschauer (2002) who says that financial planning professionals and university faculty must cooperate to improve financial planning education. Universities have a significant role to play in the development of the profession in creating decision models through research and disseminating that research to practitioners which further develops the body of knowledge and delivers competent advice to clients (Warschauer 2002).

A review of the literature on the accounting profession reveals similar views about the importance of universities working closely with the profession. Garrick et al. (2004) argue that universities can no longer afford to maintain an ivory-tower approach. This is especially true in the era of the "knowledge society" (Stehr 1994; Barnett 2003 cited in Garrick et al. 2004). The authors argue that universities are no longer the monopoly-holder in the production and validation of knowledge. They contend that universities should be helping to develop appropriate mechanisms for formally recognising and evaluating learning and knowledge constructed in the world of work and critically examining the longer-term implications. Kramer et al. (2005) discuss the various ways accountants as practitioners can work with university professors and students to ease the transition from classroom to practice. Examples of this include CPAs as members of university accounting advisory boards, CPAs serving as a "professor" for a day, and CPAs as guest classroom speakers. Moehrle et al. (2009) provide a detailed analysis of the impact of academic research on accounting practice. The authors summarise key contributions of academic accounting research to practice in financial accounting, auditing, tax, regulation, managerial accounting and information systems. The aim of this paper is that if this impact is more fully recognised, the practitioner community will be even more willing to invest in academe and help universities address the escalating costs of training and retaining doctoral-trained research faculty.

Goetz et al. (2005) provide a model that academics and professionals can utilise to promote students' seamless transition from academia to the professional world. The proposed model, illustrated below, shows that the reward for curriculum reform is a more efficient assimilation into the profession. This improvement can occur from the activities of educational programmes and the financial planning industry. For example techniques that bring the profession into the classroom include the use of problem-based learning such as case studies, adding additional courses such as a capstone course, and by bringing guest speakers into the classroom (Goetz et al. 2005). Techniques that bring the classroom into the profession include internships, part-time jobs, shadowing, establishing a financial planning counselling service and mentoring relationships with professionals (Goetz et al. 2005).

Dator (2005) takes a novel approach in looking at universities without quality and quality without universities. Dator says that quality in universities in the past may not translate into quality into the future. Basically Dator is a futurist and canvasses some preferred future for universities. For example, he says that all major universities in all countries of the world have had but one purpose since modern times: to create an industrially and militarily strong nation-state-based, and then global, economic system. He says this could change because younger cohorts are more environmentally aware and concerned than are the older generations and will want the change. Alternatively he says formal education may be forced to become focused on sustainability when the current economic base will not be anything remotely approaching the supply and demand of a "free market".

1.2.6   A DEFINITION OF PROFESSION AND PROFESSIONALISM

This book details a phenomenographic investigation of how CFP® professionals experience the phenomenon of professionalism. As a phenomenographic study, the aim is not to apply a construct of professionalism but rather capture and describe the utterances of the participants in the study. The preceding discussion provided a construct of profession and professionalism which adheres to the traditional trait theories and hegemonic role used in the sociology of professions and included various attributes.

The literature shows that professional associations play an important role in legitimising their activities in the eyes of the public and government. Professional associations provide a forum for discourses of knowledge which promote notions and understanding of professionalism. The literature also suggests that professional associations have a role in the accountability process of their members through peer review and that this is closely related to notions of autonomy of professionals.

The literature also reveals a common body of knowledge is a trait of a profession. The literature shows evidence of the importance of a common body of knowledge in the accounting and auditing professions. There is also evidence that a common body of knowledge is being amassed in the financial planning domain.

Post-professionalism provides an alternative to how professions can be viewed. This is because the traditional hegemonies no longer explain notions of profession and professionalism. This is captured by Kritzer (1999) who sees post-professionalism as defined by the loss of exclusivity, increased segmentation of knowledge and the growth of technology in accessing information.

For the purposes of this study, traditional trait theories used in the sociology of professions as well as theories relating to the roles played by professional associations and a common body of knowledge can be organised into a list of attributes that are promoted by professionals as defining characteristics of *profession* and *professionalism*. These attributes are:

- vocational qualifications;
- a specialised (and common) body of knowledge;
- having clientele;
- a relationship with clients based on trust (fiduciary);

- professional responsibilities (acting in the public interest);
- membership of a professional association; and
- adherence to a code of ethical behaviour.

1.3   Accounting: An Historical Perspective of an Allied Profession

In order to address the primary research question posited in this book, it is necessary to investigate a number of issues, many of which are related. The accounting profession, as an allied profession to financial planning that has a much longer history dating back to the 1400s (Ying and Dong 2009), provides a credible benchmark in understanding the financial planning profession. Accounting is an allied profession to financial planning in that they share the common practice model of providing advice to clients, especially when considering the practising public accountant. Accounting also has a long history and is arguably one of the oldest established professions presenting itself after the original trinity of law, medicine and divinity. Accounting history is one of the most researched areas of accounting and therefore a lot can be gleamed that may be transferable to or at least help understand the financial planning profession. Much has been written on the history of accounting. For the purposes of this research study, accounting history has relevance to the extent that it is an allied profession to financial planning and many of the experiences of accounting history may be transferrable to financial planning. The following review of accounting history will be limited to those aspects which have relevance to the development of the financial planning profession.

The first body of US professional accountants was the Institute of Accounts formed in 1882. Membership was open to any accountant passing its admission test. The Institute's main function was the education of accountants. Several other bodies were founded from 1882 onwards. One such body was the American Association of Public Accountants (1887) which was concerned solely with a public accountancy membership. Its structure and constitution were patterned on the UK chartered accountancy model, and its membership initially comprised 31 individuals based in the north-east United States (Lee 1995). Early US accountants were concerned to demonstrate publicly their high professionalism in terms of education, training and ethics (Carey 1969). Much of this concern was due to external criticism of accounting and auditing standards, and internal concern about the variety of entry standards of state societies. A need for overall control was perceived and, in 1902, the Federation of Societies of Public Accountants was formed. It merged with the Association in 1905, was renamed as the Institute of Certified Public Accountants in the United States in 1916, and further changed to the American Institute of Accountants in 1917. The Institute attempted to provide uniformity in professional standards to enhance the title "certified public accountant", seek new areas of service for its members (particularly in the governmental sector), and work with regulators to standardise accounting practice.

The accounting profession arguably is one of the oldest of all professions. This has been attributed to the development of industry and business contributing to the application of accounting principles dating back to the fifteenth century (Ying and Dong 2009). The eighteenth and nineteenth centuries witnessed an increase in government support and regulation which helped spawn the development of the accounting profession and accounting institutions and as businesses grew in scale and capital during the nineteenth century and the early part of the twentieth century, so did accounting techniques and systemised accounting theory (Ying and Dong 2009). The Great Depression of 1929–31, for example, gave impetus to the construction of regulation and rules by the US government, the accounting profession and academe. The United States was the first to apply generally accepted accounting principles (GAAP) and also set up the Securities and Exchange Commission.[3] 1973 saw the first efforts at the internationalisation of accounting with the formation of the International Accounting Standards Committee (IASC), two days before the Financial Accounting Standards Board (FASB) (Ying and Dong 2009). And since that time we have seen the continued development of international rules and accounting standards.

What these historic events tell us is that accounting responded and adapted to war, regime change, economic depression and other political and social factors (Ying and Dong 2009). We have seen the same with the global financial crisis of 2007–9. Governments provided immediate intervention by bankrolling major financial institutions and some writers were calling for better regulation (Subrahmanyam 2009). This was not just restricted to banks but also broker-dealers or investment banks because of their dealings with derivative financial products. Fetisov (2009) recommended a flexible countercyclical system of prudential regulation.

Wilkerson Jr. (2010) sees the past decade as being a difficult period in the history of the accounting profession in the United States. He argues that the challenging environment provides an opportunity for the accounting academy, acting as "trustees" for the integrity of the profession, to play a significant role in sustaining and enhancing the profession's status *as a profession*. Generally, accounting educators play this role in two ways: through our practice-related scholarship and through our teaching. This paper (Wilkerson Jr. 2010) draws on a recent comparative study of peer professions to offer insights to accounting educators as we seek to sustain the accounting profession specifically through our teaching. The paper makes two specific recommendations – first, accounting students should be required to experience and reflect on the meaning and demands of professional accounting practice as a central, continuing feature of their accounting studies; and second, they should be required to participate in significant clinical learning experiences as part of their accounting studies.

1.3.1   GATEKEEPING ROLE

A study using secondary sources was carried out by Lee (1995), in which he reviewed the nature of professionalisation; the birth of the accountancy profession; the establishment and defence of professionalisation; and a retrospect and prospect. The most obvious feature of early UK professionalisation is the pursuit by accountants and their institutions of economic self-interest in the name of a public interest. Use of entry, examination and training requirements, lobbying over legislative matters, defending the exclusive use of professional designations and attempting statutory registration each illustrate this

---

3   Committed to preventing another "Great Crash of '29", the SEC's mission was to ensure the integrity of financial markets. Namely, the companies that issued the stock, and the brokers who sold the stock, had to disclose all relevant information to stock customers. By providing a watchful eye over the securities marketplace and placing investor interests first, the SEC revitalised investor confidence. See http://www.pbs.org/moyers/journal/10122007/sec.html [accessed 3 June 2010].

point. A similar pattern emerged in the United States in the late 1880s, although the specific rationale for professionalisation was different from that of the Scots chartered accountants. For example, Walker (1990) and Kedslie (1990) point to the strengthening of the Scottish professionalisation process by entry, education, examination and training requirements. Several writers (Brown 1905; Howitt 1966) identify a similar sequence of professionalisation occurring in England, with the formation of local societies of accountants in the 1870s. However, unlike the Scottish formation, the English movement appears to have been little more than a series of copy-cat events as local accountants sought the credibility and authority of Scottish chartered accountants. According to Howitt (1966), the Institute proceeded quickly to impose standards of entry, examination and training, and was involved in influencing changes in law relating to accounting for bankruptcies and municipal auditing. Of particular concern was the Institute's requirement of an apprenticeship system, and the restriction of the activities of its members to those of public accountancy. In contrast, Society membership was UK-wide with regional organisations and members in both public and private sectors of the economy. An examination system was initiated, and specific professional designations were agreed. There also appears to have been a desire that the Society influence legislation affecting accountancy work (Garrett 1961).

The subsequent history of the UK accountancy profession is characterised by a form of unity among the royal chartered bodies, despite pre- and post-foundation English concerns regarding centralisation of power in London. This was characterised by a proliferation of bodies serving different membership needs and occupying traditionally competitive geographical locations, the specific use of the title chartered accountant by members of the chartered bodies to create exclusiveness and economic benefit, and the organisational aggressiveness of latecomers to the professional accountancy market. Statutory registration of suitably qualified individuals to practice accountancy was seen by the leaders of the competing bodies as the most sensible way of protecting the public interest against substandard accountants. It also presumably assisted in a sharing of the available economic pie by a restricted number of accountants. Many registration attempts in the form of parliamentary bills were made by chartered and incorporated bodies (Lee 1995). Lee (1996) examined the 1853 formation of the Institute of Accountants in Edinburgh (IAE) and its 1854 incorporation under charter as the Society of Accountants in Edinburgh (SAE), which he argues signals the origins of sustained institutionalised professional accountancy, and therefore has considerable historical significance in helping to explain the professionalisation process in public accountancy since the mid nineteenth century.

The 1980s and 1990s witnessed a proliferation of studies of professionals, professions and processes of professionalisation (Cooper and Robson 2006). The theoretical engagement of the studies during this time moved considerably beyond earlier trait and functionalist approaches that seemed to be characterised by an uncritical acceptance of professionals' self-accounts (Cooper and Robson 2006). The authors argue that during this period the actions of professionals and regulators are no longer rationalised by reference to public interest explanations but rather by the need for closure and so secure professional legitimacy and status within particular markets. A common position in the accounting literature is to examine the process of professionalisation and accounting and audit regulation through the context of organisations such as standard setting bodies, regulatory agencies of government and supra-national regulatory bodies as if only these institutions matter (Cooper and Robson 2006). Professional closure is often discussed in relation to education practices and struggles between the state and professional associations about regulations over practice rights and, similarly, professional regulation is typically viewed as involving struggles over accounting and audit laws and standards (Cooper and Robson 2006). This illustrates that the focus is on the relationship between professional bodies, standard setters and the government regulators. This situation mirrors what can be observed with financial planning. Financial planning is heavily controlled by the professional bodies such as CFP Board of Standards in the United States, FPSB, FPA Australia and IFPHK.

The accounting profession developed initially along distinct paths in the United States and UK. The US system was founded on accreditation by the state, and provided effectively for certified public accountants an economic monopoly in the name of the public interest Lee (1995). By comparison in the UK, the profession was being developed and controlled by the various professional bodies which could not provide the same monopoly as in the United States. What was similar in the UK and United States, however, was the phenomenon of economic self-interest driving the professionalisation process in the name of public interest (Lee 1995). In a study covering the period 1963–94 Lee (1997) contended that elite accounting academics (defined by those holding doctoral qualifications) were the gatekeepers to knowledge and reputation through their editorial roles with elite journals, and had the capacity to influence significantly the reproductive order of the academy. Lee (1997) also found for the non-elite journals there was evidence of the presence of elite academics, not so much as gatekeepers but more as image-makers in providing perceptions of elitism in the area of academic publishing. This present study is interested in the ways CFP® professionals experience the professionalism of financial planners and whether these groups identify a similar gatekeeping role for financial planners.

1.3.2   THE IMPORTANCE OF INTERNATIONAL EDUCATION STANDARDS FOR ACCOUNTING

Prescribing education requirements and standards has been one of the main pillars in the development of financial planning as a distinct field of endeavour. If we look at the work of FPSB, education and certification are significant parts of their work programme. During 2010, FPSB formed several working groups including an Education Panel aimed at developing guidance documents and approaches for how FPSB members and educational institutions can use FPSB's Curriculum Framework to deliver financial planning education courses in preparing candidates for the CFP® certification assessment program (FPSB 2010i). Setting international education standards has also been an active area of endeavour within the accounting profession.

It is not necessary to investigate the importance and role of international education standards for the accounting profession over a long period of time. There is evidence in more recent times of the role education standards plays in developing the accounting profession. For example, a study undertaken by Needles and Powers (1990) compared 17 models of accounting education published by seven organisations over the preceding 23 years. The study concluded that changes in the recommended objectives and structure of accounting education over this period of time have been minimal; a common body of knowledge has been broadly defined in terms of hours; consensus appears to have been reached on the need for a broad general education for accountants; the common body of knowledge has changed little with continued emphasis on the traditional areas of financial accounting, managerial accounting, auditing, systems and tax; and most of models studied focused on the topical content rather than the learning process or educational strategies to be employed in achieving the education outcomes.

Boyd et al. (2009) identify the need for highly sophisticated training and specific certification as mandatory in the context of globalisation and the growth and complexity of both domestic and international bodies requiring accountants. Students seeking career positions in the field of accounting are amazingly left without the easy access to certification that one might think would be readily available. Interest in, and the quest for, certification is domestic and international and across all study fields. To be fully prepared a well-equipped accountant today will be cross-functional and have proof of his or her knowledge in the form of certifications in other fields as well as being multinational by holding certifications issued in countries where he or she practises or travels. Currently, because the field is being transformed so rapidly by world events and the economy, students, as well as practitioners, need more easily accessible information on what certifications are available and how to achieve them (Boyd et al. 2009).

The International Association for Accounting Education and Research (IAAER) in cooperation with the Southern African Accounting Association (SAAA) and the International Federation of Accountants (IFAC) hosted a Globalization Roundtable in Durban, South Africa. The Roundtable devised six International Education Standards (IES) (Needles Jnr 2005). The IES covered issues such as entry requirements, content of education programmes, professional skills, professional values, ethics and attitudes, practical experience and assessment of professional capabilities and competence. A further IES on continuing professional development was subsequently developed (Needles Jnr 2005). This parallels the work of ISO in the development of the Personal Financial Planning Standard (International Organization for Standardization 2005), and the work that has been undertaken and is ongoing by FPSB. Saville (2007) argues that International Education Standards establish global benchmarks for pre-qualification education and continuing professional development for professional accountants. Saville (2007) says the goal of professional accounting education is to produce competent professional accountants. This is also the goal of professional financial planning standards. Munter and Reckers (2009) look at the results of a survey conducted by the Education Committee of the American Accounting Association and KPMG on the state of education in the United States in 2008. What is noteworthy is the shift of accounting standards in the United States from the generally accepted accounting principles (GAAP) to the International Financial Reporting Standards (IFRS). However the findings suggest that faculty will not be able to implement the IFRS into the curricula due to a time lag in changes to textbooks and necessary retraining.

In Australia Hor and Juchau (2005/2006) analysed attempts to internationalise accounting curriculum. Their study focused on the approaches utilised in internationalising the accounting curriculum, the state of separate international accounting courses; the perceived relative importance of international accounting topics to be integrated in the financial accounting curriculum; the reasons preventing the internationalising of the accounting curriculum; and the expected future demand for international accounting education. The authors found that the integration approach to internationalising the accounting curriculum where international accounting topics were integrated into the existing curriculum is the most commonly used approach by Australian educators. Financial planning curriculum on the other hand does not need the same kind of integration of international financial planning topics. Financial planning curriculum typically covers areas such as the process of financial planning, insurance planning, investment planning, retirement planning, taxation planning, estate and succession planning and the preparation of a comprehensive financial plan for a client. Within each of these broad areas are many separate topics. The CFP Board of Standards publishes a comprehensive topic list to assist candidates in preparation for the CFP® certification exam (CFP Board of Standards 2010). Although the fundamentals of personal financial planning are the same in any country and hence member organisation of FPSB, many aspects will be country-specific such as regulation, laws (e.g. taxation) and how financial products are structured and offered.

The accounting profession also provides evidence of a link between global accounting standards and global accounting education standards. Barth (2008) identifies challenges and opportunities created by global financial reporting for the education and research activities of US academics. In terms of education, after overviewing the relation between global financial reporting and US GAAP, it offers suggestions for topics to be covered in global financial reporting curricula and clarifies common misunderstandings about the concepts underlying financial reporting. Relating to research, it explains how and why research can provide meaningful input into standard setting, and identifies questions that can motivate research related to topics on the International Accounting Standards Board's technical agenda and to the globalisation of financial reporting. It would be expected that a similar link or relationship exists between FPSB's global financial planning standards and global financial planning education standards. FPSB's certification standards also include practice standards that detail related practice standards for each of the six steps in the financial planning process.

1.3.3   THE ROLE OF THE ACCOUNTING PROFESSION IN ACCREDITATION

Lock (1999) notes that accreditation in business education emerged in the United States with the gradual extension of the functions of the American Assembly of Collegiate Schools of Business (AACSB). His paper traces the development of accreditation processes in the United States, the UK, across the European Union and Central and Eastern Europe. It also explores the implications of accreditation and recognition systems for providers and consumers of business qualifications, whether employers or prospective students.

Brown Jr. and Balke (1983) surveyed accounting departments to determine attitudes towards seeking accreditation from the American Assembly of Collegiate Schools of Business (AACSB). Results indicated a strong interest in seeking accreditation. Needles and Powers' (1990) study compared 17 models of accounting education published in the 23 years preceding 1990. The findings suggest that there was little change in the curriculum and the body of knowledge over that time, and that it was generally agreed that accountants required a more general education including developing communication skills.

Goddard (2002) provides an analysis of the examination topic areas of the Chartered Institute of Public Finance & Accountancy (CIPFA) in 1976, 1989 and 1999, and that of its predecessors, the Institute of Municipal Treasurers and Accountants (IMTA) 1929 and the Corporate Treasurers and Accountants Institute (CTAI) 1903. Gaskell and Ashton

(2008) take a different perspective by examining the conflict between regulation and the traditional liberal model of the professions, and how this prohibits the development of a profession – in the case a financial services planning professional in the UK. Higley and Baker (1987) undertook a survey of AACSB-accredited colleges offering the CPA exam in the United States. The survey instrument used was a questionnaire adopting a series of questions to elicit responses around three major themes. A similar approach will be used in this research proposal to elicit responses from affiliate member organisations of FPSB. In more recent times, the requirement of 150 hours of education for membership of the American Institute of Certified Public Accountants (CPA) was an outcome of legislative activity (Reckers 2006). As a result the National Association of State Boards of Accountancy (NASBA) attempted to change the curriculum requirements for CPA examination candidates in a proposal related to the 150-hour rule which was rejected by a majority of practitioners and academics (Reckers 2006).

1.3.4   A WORD OF CAUTION: PREJUDICE IN VIEWING HISTORY

Botzem and Quack (2009) look at the bias towards viewing accounting history from an Anglo-American perspective. They do this by reviewing Camfferman and Zeff's (2007) article on financial reporting and global capital markets and by reviewing the history of the international accounting standards committee 1973–2000. The weakness of Camfferman and Zeff's contribution is their bias towards the norms, principles and interests predominant in Anglo-American accounting traditions. In writing their history they contribute to redefining the dominant paradigm of private self-regulation, which seeks to create capital-market-oriented standards that, above all, consider the information needs of large multinationals, institutional investors and analysts, and not least the interests of global auditing firms. The dominance of the Anglo-American logic among today's privately organised standard setters seems to confirm their way of telling the story. Funnell (1996) attempts to reconcile the different approaches of "old" accounting history and new or alternative accounting history.

> *The days are long gone when one could refer to accounting history in some sort of generic and all-encompassing sense: there are now many directions which accounting history can take in content, epistemology and methods (Funnell 1996, p. 38).*

Napier (2006) traces the history of accounting through articles published in the *Accounting, Organisations and Society Journal*. For example, Thompson (1991, cited in Napier 2006) reviews original documents and contemporary literature of the fifteenth and sixteenth centuries and provides an analysis of Pacioli's *Summa de Arithmetica* (and some subsequent writings on double-entry) in terms of rhetoric with the conclusion that Pacioli's exposition of double-entry gained its significance from being the first printed book on double-entry rather than merely its first exposition. Tinker et al. (1982, cited in Napier 2006) compares positivism with historical materialism from the thirteenth century to the twentieth century and provides a brief history of value theory, identifying alternative ways of conceptualising value. He argues that accounting takes for granted a "marginalist" notion of value, identifies the social ideology underpinning accounting thought, and speculates on alternative directions that accounting could follow if different notions of value were applied.

2 *The Emergence of a New Profession: Financial Planning*

2.1 What this Chapter is About

The aim of this chapter is to chronicle the history of financial planning, particularly as evidenced through the development of the CFP® and CERTIFIED FINANCIAL PLANNER™ marks. The chapter examines the development of financial planning through the CFP® certification process in the United States, Hong Kong and Australia. The importance of the role played by the Financial Planning Standards Board in recognising another 22 countries outside the United States as CFP® certifying bodies is covered. The chapter will also canvass the emergence of an International Organization for Standardization (ISO) standard on personal financial planning and allow the reader to assess whether this has enhanced or hampered the development of professional financial planning standards. Over the relatively short history of personal financial planning, not a lot of academic research has been done on the profession. This chapter will conclude by considering some of the studies that have been carried out.

2.2 Financial Planning: An Historical Perspective

In order to understand how CFP® professionals experience the professionalism of financial planners, it is necessary to understand the history of financial planning. An analysis of the historical development of financial planning will identify its path along a continuum towards how the occupation is viewed today. Freidson (1986, pp. xiv–xv) captures the essence of this when he says:

> both historical and contemporary studies are essential for a full understanding of the world, the one to follow the course of various streams of events flowing toward the present and the other to examine the contemporary pool into which all those separate streams flow.

The CFP® designation is owned and controlled by the CFP Board of Standards in the United States and by the Financial Planning Standards Board outside the United States. This book is delimited to a study of CFP® professionals from Australia, Hong Kong and the United States. The CFP® and CERTIFIED FINANCIAL PLANNER™ marks are owned by the CFP Board of Standards and FPSB outside the United States. The practice of financial planning is not restricted to the countries comprising FPSB affiliate organisations, it is also practised in other countries outside the control of FPSB, most notably in Europe. Financial planning in Europe has largely developed independently of the United States and the other countries which have supported the CFP® certification process. The European Financial Planning Association (EFPA) lays claim to being the first truly European non-government organisation with industry accepted professional, educational, examination and the ethics standards for financial services professionals across Europe (European Financial Planning Association 2010). It plays a role similar to the CFP Board of Standards in the United States and is also similar to affiliate member organisations of the Financial Planning Standards Board in that it accredits universities and banking and insurance institutes to offer the EFPA's European Financial Advisor and European Financial Planner educational programmes.

The scope of enquiry for this present phenomenographic study is the United States, Australia and Hong Kong. The United States is an obvious starting point for this analysis as this is where the practice of financial planning as we know it today and as expressed by the communities which support the CFP® and CERTIFIED FINANCIAL PLANNER™ marks. Australia was the first country outside the United States to embrace the CFP® mark and was the first member of the International CFP® Council[1] and hence warrants analysis from a historical perspective. The Institute of Financial Planners of Hong Kong has been chosen because of its characteristic "East meets West" culture and society.

Financial planning has a relatively short history with its origins dating back to only 1969 (Brandon Jr. and Welch 2009). Other writers such as Thompson (2002) suggest that financial planning had its roots in investment counselling, a term used to describe advice given to the blue-blooded clients of Boston and Manhattan advisors back in the 1920s. He cites Congressional hearings in 1940 on legislation to regulate investment advisors to support his contention. In contrast accounting has a much longer history dating back to at least 1494 with Pacioli's treatise on double-entry accounting (Godfrey 2006) and possibly much earlier. The next section will track the development of financial planning from 1969 to the present day and then this will be followed by a discourse on aspects of the development of the accounting profession. This will provide some useful comparisons and highlight some important distinctions in the development of the prospective professions. Financial planning has developed during a period of post-professionalism whereas accounting commenced its development during a period when there were more traditional views of profession and professionalism.

2.2.1   UNITED STATES

Brandon Jr. and Welch (2009) in their book on the history of financial planning track the development of those individuals and organisations supporting the CFP® and CERTIFIED FINANCIAL PLANNER™ marks which had its roots in a meeting in Chicago in 1969.

Other writers also track the beginnings of financial planning as a new profession from the same time period. Warschauer (2002) says personal financial planning commenced its evolution as a distinct field of endeavour from the 1970s and most probably from earlier beginnings. Eyssell (1999) says independent practitioners formed the heart of the new profession in the 1970s. They were independent because they provided advice

---

1   The International CFP Council was the predecessor organisation of the Financial Planning Standards Board. It was established by the CFP Board of Standards to deal with the growth of the CFP® mark internationally.

not linked to any particular product. It would seem that from this humble beginning, personal financial planning commenced its evolution into what defines the occupation of financial planning today. Personal financial planning has evolved from a narrow field into a profession (Eyssell 1999). Pahl (1996) identifies the Chicago meeting that took place on 12 December 1969, the purpose of which was to form two organisations – the International Association for Financial Planning (as an industry association) and the College for Financial Planning (as the educational arm). The College for Financial Planning also registered the CFP® and CERTIFIED FINANCIAL PLANNER™ marks as trademarks which licensed candidates to use the trademark (Pahl 1996).

Brandon Jr. and Welch (2009) also suggest that seeds of financial planning may have in fact commenced as early as the late 1940s with the writings of Joseph Schumpeter about "creative destruction". This was a period of great economic excitement in the United States – post-war – characterised by a radical innovation leading to a process of radical transformation. If you look at the chronology of events impacting on finance and markets in the United States (Brandon Jr. and Welch 2009), it might not be unreasonable to assert that financial planning had its beginnings in 1924 when mutual funds were introduced, or in 1933 when the Securities Act was passed.

The formation of the College of Financial Planning in 1972 was a critical event in the development of personal financial planning (Warschauer 2002) spawning many organisations such as the Certified Financial Planner Board of Standards Inc., the Financial Planning Association and the National Association of Personal Financial Advisors. Warschauer (2002) chronicles two important events as defining the "professional" era of the profession – the formation of the Certified Financial Planner Board of Standards in 1985 and the first job analysis study of CFP® practitioners undertaken by the Board in 1987. Other designations followed with the Chartered Financial Consultant (ChFC) designation in 1982 by the American College followed by the American Institute of Certified Public Accountants Personal Financial Planning Division's Personal Financial Specialist (PFS) designation in 1986 (Pahl 1996).

The CFP Board was originally called the International Board of Standards and Practices for Certified Financial Planners (IBCFP) and was founded in 1985 by the College for Financial Planning and the Institute of Certified Financial Planners as an independent, standard setting and certifying board to act in the public interest by maintaining the quality of the CFP® and Certified Financial Planner marks (Pahl 1996; Most 1999). Robert Goss as the executive director of the Institute of Ceritifed Financial Planners in 1991 was espousing the defining elements of professionalism of financial planners. Goss spoke of four elements – specialised knowledge, practitioners, the concept of a "calling" and perceived societal status (Goss 1991). In the same year, Goss became the executive director of the CFP Board of Standards (Brandon Jr. and Welch 2009).

In 1990 there was concern expressed about how financial planning was being defined with signs that practice was moving away from what was originally portrayed in the late 1970s and early 1980s (Walker 1990). The concern was that there was a move away from the single-minded focus on the financial plan to a range of other activities such as hourly counselling sessions often involving an array of ongoing fee and trail-commissions (Walker 1990). In many ways, not much has changed in the 20 years since this view was expressed. Walker (1990) was also concerned that educational institutions would not be able to deal with this emerging broader definition of financial planning. Walker (1990) felt that educational institutions would need to teach diverse areas such as asset management, retirement plan counselling, investment banking, global finance, business planning and how to interface with other professionals. Most (1999) covers threats to the CFP® mark by a growing number of non-credentialed and poorly credentialed financial planning advisors. He also mentions other more legitimate threats from credentialed financial planning advisors such as the American College's well-established Chartered Financial Consultant (ChFC) and the AICPA's Personal Financial Specialist (PFS), and to a lesser extent, the Registered Financial Consultant (RFC).

Blankinship (1996) commented on a recent survey by the CFP Board of Standards in which the term "financial planner" was the term cited most often as a professional most likely to be consulted for professional advice. He argued that this demonstrated that financial planning was beginning to be recognised as a distinct profession with skills different from the standard services such as securities, insurance, accounting, tax planning and estate planning. Although if we look at how financial planning was viewed in 2010 compared to 1996, we might argue that financial planners have all these skills as well.

2.2.2 AUSTRALIA

Gwen Fletcher, a leading Australian financial planning industry stalwart, is attributed with bringing financial planning to Australia when she visited the United States in the early 1980s (Brandon Jr. and Welch 2009). Fletcher's discussions were about the creation and establishment of an affiliated chapter of the International Association of Financial Planning (IAFP) or a new industry body for Australia. The affiliation model was rejected by Department of Corporate Affairs, the regulatory body responsible at the time for issuing licences to dealers of securities (Cowen 2006). In 1982, the world convention of the IAFP was held in Australia with Gwen Fletcher as one of the organisers. From this meeting the Australian Investment Planner's Association (AIPA) was formed from primarily independent investment advisors. In 1984 after a group of Australians attended the annual American convention of the IAFP, IAFP (Australia) was formed (FPA Australia 2001). In the late 1980s, the AIPA was conscious that many practitioners held membership in both the AIPA and IAFP (Australia). The AIPA changed its name to the Australian Society of Investment & Financial Advisers in an attempt to broaden its membership base. At the time the IAFP (Australia) had the support of the banks and life insurance companies and, in 1992, both bodies amalgamated to form the Australian FPA (Cowen 2006).

The development of a professional set of competencies can be viewed as providing a benchmark of best practice, a resource for organisational evaluation, and as a framework for exploring relationships between practice, education and training (Birkett 1996). Birkett indicated that competencies cannot be observed but can be inferred from task performance through personal attributes (1996). More specifically, he indicated that competency is a relational notion in that individual attributes (knowledge, skills, attributes) are drawn on in performing tasks in a particular work context. Thus, competency is realised in performance, but relies on a capacity to display a set of skills including both technical and behavioural skills (Jackling and Sullivan 2007). One difficulty that arises in affirming an appropriate level of competence in both technical and behavioural (generic) skills is that if these skills are acquired "off the job" then they must be affirmed "on the job". To address this issue in the financial services sector of the Australian economy, the government introduced the Financial Services Reform Act (FSRA, 2001). The FSRA aims to regulate where a client is unable to determine the competency of a financial intermediary because of lack of information or expertise. This regulation has had wide arching implications for training in the financial services industry with amendments to the Corporations Act (2001) and particularly with the introduction of Policy Statement 146 (PS 146)[2] (ASIC 2005 cited in Jackling and Sullivan 2007).

When viewed from an historical perspective, the development of financial planning education in Australia has closely paralleled the US educational model. A notable exception to this, however, is in regard to the role played by the Australian regulator (ASIC) in developing benchmark competencies that all financial planners must satisfy. While most courses investigated did satisfy requirements for placement on the ASIC training register it was still apparent that confusion existed in relation to whether courses were compliant for both knowledge areas and skills requirements. Several Australian universities currently use the phrase "full ASIC compliance", but readers are often unclear as to whether this indicates compliance with both knowledge areas and skills requirements or simply knowledge areas alone. Other institutions correctly make the distinction regarding what is necessary for compliance with specific knowledge areas and specific skills requirements. It appears that there is an innate problem with the ASIC training register in regards to the interpretation of this distinction and this problem needs to be addressed by the corporate regulator (Cowen 2006).

The body of financial planning knowledge arguably commenced its global evolution with the signing of a CFP® licence agreement with the International Association of Financial Planners (IAFP) in Australia in 1991. The IAFP in 1992 joined with the Australian Society for Investment Financial Advisers (ASIFA) to become the Financial Planning Association (FPA). Australia was soon followed by Japan as an affiliate of the CFP Board. The CFP Board then established the International CFP Council as a forum for its international licensees to discuss common issues and further foster the development of financial planning in their regions. New affiliate license agreements were being signed annually and affiliates ultimately put pressure on the CFP Board to have more say and this was achieved with the formation of the Financial Planning Standards Board which in 2004 acquired ownership and control of the CFP® and Certified Financial Planner marks outside the United States.

In Australia, of the 38 publicly funded universities, 12 offer dedicated financial planning courses. Notably, only one of these 12 is a member of the established "Group of Eight". This group represents Australia's leading universities and consists of the vice-chancellors (presidents) of: the University of Adelaide, the Australian National University, the University of Melbourne, Monash University, the University of New South Wales, the University of Queensland, the University of Sydney and the University of Western Australia. The other 11 universities delivering financial planning courses are all "younger" universities established after 1960 (Cowen 2006).

2.2.3   HONG KONG

The evolution of financial planning in Hong Kong provides an interesting perspective because of the history of Hong Kong itself and its relationship to the People's Republic of China. Hong Kong is one of the two Special Administrative Regions of the People's

---

2   Now referred to as Regulatory Guide 146.

Republic of China.[3] The handing back of sovereignty in 1997 to the People's Republic of China ended 156 years of British colonial rule. The Institute of Financial Planners of Hong Kong (IFPHK) was established as a non-profit self-regulatory organisation in 2000 (FPSB 2010e). The Financial Planning Standards Council of China (FPSCC) was established in 2004 and became a member of the Financial Planning Standards Board in 2006. In 2009, the FPSCC became FPSB China Ltd. (FPSB 2010e).

The IFPHK maintained close ties with FPA Australia during its formative years and entered into a licensing agreement with the former organisation to use intellectual property in the FPA's Diploma of Financial Planning course materials. To this end, CFP® professionals from the IFPHK provide a valid and useful participant group involved in the research presented here.

2.2.4   OTHER AFFILIATE MEMBERS OF THE FINANCIAL PLANNING STANDARDS BOARD

Compared to other professions such as accounting and medicine, the number of financial planners is relatively small. In 2011, FPSB reported 138,818 Certified Financial Planner professionals globally, comprised of 75,586 as FPSB Council members (outside the United States) and 64,323 in the United States (see Table 2.1 on page 29). CPA Australia alone by way of comparison reported 128,995 members in 2009 (CPA Australia 2009).

FPSB has embarked on a process of developing education and certification standards for its affiliate members. In this regard it has continued the work of its predecessor organisation, the International CFP® Council. FPSB has developed a *Financial Planner Competency Profile* which reflects what a financial planning professional does, as well as describing the full range of abilities, skills and knowledge needed to competently deliver financial planning to clients (FPSB 2010c).

FPSB affiliates have largely adopted the US CFP Board's model of registering or accrediting education providers to deliver knowledge topic areas which prepare individuals for the CFP® certification examination requirement. These knowledge topic areas essentially represent the body of knowledge of financial planning in the region of FPSB affiliate member. The knowledge topic areas typically cover generic areas such as the process of the financial planning and those characteristics of specialist knowledge areas that are generic in nature such as the principles of insurance, principles of investment or specific concepts such as risk and return, time value of money and so forth. The topics also mirror the practice of personal financial planning in the affiliate's own country. This particularly relates to types and characteristics of financial products, legislation and regulation that may affect taxation considerations, estate planning and retirement planning strategies.

Many FPSB affiliates have registered private education providers to deliver their CFP® education programmes (FPA Malaysia 2010; FPA Singapore 2010; FPSB India 2010). In these regions the delivery of education programmes by private providers is commonplace. It is also common in these countries for young people to complete studies in overseas universities such as in the United States, UK, Australia or Canada. Other FPSB affiliates more closely mirror the US CFP Board of Standards by registering education programmes delivered by universities. The Financial Planning Association of Australia accredits

---

3   The other is Macau.

university programmes at Graduate Diploma or Masters level for advanced standing into the CFP® Certification Program. University undergraduate degrees will gain entry to the CFP® Certification Program and lesser qualifications at advanced diploma level have in the past also been recognised (FPA Australia 2010b). The Institute of Financial Planners of Hong Kong has six registered education programmes which are delivered by schools or institutes under the auspices of local universities. The University of the Free State, through its Centre for Financial Planning Law in partnership with the Financial Planning Institute of South Africa, offers formal postgraduate qualifications providing a pathway for CFP® certification (Financial Planning Institute 2010). The UK Institute of Financial Planning recognises an Advanced Financial Planning Certificate or Diploma in Financial Planning as a pathway to its fast-track CFP® certification assessment (Institute of Financial Planning 2010a).

At its Global Financial Forum in Taipei in April 2010, FPSB discussed several planned initiatives relating to the "Body of Knowledge" and "Career Path", including designing a global curriculum, supported with textbooks and course outlines, as a guide to educators (FPSB 2010f). FPSB has an opportunity to develop a compliance regime that provides assurance to the public that its affiliates are delivering the financial planning body of knowledge – global and country-specific – to a common benchmarked standard (Bruce 2007a). Whether FPSB should seize this opportunity is one of several questions that will be addressed by this book. But if FPSB does proceed down this path, then the common benchmarked standard could be an expansion of FPSB's fundamental and core financial planning competency matrix to include country-specific competencies and suitable guidance as to depth of mastery required by reference to cognitive tools such as Bloom's taxonomy and/or a recognised qualifications framework (Bruce 2007a).

Of the other affiliate member organisations of FPSB, China as one of the newest members is also one that has great potential to move the CFP® credential into the twenty-first century. Established in 2009, FPSB China Ltd. assumes all of the rights and responsibilities originally given to the FPSCC (its predecessor organisation) to establish, uphold and maintain practice standards and code of ethics in the field of financial planning; to accredit and authorise educational institutes to offer professional training; to organise and operate uniform professional certification examination; to license certificates to eligible professionals; and to offer re-education and re-certification to professionals so that the public values, has access to and benefits from competent and ethical financial planning (FPSB 2010e).

Japanese businessmen with their business contacts in the United States first heard of financial planning in the 1970s (Brandon Jr. and Welch 2009). The Japan Association of Financial Planners (JAFP) was established in November 1987, and introduced CFP® certification to Japan in May 1992. The JAFP's purpose is to promote financial planning to the general public and foster financial planners as financial planning professionals (FPSB 2010e). The JAFP first began offering the designation Affiliated Financial Planner (AFP) to its members, but the JAFP's founders soon realised that the CFP® designation represented a more advanced level of certification (Brandon Jr. and Welch 2009). Today the JAFP is one of the largest FPSB affiliate members with over 16,000 CFP® certificants. This compares with over 136,000 who hold the intermediate-level AFP designation (Brandon Jr. and Welch 2009).

An influential development in the regulation of personal financial services in the UK was Gower's (1984) review of investor protection. This investigation laid the foundations for the deregulated market for financial services within a codified, self-regulatory, light touch, statutory framework. The notion that both the thrifty and adventurous could share the benefits of the free market found expression in the Financial Services Act (1986). This view of financial services regulation was conceived in terms of sustaining efficient markets populated by well-informed consumers receiving advice from competent firms and employees (Gower 1984).

The Institute of Financial Planning (IFP) is a not-for-profit professional body established in 1986 (Institute of Financial Planning 2010b). While there are over 126,000 CFP® professionals globally, only 1,000 reside the UK (Institute of Financial Planning 2010b). Gaskell and Ashton (2008) argue that financial planning is not in its own right recognised as a profession in the UK, despite the fact that many of the characteristics of personal financial services lend themselves to an environment of professional advice. In defining a *profession*, Gaskell and Ashton (2008, p. 160) use a definition proposed by Clarke (2000): "an occupational group which achieves market closure and autonomy on the basis of a successful claim to the expertise and the delivery of a service based upon it in an area of vital social importance". It is reported that the current regulatory underpinnings of the UK financial services industry require major modification before a profession of personal financial advisors can emerge. Further, survey evidence indicates personal financial planning practitioners view the current form of financial services regulation as impeding these developments (Gaskell and Ashton 2008).

Malaysia is significant because, in September 2003, the Malaysian parliament approved an amendment to the Securities Act 1983 (SIA), requiring that all who hold themselves out to be financial planners apply for an investment advisor's licence before 31 August 2004 and must hold a professional designation (Garrison 2004). The Certified Financial Planner (CFP®) and Chartered Financial Consultant (ChFC) marks have been nominated as the designations. Formed on 13 December 1999, the Financial Planning Association of Malaysia (FPAM) is a non-profit organisation with a mission to raise the standards of competency and ethical practice of qualified financial planners in Malaysia and to educate the public on the benefits of financial planning. The FPAM is represented by a group of corporate and professional individuals representing diverse financial services industries such as insurance, unit trusts, banking, legal services, stockbroking, accounting services and asset management (FPSB 2010e).

China first introduced financial planning by training bank employees in personal finance. This proved to be successful and after initially training a group of 180 people, the second group comprised 300 bank employees. The banks soon realised the potential for this and financial planning under the CFP® certification brand has literally taken off in China (Brandon Jr. and Welch 2009). China grew its CFP® membership by 19 per cent in the first quarter of 2010 (FPSB 2010g) and has been able to leapfrog Australia's CFP® professionals in less than four years.

Table 2.1 shows the growth in the number of CFP® professionals globally including the United States and the member organisations of FPSB (FPSB 2013; FPSB 2010b #232; FPSB 2012 #514). This shows the number of affiliate organisations numbering 24 in 2012 representing over 80,581 CFP® professionals with a further 67,241 in the United States making a combined total of 147,822 CFP® professionals globally. Australia had 5,437 CFP® professionals in 2012, which had remained static for the last five years. Hong Kong reported 4,700 CFP® professionals in 2012 which has steadily grown annually from 88 in 2001 with 2009 the only year reporting negative growth.

Table 2.1   Growth rates of relevant FPSB affiliate members

Year	Australia	Hong Kong	United States	Total FPSB territories*	Total
1996	782	—	30,129	1,652	31,781
1997	1,030	—	31,939	7,106	39,045
1998	1,480	—	33,120	10,231	43,351
1999	2,162	—	34,656	17,971	52,627
2000	3,011	—	36,307	22,282	58,589
2001	3,885	88	38,408	27,403	65,811
2002	4,725	334	40,375	33,243	73,618
2003	5,198	996	42,973	40,685	83,658
2004	5,336	1,422	45,755	43,935	89,690
2005	5,310	1,929	49,117	47,432	96,549
2006	5,308	2,293	53,031	51,921	104,952
2007	5,524	2,776	56,511	55,328	111,839
2008	5,430	3,389	58,830	59,676	118,506
2009	5,588	3,384	60,634	65,382	126,016
2010	5,575	4,171	61,950	71,805	133,756
2011	5,492	4,475	64,323	75,586	139,909
2012	5,437	4,700	67,241	80,581	147,822

Note: * This includes all 24 countries outside the United States.
Source: Extracted from http://www.fpsb.org/component/content/article/64.html [accessed 14 June 2013].

2.3   International Organization for Standardization (ISO)

An examination of the work undertaken by the International Organization for Standardization through Technical Committee 222, *Personal Financial Planning* is important not only in adding to the global body of knowledge of financial planning, but also because of the way this standard came about. The work commenced in 2001 and concluded with the publication of ISO 22222:2005 *Personal Financial Planning – Requirements for Personal Financial Planners* in 2005.

Significantly, representatives from the CFP Board's International CFP Council (FPSB's predecessor organisation) met with the European Commission in 1999 to discuss the adoption of CFP® certification. The Commission recommended that CFP® certification would carry more weight if it was associated with the International Organization for Standardization (Brandon Jr. and Welch 2009).

Two years later, in Atlanta, a group of technical experts was assembled to form the inaugural technical committee – ISO TC222. The meeting was held immediately after the CFP Board of Standard's International CFP Council meeting and comprised technical experts from many of the CFP Board's affiliate organisations. There were some notable exceptions, particularly the UK experts who did not belong to the CFP Board affiliate organisation, the Financial Planning Institute. The United States had wide representation, with technical experts with an accounting bias being prevalent.

The inaugural technical committee was established and quickly five work groups were formed mirroring the CFP Board's certification requirements of *process of financial planning, education (competences), ethics* and *experience.* These work groups were divided further into work items with work item leaders appointed. This provided an effective way of developing the standard with relatively small groups working simultaneously on the aspects which would ultimately comprise the full published standard.

ISO standards are voluntary, but serve many purposes including safeguarding consumers, and users in general, of products and services (International Organization for Standardization 2010). In many ways, the consumer protection aspect of ISO has been the principal driver for a personal financial planning standard. This echoes the primary role of regulators in this field, such as the Australian Securities and Investment Commission (ASIC 2010).

The global body of financial planning knowledge is embedded in ISO 22222:2005 *Personal Financial Planning – Requirements for Personal Financial Planners.* The standard describes both the context and process of personal financial planning. The process includes (but is not limited to) the same six-step process espoused by the CFP Board of Standards and FPSB and all its 24 affiliate organisations as underpinning CFP® certification. The general and specific requirements for competence are all described. The specific requirements cover each of the six steps and are broken down into knowledge/understanding and skills. The standard describes further ethical principles and experience requirements – both of which are not incompatible with requirements for CFP® certification.

The team of technical experts assembled to develop the ISO standard on personal financial planning has not determined anything markedly different from the standards which underpin the CFP® and Certified Financial Planner marks. An examination of FPSB's Global Competency Profile (FPSB 2010c) shows a high degree of compatibility with ISO 22222:2005. Both documents are equally informative to curriculum writers. Both documents attempt to incorporate the notion of degrees of knowledge or competence with the ISO standard's reference to the "hierarchy of thinking" broken down into *knowledge, understanding, application, analysis* and *evaluation* (International Organization for Standardization 2005). FPSB's Competency Profile uses a matrix to distinguish between financial planning functions of *collection, analysis* and *synthesis.* FPSB's Global Competency Profile through a comprehensive matrix arguably provides more detailed analysis of the financial planning competencies than the ISO standard. The most important point of differentiation between the two standards is one of the depth in which the knowledge areas or competences need to be mastered. The ISO standard is benchmarked against level 8 of the Scottish Credit and Qualification Framework. Level 8 is described as higher national diploma or diploma in higher education. To provide some context, level 9 is an ordinary degree, level 10 is an honours degree and/or graduate diploma, level 11 a master's degree and level 12 a doctorate (International Organization for Standardization 2005). FPSB has benchmarked its CFP® certification standard at upper division undergraduate or master's degree level (FPSB 2010d).

It is worth noting that a sticking point during the development of the standard was the issue of third-party accreditation. A fundamental principle of the ISO process is that it is only concerned with the setting of a standard, not with how that standard is accredited and enforced. This meant that individuals could self-accredit themselves against ISO 22222:2005 and hold themselves as meeting the ISO standard. This was contrary to process of certification followed and applied by FPSB and its affiliate member organisations. Despite, these objections ISO 22222:2005 was voted on in November 2005 with 12 positive votes from 16 countries and later published (Brandon Jr. and Welch 2009).

2.4 Studies in Financial Planning Professionalism

Very little is known about financial planning as a profession, the underlying theories of either financial planning, or the competence or professionalism of financial planners. A significant research study was undertaken in Australia (Smith 2009), however, that investigated professionalism and ethics in financial planning. This study focused on the relationship between organisational environment and culture and the ethical decision-making of financial planners. The findings of this study, among other things, identified patterns of unethical behaviour. The study proposed here is different from that of Smith (2009) in that it will take a second-order perspective by understanding the phenomenon of *professionalism* through the eyes of those people closely involved in the CFP® certification process. This research study will therefore be located in the current literature as contributing to the knowledge of "profession", "professionalism" and the professionalism of financial planners. A review of the literature on the closely allied profession of accounting provides a useful benchmark from which to understand historical perspectives of financial planning.

A study was carried out in Australia (Murphy and Watts 2009) which surveyed 78 financial planners in the North Shore area of Sydney. The aim of the study was to test attributes of professionalism against the attitudes of professionalism of the surveyed financial planners. The main findings suggest that this group of financial planners failed to exhibit a satisfactory level of professionalism against attributes measured (Murphy and Watts 2009). This finding was consistent for all the attributes of public/ societal responsibility, a systematic body of knowledge, professional authority and ethical responsibility. Sanders (2010) takes a transdisciplinary approach to considering how a profession is defined and established in the Australian financial planning sector. This definition is in the context of challenging community, regulatory, market and professional conditions for trust in financial services arising from a post-"global financial crisis" environment. The study identified that professionalisation of financial planning is an issue of public significance, and concluded that it is the best means to address the increasing financial inequality in Australian society and the emergent risks inherent in the financialisation of Australian society (Sanders 2010).

Some of the considerations of this research study relating to the individual (CFP® professional) were that CFP® professionals are confident in their own professional competence and trustworthiness, that there is a lack of confidence in the quality of professionalism of the wider cohort of financial planners, and financial planners generally are unable to differentiate those who are "professional" from those who are not (Sanders 2010). These findings have applicability to most countries with developed economies such as the United States and Hong Kong as the other countries in focus in this present study. Another Australian study has measured the organisational commitment and professional commitment of financial planners in Australia (Clayton et al. 2007).

The study found that females demonstrated a statistically significant higher level of organisational commitment than did their male counterparts, however there was no difference between their levels of professional commitment. The study also found that financial planners employed for a period of over three years showed no difference in their levels of organisational commitment or professional commitment than those employed for a period of less than three years (Clayton et al. 2007).

3 *Financial Planning Professionalism Case Studies*

3.1   What this Chapter is About

The aim of this chapter is to describe three case studies of financial planning professionalism. These case studies have been chosen to provide background to this present research study and include Australia, Hong Kong and the United States. These countries have been chosen because they represent exemplars of CFP® certification as espoused by the Financial Planning Standards Board (for Australia and Hong Kong) and the CFP Board of Standards (for the United States).

Research participants for this study have been chosen from the Financial Planning Association of Australia, the Institute of Financial Planners of Hong Kong and the United States CFP Board of Standards.[1] The Financial Planning Association of Australia and the Institute of Financial Planners of Hong Kong are affiliate members of the Financial Planning Standards Board. These financial planning professionalism case studies are included to provide the reader with background to the context in which research participants in each of the three countries operate. This is important, as although each of the research participants are CERTIFIED FINANCIAL PLANNER™ professionals and adhere to the same global CFP® certification standards, there are nevertheless important differences. Each of the case studies will provide and the professional membership and/or standard setting body and the relevant CFP® certification requirements in each country.

The next section provides a discussion on the regulatory environment in Australia and the requirements for CFP® certification.

3.2   Australia

The Australian federal government has been active in the area of financial services regulation. Aspects of how the activities of financial advisors are regulated, particularly current regulatory reforms under the *Future of Financial Advice*[2] package of reforms are playing out in the Australian environment. The breadth and depth of regulation is

---

1   In the United States, individual CFP® professionals are licensed to hold the CFP® mark from the CFP Board of Standards and many, but not all, will be members of the Financial Planning Association (FPA). For the purposes of this study, US research participants are also members of the FPA.

2   The *Future of Financial Advice* package was released in April 2010, announcing a number of reforms designed to deliver improved quality of advice and enhanced retail investor protection (Australian Government 2011).

of interest to this present study to the extent that it may influence the experience of professionalism for CFP® professionals.

The other area of interest for this present study is the requirements for CFP® certification in Australia. This study has been delimited to investigate the conceptions of professionalism for CFP® professionals only. In Australia all financial advisors providing advice on retail financial products must be licensed under corporations law which is administered by the Australian Investments and Securities Commission. Financial advisors certified against the CFP® certification prescribed by the Financial Planning Association of Australia have to meet additional requirements prescribed by the FPA. What these standards are and what is required to become a CFP® professional and to maintain certification in Australia is important in investigating conceptions of the professionalism of financial planners.

3.2.1   REGULATORY ENVIRONMENT

Financial services regulation in Australian is complex and financial planners in Australia are subjected to a more stringent regulatory regime than either Hong Kong or the United States. The Australian financial system has undergone significant change resulting from the Wallis Inquiry in 1996 and leading to the Financial Services Reform Act 2001 (Cth) (Taylor et al. 2010).

There are three main regulatory agencies in Australia which are referred to as the "three pillars". These are the Reserve Bank which is responsible for monetary and banking policy, the stability of the Australian banking system; the Australian Prudential Regulation Authority (APRA) which is responsible for the prudential regulation and depositor protection of banks, credit unions and building societies under the Banking Act, as well as insurance companies and superannuation funds; and the Australian Securities and Investments Commission (ASIC) which is Australia's corporate, markets and financial services regulator and supervises consumer protection in the financial services sector. ASIC has responsibility for monitoring and reviewing the Electronic Funds Transfer Code of Conduct. ASIC is also responsible for registering companies, issuing Australian financial services licences and monitoring fundraising.

Other regulatory agencies include the Australian Competition and Consumer Commission (ACCC) which administers competition, fair trading and consumer protection laws; the Australian Taxation Office (ATO) which is the government's principal revenue collection agency; the Australian Transaction Reports and Analysis Centre which is Australia's anti-money-laundering and counter-terrorism financing regulator and specialist financial intelligence unit; and the Australian Securities Exchange (ASX) which operates the Australian Stock Exchange and Sydney Futures Exchange, as well as monitoring the compliance of market participants (brokers) and listed entities with its Operating Rules.

ASIC has the most influence on the role of financial planners in Australia. ASIC administers several Acts of Parliament including the Corporations Act 2001 (Cth). The Corporations Act 2001 (Cth) introduced a single licensing regime for financial sales, advice and dealings in relation to financial products and requires consistent and comparable financial product disclosure. ASIC issues Regulatory Guides (RGs) which provide guidance to regarding the laws which ASIC administers.

There have been a number of Australian government inquiries which have impacted financial services in recent years including the Parliamentary Joint Committee on Corporations and Financial Services (known as the Ripoll Report); the Henry Review which looked at the taxation system; the Harmer Review which looked at issues around retirement and pensions; and the Cooper Review which looked into superannuation. The most significant government review in terms of the impact on financial planners was the Bowen Review.[3] The Bowen Review was effectively the government's repose to the Ripoll Report and resulted in *Future of Financial Advice* Information Packs being released in April 2010 and April 2011 respectively.

After extensive consultation from the reforms announced in April 2010, the second Information Pack announced in April 2011 provided the following clarification:

A prospective ban on up-front and trailing commissions and like payments for both individual and group risk within superannuation from 1 July 2013.

A prospective requirement for advisers to get clients to opt-in (or renew) their advice agreement every two years from 1 July 2012.

A prospective ban on any form of payment relating to volume or sales targets from any financial services business to dealer groups, authorised representatives or advisers, including volume rebates from platform providers to dealer groups.

A prospective ban on soft dollar benefits, where a benefit is $300 or more (per benefit) from 1 July 2012. The ban does not apply to any benefit provided for the purposes of professional development and administrative IT services if set criteria are met.

Expanding a new form of limited advice called scaled advice, which can be provided by a range of advice providers, including superannuation trustees, financial planners and potentially accountants, creating a level playing field for people who provide advice. Scaled advice is advice about one area of an investor's needs, such as insurance, or about a limited range of issues.

A limited carve out from elements of the ban on conflicted remuneration and best interests duty for basic banking products where employees of an Australian Deposit-taking Institution (ADI) are advising on and selling their employer ADI's basic banking products. Basic banking products are basic deposit products (e.g. savings accounts), first home saver account deposit accounts and non-cash payment products (e.g. travellers' cheques and cheque accounts).

The Government will explore whether the term "financial planner/adviser" should be restricted under the Corporations Act 2001 (Corporations Act). (Australian Government 2011, p. 2 of 7)

The Financial Planning Association of Australia has developed a "Professional Framework" which is intended to operate along government regulation and inform Australian Financial Services Licence Holders ("licensees") compliance requirements (FPA Australia 2011). These regulatory obligations are depicted in Figure 3.1 on the next page.

---

3   The Bowen Review resulted in a report created by the Hon Chris Bowen, Minister for Human Services, Minister for Financial Services, Superannuation and Corporate Law.

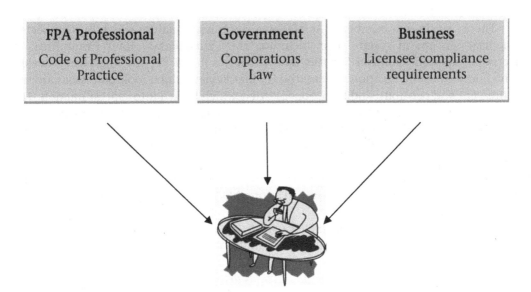

Figure 3.1   Graphic depicting regulatory obligations in Australia
Source: Adapted from FPA Australia's "Professional Framework".

Section 911A of the Corporations Act 2001 (Corporations Act) stipulates that financial services businesses, including those who provide financial product advice, must hold an Australian Financial Services Licence (AFSL). As part of its responsibility for regulating the financial services industry, licences are issued and monitored by ASIC. Section 766A of the Corporations Act states that the provision of a financial service includes the following:

- providing financial product advice;
- dealing in financial products;
- making a market for financial products;
- operating a registered scheme; or
- providing a custodial or depository service.

Unless a financial planner is a holder of an AFSL, they must be authorised by a licensee to provide advice on retail financial products.

Given this licensing regime, there are a number of business practice models in Australia. Financial planners may be salaried employees of a large financial services organisation such as a bank, or they may be contracted authorised representatives of such an entity; or they may be contracted financial planners of a mid-sized, non-aligned entity; or they may be stand-alone financial planners in a boutique licensee (Taylor et al. 2010).

ASIC's RG 146 specifies generic knowledge areas, specialist knowledge areas and skill requirements all in the context of product advice. Knowledge requirements comprise generic knowledge and specialist knowledge. Generic knowledge covers areas such as the economic environment, operation of financial markets and knowledge about financial products. Among the specialist knowledge areas, financial planning is listed as covering theories behind the use of the products listed above as well as issues such as the legal environment, taxation and estate planning. The skill requirements are also shown in Table 3.1. The intent is that advisors should be able to apply appropriate skills to their activities and the products and markets in which they operate (ASIC 2008). However, advisors providing general advice only are not required to demonstrate they have these skills requirements (ASIC 2008).

3.2.2   CERTIFICATION ENVIRONMENT

A review of the Financial Planning Association of Australia's website[4] reveals the requirements of an undergraduate degree, master's degree or doctorate, completion of CFP® certification programme Modules 1 to 5, a minimum of three[5] years' approved practitioner experience including Authorised Representative status for 12 months prior to application and agreement to adhere to the FPA Code of Ethics, Rules of Professional Conduct and Practice Standards. These four initial certification requirements are referred to as the four Es – education, examination, experience and ethics. Table 3.1, on page 46, summarises the requirements for CFP® certification in Australia.

FPA Australia has also modelled FPSB's notion of a Professional Framework by developing its own structured professional framework. The professional framework consists of three pillars of professionalism comprising professional membership, professional conduct and professional accountability. Professional membership entails entry, education and experience requirements. Professional conduct entails compliance, conduct, continuing professional development and supervision requirements. Professional accountability entails complaints and disciplinary systems. FPA Australia then links this professional framework to stakeholder trust and outcomes. Stakeholder trust is embodied in member trust, regulator trust and community trust leading to outcomes of professional standing (FPA Australia 2007).

FPA Australia is cognisant that professional education is an important ingredient in establishing the professional reputation and integrity of its members. FPA Australia released a White Paper, titled *Education Expectations for Professional Financial Planners*, during its national conference in November 2009 seeking stakeholder feedback. At its 2010 national conference it announced, among other things, that from 1 July 2013 all new members of the FPA would be required to have an approved bachelor's degree (or higher) before acceptance as an Associate Financial Planner. The association already has in place the requirement of a bachelor's degree in financial planning for entry to the CFP® certification programme.

These initiatives are expected to complement changes in government regulation including the *Future of Financial Advice* reforms to be introduced from 1 July 2012, the most significant of which include the introduction of a statutory fiduciary duty requiring financial advisors to act in the best interests of their clients, and a prospective ban on conflicted remuneration structures including commissions and volume-based payments.[6]

---

4   For a complete description of CFP® certification requirements, readers can refer to http://www.fpa.asn.au/default. asp?action=article&ID=21659 [accessed 20 December 2010].

5   Modules 1 and 5 of the CFP® certification programme are compulsory. Some candidates receive exemption from Modules 2, 3 and 4. Module 5 is the CFP® Certification examination requirement.

6   See the Australian Government Treasury's *Future of Financial Advice* website for further reading: http://futureofadvice. treasury.gov.au/content/Content.aspx?doc=home.htm [accessed 8 June 2011].

FPA Australia established the Financial Planning Education Council (FPEC) in 2010 as an independent body chartered with the responsibility of raising the standard of financial planning education and promoting financial planning as a distinct learning area and a career of choice for new students and career changers (FPA Australia 2012). From July 2013 FPEC will specifically have the power to approve individual programmes that satisfy requirements for admittance to the CFP® certification programme. This power was presented in a consultation paper to education providers and other stakeholders in April 2012. The consultation paper outlined the proposed approach to assessment and accreditation by FPEC and sought feedback on a number of proposals. The proposals comprise a number of standards such as on the curriculum framework, ensuring student learning outcomes, assessment approach and methodology (FPA Australia 2012).

Australia's Financial Planning Education Council's process for assuring learning outcomes of students undertaking financial planning courses comprises three key aspects of planning, learning and measuring. Learning objectives are mapped from subjects to an overall course design which ensures that content knowledge and generic skills are embedded in the course and clearly reflect the learning objectives through assessment. Strengths and weaknesses are identified in the initial accreditation process with the expectation that an education provider will employ appropriate continual improvement processes to address the weaknesses for subsequent accreditation (FPA Australia 2012).

3.3   Hong Kong

Regulation in Hong Kong is concerned with the integrity of the markets through the Hong Kong Monetary Authority (HKMA), the Securities and Futures Commission (SFC), the Office of the Commissioner of Insurance (OCI) and the Mandatory Provident Fund Schemes Authority (MPFA). Recent reforms have moved the regulation of the activities of advisors closer to regulation in Australia. Financial advice in Hong Kong is primarily concerned with selling either insurance or investment products. This aspect is of interest to this present study in understanding how CFP^CM professionals in Hong Kong experience professionalism.

The other area of interest for this present study is the requirements for CFP^CM certification in Hong Kong. This study has been delimited to investigate the conceptions of professionalism for CFP^CM professionals only and therefore the influence of CFP^CM certification and membership to the Institute of Financial Planners of Hong Kong is of interest to this study. CFP^CM certification requirements of Hong Kong and Australia are prescribed by the Financial Planning Standards Board against a common standards framework. What these standards are and what is required to become a CFP^CM professional and to maintain certification in Hong Kong is important in investigating conceptions of the professionalism of financial planners.

3.3.1   REGULATORY ENVIRONMENT

The Financial Services Regulator of Hong Kong was established under the Hong Kong Monetary Authority Act 1970. The Financial Services Regulator of Hong Kong supervises, and at all times regulates and inspects, all financial-related institutions within its covered area of responsibility.

The HKMA is the government authority in Hong Kong responsible for maintaining monetary and banking stability. Its main functions are:

- maintaining currency stability within the framework of the Linked Exchange Rate system;
- promoting the stability and integrity of the financial system, including the banking system;
- helping to maintain Hong Kong's status as an international financial centre, including the maintenance and development of Hong Kong's financial infrastructure;
- managing the Exchange Fund (Hong Kong Monetary Authority 2011).

The government of the Hong Kong Special Administrative Region (HKSAR) abides by the principle of keeping intervention into the way in which the market operates to a minimum and has endeavoured to provide a favourable environment in which business operates (Hong Kong Special Administrative Region Government 2010). At the end of July 2010, there were 146 licensed banks, 22 restricted licence banks and 27 deposit-taking companies in Hong Kong, together with 70 local representative offices of overseas banking institutions (Hong Kong Special Administrative Region Government 2010). Apart from the stock market and the futures market, there is also an active over-the-counter market which is mainly operated and used by professional institutions and trades swaps, forwards and options in relation to equities, interest rates and currencies. The introduction of the Mandatory Provident Fund (MPF) System in December 2000 has generated significant amounts of retirement assets, adding impetus to the further development of the financial markets. As contributions are mandatory, the government has built into the MPF System a multiplicity of measures to ensure that MPF assets are safe and secure. The measures include stringent criteria for the approval of MPF trustees; prudential supervision to ensure compliance with standards and regulations; smooth and transparent operation of schemes; as well as a compensation fund mechanism to make good losses caused by illegal conduct. Hence, apart from creating new and additional demands for investment products, the MPF System also contributes to greater stability in the financial markets (Hong Kong Special Administrative Region Government 2010).

The principal regulators are the Hong Kong Monetary Authority (HKMA), the Securities and Futures Commission (SFC), the Office of the Commissioner of Insurance (OCI) and the Mandatory Provident Fund Schemes Authority (MPFA). They are responsible respectively for regulation of the banking; securities and futures; insurance and retirement scheme industries (Hong Kong Special Administrative Region Government 2010). The government is not involved in the day-to-day regulation of the securities and futures industry. The SFC, established in 1989, is an autonomous statutory body responsible for administering the laws governing the securities and futures markets in Hong Kong and facilitating and encouraging the development of these markets. Established as an office within the government structure, the OCI administers the legislation governing the operation of insurance companies and insurance intermediaries in Hong Kong. Hong Kong maintains a three-tier system of deposit-taking institutions, namely, licensed banks, restricted licence banks and deposit-taking companies. They are collectively known as authorised institutions (AIs) under the Banking Ordinance. AIs may operate in Hong Kong as either locally incorporated companies or branches of foreign banks (Hong Kong Special Administrative Region Government 2010).

The main role of the Financial Services Regulator of Hong Kong (FSRHK) is to protect the integrity and stability of the non-bank financial services sector and by so doing protect the interest of investors and consumers. The FSRHK regulates non-bank financial institutions whose roles are to channel funds from lenders to borrowers by accepting long-term or specialised types of deposits and by incurring liabilities on their own account through the issuing of bills, bonds or other securities. Such institutions often specialise in lending to particular types of borrowers and in using specialised financial arrangements such as financial leasing, securitised lending and financial derivatives. As a government authoritative body in terms of the financial services sector, the FSRHK from time to time develops financial regulations that directly apply to the administration of Hong Kong's banking institutions, trust companies, insurance companies and investment business. In addition, as required by the relevant financial services legislation, the FSRHK provides specific reports on its activities to the Department of Finance on an annual basis (Financial Services Regulator of Hong Kong 2011a).

The *Capital Markets and Services Act 2007* (CMSA) repealed the *Securities Industry Act 1983* (SIA) and the *Futures Industry Act 1993* (FIA). The CMSA, which took effect on 28 September 2007, introduced a single licensing regime for capital market intermediaries. Under this new regime, a capital market intermediary will only need one licence to carry on the business in any one or more of the following regulated activities:

- dealing in securities;
- trading in futures contracts;
- fund management;
- advising on corporate finance;
- investment advice; and
- financial planning.

Licensing ensures an adequate level of investor protection, including the provision of sufficient safeguards to protect investors from default by market intermediaries or problems arising from the insolvency of such intermediaries. More importantly, it instils confidence among investors that the organisations and people they deal with will treat them fairly, and are efficient, honest and financially sound (Financial Services Regulator of Hong Kong 2011b).

3.3.2   CERTIFICATION ENVIRONMENT

The Institute of Financial Planners of Hong Kong (IFPHK) requires candidates to develop their theoretical and practical financial planning knowledge by completing an education programme from one of its approved education providers. The education programme comprises six modules and is called the "Registered CFP^{CM} Certification Education Program". The six modules cover foundation of financial planning, insurance, investments, taxation and tax planning, employee benefits and estate planning and advanced financial planning. Some candidates may be exempted from completing part or all of "Registered CFP^{CM} Certification Education Program" if, on review of their academic transcript, they are deemed to have covered part or all of the syllabus. There is also a requirement that every candidate must possess a bachelor's degree or attain a minimum of five passes in the Hong Kong Certificate of Education Examination.

Once the education requirement has been satisfied candidates are able to sit the certification examination. The certification examination comprises four papers and is designed to test candidates' competence on specific major sections of the examination syllabus. Candidates are required to pass all four papers. The work experience varies depending upon the education background of the candidate. Candidates with a recognised bachelor's degree, three years' full-time experience or the equivalent part-time is required. If a candidate does not have a degree from a recognised college or university, six years' full-time or the equivalent part-time is required. Further, all candidates must agree to abide by the IFPHK's Code of Ethics and Professional Responsibility and disclose any investigations or legal proceedings related to their professional or business conduct.

Once candidates are certified they are required to renew their CFP^{CM} certification annually. Candidates are required to complete 15 credits of continuing professional development and report any public, civil, criminal or disciplinary actions that may have been taken against them. Table 3.1, on page 46, summarises the requirements for CFP^{CM} certification in Hong Kong.

3.4   United States

Regulation in the United States is primarily state-based. Financial planners are regulated as investment advisors by the Securities and Exchange Commission (SEC) and the states, and as such are subject to laws and regulations governing broker-dealers and insurance agents when acting in those capacities. Regulation as such is fragmented and the extent to which it may influence the experience of professionalism for CFP® professionals is of interest to this present study.

The other area of interest for this present study is the requirements for CFP® certification in the United States. This study has been delimited to investigate the conceptions of professionalism for CFP® professionals only and therefore the influence of CFP® certification and membership to the Financial Planning Association of America is of interest to this study. CFP® certification requirements of the United States are prescribed by the CFP Board of Standards. These standards formed the basis of the CFP® certification requirements prescribed by the Financial Planning Standards Board.

3.4.1   REGULATORY ENVIRONMENT

In the United States, no single law governs the activities of financial planners and as such they are regulated by different laws. Under these different laws, three types of licence are required: "Investor Adviser Representative", "Registered Representative" and "Insurance Producer". Carrying out a practice of investment advice, the sale of investment securities and the sale of insurance products requires an individual to pass an exam, affiliate with a firm and register with one or more states before conducting business. In addition to this regulation, federal and state agencies regulate marketing and the use of titles and designations that can apply to financial planners.

Importantly, there are no regulated ethical or competency standards for financial planning, although some aspects are regulated by the SEC and other bodies. Financial planners can adopt a variety of titles and designations (such as CFP® certification). The different designations can imply different types of qualifications, but the problem is that consumers may not understand or distinguish among these designations, and therefore may be unable to properly assess the qualifications and expertise of financial planners.

The Government Accountability Office (GAO) released a report to Congress on 18 January 2011 entitled *Regulatory Coverage Exists for Financial Planners, but Consumer Protection Issues Remain* (Government Accountability Office 2011). In the absence of statutory or a single definition of financial planning, the report considers financial planning broadly as a process that involves preparing plans for clients based on their financial objectives. It may also involve recommending or providing insurance products, securities or other investments. GAO confirms that the primary activities performed by a financial planner are already generally subject to regulation at the federal or state levels covering requirements applicable to investment advisers, broker-dealers and insurance agents.

One of several recommendations made in the GAO report is that the SEC incorporates into its ongoing review of the financial literacy of investors an assessment of the extent to which investors understand the titles and designations used by financial planners and any implications that lack of such understanding may have for consumers' investment decisions. In so doing, it should collaborate with state securities regulators in identifying methods to better understand the extent of problems specifically involving financial planners and financial planning services, and take actions to address any identified problems (Government Accountability Office 2011).

Further, the three major financial planning organisations in the United States – the National Association of Personal Financial Advisors, the Financial Planning Association and the Certified Financial Planner Board of Standards Inc. – have been working together for the past two years, calling for legislation that will create a national oversight board to set standards and enforce a "fiduciary duty" for financial planners.

In the United States, broker-dealers and investment advisors are highly regulated, but broker-dealers and investment advisors are subject to different standards under federal law when providing investment advice about securities. These differences are confusing to retail investors who are not generally aware of these differences or their legal implications.

Section 913 of Title IX of the Dodd-Frank Wall Street Reform and Consumer Protection Act of 2010 (the "Dodd-Frank Act") requires the US Securities and Exchange Commission (the "Commission") to conduct a study (the "Study") to evaluate the effectiveness of existing legal or regulatory standards of care for providing personalised investment advice and recommendations about securities to retail customers; and whether there are legal or regulatory gaps, shortcomings or overlaps in legal or regulatory standards in the protection of retail customers relating to the standards of care for providing personalised investment advice about securities to retail customers.

Financial planners are not currently regulated as financial planners by either state or federal government. Many financial planners however are regulated by the states through subsets of financial planning such as insurance and taxation. The Securities and Exchange Commission (SEC) and most states have requirements for people who give investment advice, which would include many financial planners.

3.4.2   CERTIFICATION ENVIRONMENT

CFP® professionalism is initiated through a certification process where eligible candidates meet the requirements prescribed by the appropriate professional body. For candidates within the United States, the certifying body is the CFP Board of Standards. Outside the United States, the Financial Planning Standards Board licenses its affiliate members to certify individuals against CFP® certification requirements. This section describes what is currently prescribed as the certification requirements to become a CFP® professional in the United States.

It is important to distinguish between CFP® professionalism and certification in the United States compared to the rest of the world. The CFP® and CERTIFIED FINANCIAL PLANNER™ marks were initiated in the United States and the CFP Board then constituted the International CFP Council to deal with the burgeoning number of countries outside the United States with an interest in CFP® certification (which has now morphed into FPSB). The CFP Board owns the rights for the CFP® and CERTIFIED FINANCIAL PLANNER™ marks in the United States and entered into an agreement with FPSB on 1 December 2004 for FPSB to purchase the marks outside of the United States (Brandon Jr. and Welch 2009). From that point the two organisations have gone their separate ways, although they are both promoting the same mark of professionalism to the profession and to the general public. FPSB's core focus is growing the "brand" internationally, whilst the CFP Board stays focused on growing the "brand" in the United States.

CFP Board of Standards

The CFP Board of Standards has what is commonly referred to as the four Es of *education*, *examination*, *experience* and *ethics* as requirements of their certification process.

Before applying for the CFP® Certification Examination, candidates are required to complete education requirements through one of three paths: complete a CFP Board-Registered Education Program;[7] apply for Challenge Status where certain degrees and professional credentials fulfil the educational requirement;[8] request a Transcript Review where certain industry credentials recognised by the CFP Board, or the successful completion of upper-division level college courses, may satisfy some or all of the education requirements set by the CFP Board. Finally, a bachelor's degree (or higher), or its equivalent, in any discipline, from an accredited college or university is required to attain CFP® certification. The bachelor's degree requirement is a condition of initial certification; it is not a requirement to be eligible to take the CFP® Certification Examination.

When candidates have demonstrated they have completed recognised education requirements, they are required to take the CFP® Certification Examination. This is a 10-hour exam taken in three separate sessions, designed to test application of financial planning knowledge to client situations. At least three years of qualifying full-time work experience are required for certification. Qualifying experience includes work that can be categorised into one of the six primary elements of the personal financial planning process. Experience can be gained in a number of ways including: the delivery of all, or

---

7   There are more than 300 academic programmes at colleges and universities across the country from which to choose. These programmes include credit and non-credit certificate programmes, undergraduate and graduate degree programmes. They use various delivery formats and schedules, including classroom instruction, self-study and online delivery. Many of the CFP Board's Registered Programs also offer in-house educational programmes for individual companies.

8   Academic degrees and credentials that fulfil the educational requirements include: Certified Public Accountant (CPA), licensed attorney, Chartered Financial Analyst® (CFA®), Doctor of Business Administration, Chartered Financial Consultant (ChFC), PhD in business or economics, and Chartered Life Underwriter (CLU).

of any portion, of the personal financial planning process to a client; the direct support or supervision of individuals who deliver all, or any portion, of the personal financial planning process to a client; teaching all, or any portion, of the personal financial planning process. Finally candidates for CFP® certification must pass CFP Board's *Candidate Fitness Standards*.[9] These, for example, cover conduct that is presumed to be unacceptable such as one personal or business bankruptcy filed within five years prior to completing the CFP® Certification Application. CFP® professionals are required to renew their licence every two years when they must produce evidence that 30 hours of acceptable continuing education has been completed.

The mission of Certified Financial Planner Board of Standards, Inc. (CFP Board) is to benefit the public by granting the CFP® certification and upholding it as the recognised standard of excellence for personal financial planning. The CFP Board's formation took place relatively early in the development of the movement that became known as the financial planning profession. The CFP Board was founded on 17 July 1985. The idea that people could benefit from professional assistance from a profession that integrated knowledge and practices from the many often-fragmented areas of the financial services industry developed soon after the Second World War, as new financial products and services evolved to meet the needs of Americans. This movement experienced a watershed event on 12 December 1969, when 13 men met in Chicago and outlined the first steps needed to establish these integrated practices as a new profession called financial planning. At the meeting, resolutions were made to create a membership organisation named the International Association for Financial Planners (IAFP) and a new educational institution that would be named the College for Financial Planning (CFP Board of Standards 2011).

The Financial Planning Association (FPA®) claims to be the largest membership organisation for personal financial planning experts in the United States and includes professionals from all backgrounds and business models (Financial Planning Association (USA) 2011).

On 1 January 2000, members of the Institute of Certified Financial Planners (ICFP) and the International Association for Financial Planning (IAFP) took a step forward, combining forces to create the Financial Planning Association® (FPA®). The FPA is the leadership and advocacy organisation connecting those who provide, support and benefit from professional financial planning. In 2001, September 11 created a challenging environment for the entire world. Stemming directly from the terrorist attacks on the United States, the FPA created its National Planning Support Center on 8 October 2001. The immediate focus of the Support Center was to offer pro bono financial planning assistance to families, individuals and businesses directly affected by the attacks. Since then, with generous assistance from the Foundation for Financial Planning, the Support Center has expanded its public service to disaster-related victims and military personnel. With the National Planning Support Center in place, the FPA realised the need to expand its resources to the broader public. A new consumer website was created to help individuals learn about the value of financial planning. It offers interactive tools including educational seminars, literature, audio casts, checklists, an email hotline, a financial planner search service and more (Financial Planning Association (USA) 2011).

---

9   Candidate Fitness Standards can be accessed at http://www.CFP.net/become/fitness.asp [accessed 20 December 2010].

In the United States, to obtain the CFP® designation, individuals have to complete a registered education programme[10] and complete the CFP® Certification Examination. The CFP Board also has a requirement of a bachelor's degree (or higher), or its equivalent, in any discipline, from an accredited college or university to attain CFP® certification (CFP Board of Standards 2011). At the centre of CFP Board's CFP® certification requirements are the four Es – examination, education, experience and ethics (CFP Board of Standards 2011). Examination refers to the CFP Board's comprehensive certification examination, which tests the individual's knowledge on various key aspects of financial planning. Candidates must complete 30 hours of continuing education every two years to stay current in financial planning knowledge, including ethics. Candidates must acquire three years of financial planning-related experience before receiving the right to use the CFP® marks. Candidates must voluntarily ascribe to CFP Board's code of ethics and additional requirements as mandated.

Financial Planning Standards Board

FPSB prescribes similar requirements to the CFP Board of Standards for those CFP® professionals outside the United States. The initial certification requires the four Es of education, examination, experience and ethics. The following is a summary of these requirements sourced from FPSB's website.[11] Candidates for CFP® certification must master theoretical and practical financial planning knowledge by completing a comprehensive course of study that meets standards set by FPSB. Candidates for CFP® certification must pass a comprehensive CFP® Certification Examination that assesses their ability to apply integrated financial planning knowledge to real world client situations. The examination covers the financial planning process, tax planning, employee benefits and retirement planning, estate planning, investment management and insurance. Candidates must also meet relevant work experience standards (one-year supervised experience or a minimum of three years of unsupervised practice experience) in the financial planning process prior to being awarded CFP® certification. Candidates must also agree to abide by a strict Code of Ethics and Professional Responsibility that defines their ethical responsibilities to the public, clients and employers. CFP® professionals must disclose any investigations or legal proceedings related to their professional or business conduct and agree to place the interest of clients first, act fairly, diligently and with integrity, and offer clients professional services that are objective and based on clients' needs. CFP® professionals must disclose in writing to clients information about their sources of compensation and conflicts of interest. CFP® professionals are required to maintain technical competence and fulfil ethical obligations. Every two years, they must complete at least 30 hours of continuing professional development education to stay current with developments in the financial planning profession. In addition, CFP® professionals must disclose any public, civil, criminal or disciplinary actions that may

---

10   Candidates can also apply for "challenge status" if they have a recognised credential such as CPA, CFA, or apply for a review of their academic transcript.

11   For a complete description of the FPSB's CFP® certification requirements refer to www.fpsb.org [accessed 8 June 2012.]

Table 3.1   Regulation and CFP® certification requirements for Australia, Hong Kong and the United States

	Australia	Hong Kong	United States
Regulation	The Australian Securities and Investments Commission regulates consumer protection and market conduct. The Australian Prudential Regulatory Authority regulates capital adequacy, banks, life insurance companies and superannuation funds. *Future of Financial Advice* reforms including the banning of commissions. ASIC RG 146 setting minimum training requirements for advising providing advice on retail financial products.	The principal regulators are the Hong Kong Monetary Authority (HKMA), the Securities and Futures Commission (SFC), the Office of the Commissioner of Insurance (OCI) and the Mandatory Provident Fund Schemes Authority (MPFA). They are responsible respectively for regulation of the banking; securities and futures; insurance and retirement scheme industries (Hong Kong Special Administrative Region Government 2010). The government is not involved in the day-to-day regulation of the securities and futures industry.	No single law governs the activities of financial planners. Financial planners are primarily regulated as investment advisors by the SEC and the states, and as such are subject to laws and regulations governing broker-dealers and insurance agents when acting in those capacities.
Education	Candidates complete an approved undergraduate or postgraduate course as entry to the CFP Certification Program. A Transcript Review process is available for some candidates who have completed a finance-related degree that has not been approved by the FPA.	Candidates must complete a comprehensive education programme from one of the approved education providers of IFPHK.	Candidates complete an education programme registered by the CFP Board of Standards (includes over 300 college and university programmes). Candidates can also apply under a Challenge Status if they hold certain credentials such as CPA or CFA. Candidates can also request a Transcript Review if they have not completed a registered education programme.
Continuing education	CFP® professionals are required to (1) complete a statement disclosing any investigations or legal proceedings relating to professional or business conduct; (2) submit a business card and business stationery for CFP® mark audit; (3) confirm 120 CPD points per triennium (min 35 points per annum) have been completed (note: no more than 50 per cent of these points can be from non-accredited CPD and three points must be specifically on ethics).	CFP® professionals must renew their certification annually, which requires a minimum of 15 credits of continuing education and reporting any public, civil, criminal or disciplinary actions that may have been taken against them.	CFP® professionals must be renewed every two years. Candidates must show 30 hours of continuing education (CE). The CE requirement includes 28 hours in the accepted financial planning topics and two hours from a pre-approved programme on the CFP Board's *Code of Ethics and Professional Responsibility or Financial Planning Practice Standards.*

Table 3.1   Continued

	Australia	Hong Kong	United States
Examination	CFP Certification Assessment (CFP 5) makes up the examination part of the CFP® Certification Program. The assessment verifies that those wishing to practice the profession of financial planning have mastered a certain level of theoretical knowledge and practical application of that knowledge.	Candidates complete the CFP^CM Certification Examination. Candidates are required to pass four papers within five years (11 exam intakes).	Candidates must complete a 10-hour exam that is divided into three separate sessions. All questions are multiple-choice, including those questions related to case problems.
Experience	Three years of financial planning experience is required. OR two years' experience in the delivery of any step in the financial planning process to a client, of which twelve months experience in providing face-to-face comprehensive financial planning advice.	Three years' full-time, or the equivalent part-time (2,000 hours part-time equals one year full-time), if the candidate has an undergraduate degree from a recognised college or university. Six years' full-time, or the equivalent part-time (2,000 hours part-time equals one year full-time), if the candidate does not have an undergraduate degree from a recognised college or university.	Three years' full-time, or the equivalent part-time (2,000 hours equals one year full-time). Six months of experience must have been gained within 12 months of reporting work experience. Experience may be gained up to 10 years before or up to five years after the exam date.
Ethics	Candidates must: • disclose any involvement in any criminal, civil, self-regulatory organisation or government agency investigation or proceedings; • agree to adhere to the FPA Code of Professional Practice which includes the Code of Ethics, Rules of Professional Conduct and Practice Standards; • undertake ongoing Continuing Professional Development (CPD).	All candidates for CFP^CM Certification must agree to abide by the IFPHK's Code of Ethics and Professional Responsibility and the IFPHK's Financial Planning Practice Standards. The IFPHK also performs a background check and each candidate must disclose any investigations or legal proceedings related to their professional or business conduct.	Candidates must agree to adhere to the CFP Board's *Standards of Professional Conduct* – including the *Code of Ethics and Professional Responsibility, Rules of Conduct and Financial Planning Practice Standards* – and to acknowledge the CFP Board's right to enforce them through its *Disciplinary Rules and Procedures*.

have been taken against them during the certification period. Table 3.1 summarises the requirements for CFP® certification in the Australia, Hong Kong and the United States.

FPSB has developed a framework for financial planning professionalism. FPSB claims to work in conjunction with its members, practising CFP® professionals and subject-matter experts from around the world in creating standards for financial planning (FPSB 2010a). A review of FPSB's website suggests that this professional framework covers competency standards, ethics requirements, practice standards and certification requirements in education, assessment, experience and continuing professional development.

FPSB operates by entering into licensing and affiliation agreements with non-profit or equivalent organisations that become FPSB members who then administer the CERTIFIED FINANCIAL PLANNER certification programme. In this sense FPSB affiliate members are agents of FPSB and administer the CFP® certification programme in a country on behalf of FPSB. The intent is that FPSB's standards are consistent across all its affiliate members subject to differences due to country-specific regulations, laws and products.

The CFP® certification education curriculum is prescribed by FPSB for its affiliate members outside the United States and the CFP Board of Standards in the United States. FPSB has developed a competency profile which provides a theoretical foundation for its certification standards, particularly those related to education. The competency profile comprises abilities, professional skill and knowledge.

3.5   A Comparison of the Regulatory and Certification Environments of Australia, Hong Kong and the United States

This study has as its focus how CFP® professionals experience *professionalism*. These conceptions are of three cohorts – Australia, Hong Kong and the United States. It is important for the reader to have context in *what* is experienced with professionalism and *how* professionalism is experienced. This is provided by understanding the regulatory environment and CFP® certification requirements of each country.

The regulation of financial planners in Australia with respect to education and training requirements is more advanced than in Hong Kong and the United States. A study of the impact of minimum standards for financial advisors in Australia suggests that this may have curtailed the growth in the number of CFP® professionals in Australia (Bruce and Gupta 2011). This study attempted to understand the extent to which private providers are delivering training and education to aspiring financial planners in Australia. An analysis was carried out on the ASIC Training Register which involved a search of the number of providers listed on the Register. The ASIC Training Register enables courses to be sorted by knowledge category/location, or by knowledge category/course name for each training provider or by Tier 1/Tier 2 courses. The research was limited to the *financial planning* specialist knowledge area. The research showed that 56 per cent of courses registered on the ASIC Training Register were delivered by private education providers, 28 per cent by universities, 9 per cent by state-funded Technical and Further Education Colleges (TAFE) and 7 per cent by professional bodies (Bruce and Gupta 2011). Many of these private providers were conducting courses over a much shorter semester or term period than was being delivered in universities and TAFE colleges. In some cases courses were being conducted over a few days but were still registered as meeting the minimum training requirements. The study also analysed the growth in CFP® professionals in Australia and found that this was 31 per cent in 1998–9 and then declined to -0.05 per cent in 2004–5. Growth from 2005 to 2009 has been just below 5 per cent. This growth has slowed following the introduction of RG 146 by ASIC under licensing requirements of the corporations law; and the introduction of Diploma and Advanced Diploma programmes in the education marketplace as meeting the training requirements for financial planners (Bruce and Gupta 2011).

ASIC released a consultation paper (ASIC 2011) to seek feedback on a proposed assessment and professional development framework for financial advisors in Australia. The proposed framework was intended to enhance and maintain the competence of financial advisors and lead to improvements in the quality of advice as well as increasing consumer confidence. One of the more controversial proposals was the introduction of a national examination. The proposal was to use a module-based approach to structure the exam, with modules targeted principally at an advisor's authorisations, including compulsory core modules to be prescribed, with other modules used to demonstrate competence for relevant authorisations (ASIC 2011). All advisers, whether new or existing, would be required to pass the exam aimed at improving the trust and confidence and the professionalism of the whole industry. The proposal would require advisers to either receive a pass/fail grade or a graduated result (pass, credit, distinction) when taking the examination (ASIC 2011).

Regulation of the activities of financial planners in both Hong Kong and the United States has not reached the same maturity as we see in Australia. In Hong Kong, a capital market intermediary only requires one licence to carry on the business in any one or more of the regulated activities, including dealing in securities; trading in futures contracts; fund management; advising on corporate finance; investment advice; and financial planning.

While in the United States some activities of financial planners are regulated, consumers rely on the value of the designation that a financial planner holds. There are numerous designations and they each reflect varying standards. The GAO, in its January 2011 report, fell short of recommending regulation of education and training standards in favour of the SEC including consumer understanding of the various designations as part of its ongoing review.

4 *Phenomenography*

4.1 What this Chapter is About

The aim of this chapter is to explain the selection of phenomenography as the most appropriate research method to investigate the phenomenon of *professionalism* as it is experienced by CFP® professionals.

The chapter will discuss the research methods that are typically used in PhD theses and explain the choice of a qualitative approach as being most appropriate for this study. This is followed by a description of phenomenography within qualitative research models and its relevance in investigating conceptions of the professionalism of financial planners. Phenomenography has its origins in the 1970s and has now emerged as a widely popular research methodology (Entwistle 1997). The chapter will clarify the difference between *phenomenography* and *phenomenology* and will outline the major elements of phenomenographic research including conception, experience and structure of awareness. The results of phenomenographic studies including categories of description and outcome space will then be explained. The chapter will also illuminate recent discussion about variation theory as it relates to the "new" phenomenography (Pang 2003) and its relevance to the phenomenographic approach taken in this current study. This is followed by a critical review of phenomenography perspectives on the structure of conceptions. The chapter concludes by explaining the perspective on the structure of conceptions taken in this study.

4.2 Research Method: The Case for Qualitative Enquiry

This section provides an overview of different research methods as a process of determining the most appropriate research methodology for this study.

Creswell and Miller (1997), in exploring the methodologies that guide student research in the social sciences and education, assess the four research methodologies of positivist (or quantitative), qualitative (or interpretive), ideological (such as post-modern thinking or feminist perspectives) and pragmatic (combining quantitative and qualitative approaches). The positivist approach views knowledge as external to the individual, that knowledge is objective and does not depend on the perception of any one individual (Creswell and Miller 1997). In following a positivist approach, researchers are focused on how individuals make sense of the subject matter being researched. With qualitative research, each qualitative method is a specific way of thinking about data and using techniques as tools to manipulate data to achieve a goal (Atieno 2009). Ideological methodologies rely on knowledge which is either internal or external and negotiated among individuals. Researchers either build or use a theory to explain the subject matter being investigated (Creswell and Miller 1997).

Increasingly researchers are adopting a mixed method combining qualitative and quantitative approaches where knowledge is viewed as being both external to the individual and residing in the individual (Creswell and Miller 1997). Mixed methods can strengthen research findings because data is examined from different perspectives (Pole 2007). Numerous writers have been positing the virtues of adopting a pragmatic approach to research by combining quantitative and qualitative methods (Onwuegbuzie and Leech 2005; Pole 2007; Onwuegbuzie et al. 2009). They argue that there is a false dichotomy between quantitative and qualitative research. For example, positivists claim that the essence of science is objective verification, and that their methods are objective, yet disregard the fact that many research decisions are made throughout the research process that precede objective verification decisions (Onwuegbuzie and Leech 2005). A combination of both methods can build on the strengths and eliminate the limitations of each model (Pole 2007). Although researchers tend to label themselves as either positivist or interpretive researchers, there are an increasingly groups of researchers who are interested in blending the two traditions, attempting to get the advantages of each (Atieno 2009).

A study was carried out in 2005 (Meyer et al. 2005) which explored Australian and South African students' conceptions of research from two complementary research perspectives. Open-ended written responses to questions aimed at soliciting variations in conceptions of what research is, were analysed using a qualitative methodology to isolate what was referred to as "categories of description". These conceptually discrete, although not necessarily conceptually independent, qualitative dimensions of variation suggested by the analysis were then analysed using quantitative methods to see whether these sources of variation also exist in a statistical sense. Empirically, and in terms of additional psychometric considerations, there was support for five of the eight dimensions of variation (Meyer et al. 2005). This study demonstrated an innovative way of combining both qualitative and quantitative approaches to provide deeper analysis and deeper meaning to the research.

Quantitative methods assess the statistical significance of relationships between variables, and have a high degree of statistical validity and reliability, and therefore are suitable for examining or assessing individuals in the context of theory based on large numbers of observations (Perl and Noldon 2000). According to Carr (1995), quantitative research is congruent with the traditions of how research is carried out in education institutions. In this sense, researchers have over the years adopted quantitative methods as part of a legitimising process among their peers. The core belief system within academe has propagated the idea that quantitative data are of higher quality and that the knowledge produced from quantitative research is more valid (Guba and Lincoln 1994). This attitude has acted as a barrier to researchers who have been persuaded by peer pressure to adopt quantitative approaches rather than qualitative.

Examples of qualitative methods include interviews, observation, focus groups, document analysis and theoretical methods (Nicholls 2009). Qualitative research can produce valuable, detail-oriented data through careful description of behaviours, events, situations and interactions because it emphasises processes that can be rigorously examined. In addition, qualitative research allows researchers to answer questions related to issues that cannot be addressed by quantitative methods (Gaytan 2007). The designs of qualitative research allows for simple descriptive analyses or more sophisticated prediction, significance testing, strength of relationship, and other complex types of analyses (Perl and Noldon 2000). Qualitative research methods are preferred when the researcher does not have a firm idea of what form the results can take (Levy and Ben-Ari 2009).

> *Qualitative research is not just a matter of performing techniques on data; rather, each qualitative method is a specific way of thinking about data and using techniques as tools to manipulate data to achieve a goal (Atieno 2009, p. 15).*

Qualitative methods are highly appropriate for questions where pre-emptive lessening of the data will prevent discovery. The researcher needs methods which will allow for discovery and for the analysis of the complex nature of actual experience and individual's interpretation of this experience (Atieno 2009). Qualitative research methodologies are based on interpretive, verbal descriptions rather than on statistical or numerical measurements (Gaytan 2007). Although qualitative methodologies are potentially more time-consuming and expensive, they capture what is important rather than what is easily measurable (Gaytan 2007). This is what is being researched in this present study by capturing the utterances of CFP® professionals.

One of the criticisms of qualitative research is the issue of generality. This is because, due to the unique nature of the research, it is difficult to generalise to other research settings (Huberman and Miles 1983; Firestone 1987; Atieno 2009).

> *This is because the findings of the research are not tested to discover whether they are statistically significant or due to chance (Atieno 2009, p. 17).*

Data reduction also poses a challenge for the qualitative researcher. This arises because field data is not immediately transferred into numeric or alphanumeric forms but exists as masses of words held onto as the researcher seeks to find qualitative evidence (Huberman and Miles 1983). Quantitative research has been criticised from the positivist's perspective that the researcher's viewpoint must be separate from the research itself to ensure the research is value neutral (Hara 1995). Carr and Kemmis (1986) argue that in relation to education, quantitative research fails to acknowledge the intrinsic relationship between aims, policies and methods.

Chang and Hsieh (1997) carried out a study on management doctoral dissertations in Taiwan between 1988 and 1994. Over that period the authors saw a decline in the number of dissertations which relied on surveys and simulation and an increase in those using logical argument, experimental design, mathematical modelling and case studies (Chang and Hsieh 1997). The authors also found that over half the dissertations used causal research methods followed by descriptive methods and exploratory research methods (Chang and Hsieh 1997).

This present study seeks to understand how CFP® professionals experience the phenomenon of *professionalism*. The interest of the researcher is in understanding how CFP® professionals experience their world of professionalism rather than prescribing criteria or characteristics of professionalism and analysing responses by way of a questionnaire or similar data collection method. In order to capture and understand how CFP® professionals experience *professionalism*, qualitative research has been chosen as the most appropriate research methodology.

The next section will discuss phenomenography as a research method and justify its application as the most appropriate qualitative approach for this study. Phenomenography appeals to this researcher as the method best able to investigate the conceptions of the professionalism of financial planners. Phenomenography is best described as a:

> *research method adapted for mapping the qualitative different ways in which people experience, conceptualise, perceive, and understand various aspects of, and phenomena in, the world around them (Marton 1986, p. 31).*

The group in this study being CFP® professionals as defined by the standards set by the CFP Board of Standards in the United States and the Financial Planning Standards Board (FPSB) outside the United States. FPSB prescribe standards for its affiliate members of which FPA Australia and the Institute of Financial Planners of Hong Kong have relevance here. Thus, in this convergent study, the main aim is to understand the different ways that CFP® professionals from Australia, Hong Kong and the United States experience the phenomenon, and this will provide an understanding of what these groups may have in common in how they experience professionalism.

4.3   What is Phenomenography?

Stated simply, phenomenography is an interpretive research method used to investigate and describe the qualitatively different ways in which a group of people experience a particular phenomenon. As an interpretive research method, phenomenography is therefore a qualitative research method and as such provides an alternative to the positivist standard that prevailed prior to the 1970s. Phenomenography is a qualitative research approach that allows the researcher to look at the experiences people have of a particular phenomenon, such as looking at the variation in conceptions of the professionalism of financial planners which is the focus of this present study.

The term "phenomenography" was first used by Sonnemann (1954) in an attempt to distinguish between the phenomenologies of Karl Jaspers and Martin Heidegger, as applied within psychopathology. But this usage has little to do with phenomenography as we know it today. According to Marton (1994) phenomenography has its roots in a set of studies of learning among university students carried out at the University of Göteborg, Sweden, in the early 1970s in exploring "how" and "what" students learned. According to Pang (2003) "phenomenography" as a term was created in 1979 and appeared in the work of Marton (1981). Trigwell (2006) provides a definition of phenomenography by showing how phenomenography differs from other research approaches:

> *The essence of the phenomenographic research approach is that it takes a relational (or non-dualist) qualitative, second-order perspective, that it aims to describe the key aspects of the variation of the collective experience of a phenomenon rather than the richness of individual experiences, and that it yields a limited number of internally related, hierarchical categories of description of the variation (2006, pp. 368–9).*

Phenomenography as a research tradition is located broadly within an interpretive epistemological orientation and focuses on the variation in how a phenomenon is experienced by a group of individuals. Phenomenography is underpinned by, amongst other things, a focus on the relational nature of human experience, a non-dualistic ontological perspective, an explicit focus on the experience of phenomena, and the adoption of a second-order perspective. The research outcome is a set of categories that describe the qualitatively different ways of experiencing that phenomenon, and are logically related in structure and meaning. The categories are not descriptive of how individuals perceive the phenomenon – rather they describe the phenomenon at the collective level. Learning, in the phenomenographic tradition, points to coming to discern phenomena in new and more powerful ways (Collier-Reed et al. 2009).

Phenomenography is research which "aims at description, analysis, and understanding of experiences" (Marton 1981, p. 180). Marton (1981) positioned this as a relatively distinct field of inquiry which he labelled phenomenography:

> The phenomenographic perspective does not depict learning in terms of mental models (for example, the cognitive science perspective) or as something that is formulated outside of a person in some social milieu (for example, the situated cognition perspective) instead, phenomenography draws upon Brentano's (1973) notion of intentionality to characterize a non-dualist model of experience (Linder and Marshall 2003, p. 272).

In this sense, phenomenography takes a different epistemological perspective than other learning models which have their origins in psychology, cognitive sciences and other forms of constructivism.

Phenomenography is described by Marton (1986, p. 31) as:

> a research method adapted for mapping the qualitatively different ways in which people experience, conceptualise, perceive, and understand various aspects of, and phenomena in, the world around them.

A fundamental assumption underlying phenomenographic research is that there are a finite number of qualitatively different understandings of a particular phenomenon (Marton 1981; Bruce et al. 2004). Phenomenography therefore "focuses on reflected-on experience, meaning that the emphasis is on the experience as described" (Greasley and Ashworth 2007, p. 821). This means that phenomenography does not study the cognitive process behind the experience nor any pre-reflective assumptions in the verbalised experience of the phenomenon (Greasley and Ashworth 2007). This is important as the role of the phenomenographer is to capture the experience of a phenomenon as it is experienced by the research participant. Therefore it does not matter if the research participant exaggerates or embellishes their utterance of how they experience the phenomenon, as this exaggeration or embellishment is how they experience the phenomenon in question.

Although phenomenography developed from empirical studies of learning in higher education focussed on the experience of learning, other applications of phenomenography have also emerged. Other studies have focussed on finding the main differences in which predominant phenomena, concepts and principles in specific fields are understood (Renström et al. 1990). According to Marton (1981) the knowledge interest of pure phenomenography describes conceptions of the world around us in a way that we can understand the collective mind of the many different ways we make sense of the world. Although the analysis is comprised of individual utterances from a selection of a particular cohort, it is the collective experience that phenomenography captures. Phenomenography is based on the knowledge that a particular cohort experiences a phenomenon in a qualitatively limited number of ways. So although a group may have a population of several hundred, or several thousand or more, it is only necessary to interview or observe a very small number of that group to uncover the different ways the phenomenon is experienced.

Svensson (1997) posited that the theoretical foundations of phenomenography assumes that knowledge has a relational and holistic nature. Svensson (1997) contends that the theoretical assumptions of phenomenographic research are as follows:

- *conceptions are the central form of knowledge;*
- *scientific knowledge about conceptions (and generally) is uncertain;*
- *descriptions are fundamental to scientific knowledge and about conceptions (and generally);*
- *scientifically knowledge about conceptions is based on exploration of delimitations and holistic meanings of objects as conceptualised; and*
- *scientific knowledge about conceptions (and generally) is based on differentiation, abstraction, reduction and comparison of meaning (p. 171).*

In answering my research questions, I will adopt a qualitative approach. This is essentially a qualitative study to gain an understanding of how CFP® professionals conceive or think of their professionalism. The primary orientation of this research study is a towards an interpretive perspective where the focus of the research is describing the distinctively different ways people experience a phenomenon in a way that each utterance is understood from a participant's experience of the phenomenon (Booth 1992).

Phenomenography emphasises the experience as described which sets aside both the study of the cognitive process behind the experience and any pre-reflective, taken-for granted assumptions in the experience of a phenomena (Greasley and Ashworth 2007). The primary research orientation of phenomenography is therefore to address the questions of the different ways of experiencing a phenomenon and how these ways are related to each other (Pang 2003). The primary research focus of this present study is to understand the different ways *professionalism* is experienced by CFP® professionals from Australia, Hong Kong and the United States. This will provide three separate phenomenographic studies and will enable a discussion between the similarities and differences in how professionalism is experienced from a transnational perspective.

Pang (2003) points out that although most phenomenographic studies have been conducted on the content of learning and student's conceptions of the various content domains, phenomenographic research has also been applied to the study of phenomena outside of the educational context such as conceptions of political power, conceptions of death and a study of Nobel laureate views of scientific intuition. Phenomenography has also been applied to recent research studies in areas such as looking at the understanding of competence (Ramritu and Barnard 2001; Huntly 2003), understandings of ethics (Stoodley 2009) and applying phenomenography to nursing research (Sjöström and Dahlgren 2002). Phenomenography has also been applied as a research method in management research (Osteraker 2002).

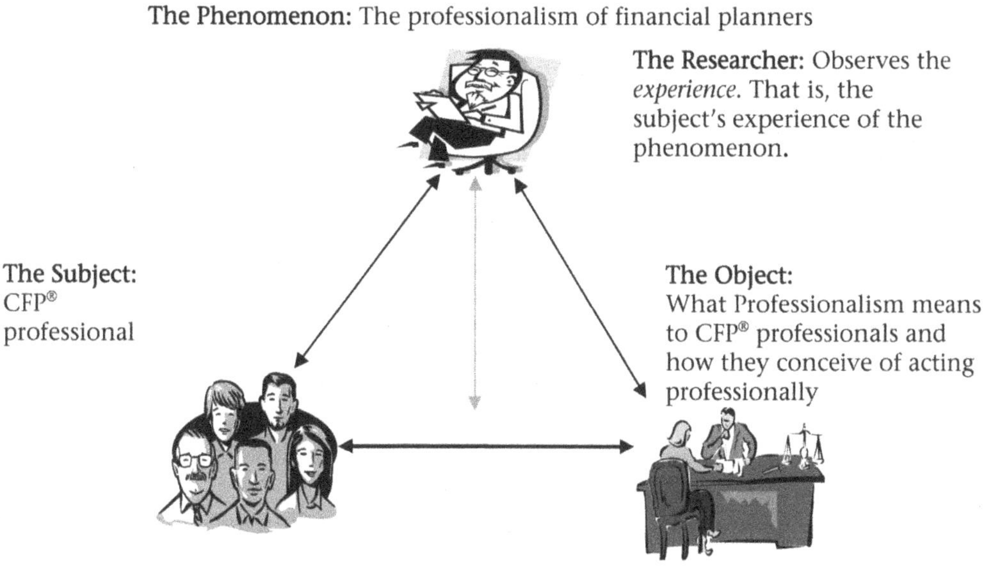

The **Phenomenon:** The professionalism of financial planners

The Researcher: Observes the *experience*. That is, the subject's experience of the phenomenon.

The Subject: CFP® professional

The Object: What Professionalism means to CFP® professionals and how they conceive of acting professionally

Figure 4.1   An illustration of the second-order perspective used in phenomenography

Source: Adapted from Berglund (2002) and Edwards (2005).

4.3.1   SECOND-ORDER PERSPECTIVE

In considering reality, Marton (1981) talks about "first order" and "second order" perspectives. Statements are made about the world as experienced and these are made from a first-order perspective. A first-order research question might ask "why some financial planners are more professional than others". A second-order perspective on the other hand looks at the *ways* of experiencing the world. A second-order research question might ask "what people think about why some financial planners are more professional than others" (Marton 1981). The challenge for the phenomenographer in adopting a second-order perspective is that in every stage of carrying out the research, including posing the research questions, gathering data, analysing the data, the researcher has to do this through the subject's eyes – to live the experience vicariously (Marton and Booth 1997).

Figure 4.1 illustrates the second-order perspective that a phenomenographer must take. In this present study, the researcher is compelled to observe the experience of CFP® professionals in how they experience the phenomenon of the *professionalism* of financial planners. This observation is by means of digital recordings of the research participant's utterances. The researcher makes no judgment or interpretation of these utterances and must bracket any preconceived notion or previous experience on the phenomenon in question.[1]

---

1   The concept of bracketing and how it is applied in this present study is discussed in Chapter 5.

4.3.2   PHENOMENOGRAPHY IS NOT PHENOMENOLOGY

There are similarities in the epistemological foundations of phenomenography and phenomenology (Marton 1981) but they are not part of the same research tradition (Svensson 1994). Both phenomenography and phenomenology investigate experience as the subject of study, but they differ in their intent. Phenomenology seeks to capture the richness of experience through description of a person's life world. Phenomenography on the other hand seeks to capture the critical aspects of the ways of experiencing the world that make people able to handle it in more or less efficient ways (Marton and Booth 1997). Researchers in both traditions seek to reveal the nature of human experience and awareness in order to understand conceptions of reality (Marton and Booth 1997). Phenomenology was founded by a number of German philosophers led by Husserl[2] who considered phenomenological reduction as suspending one's beliefs concerning the existence of perceptual objects in order to focus on their intrinsic properties or essences (Richardson 1999).

However, there are a number of differences between the two research traditions. Phenomenography is different from phenomenology in that is only considers "second-order" perspective. According to Marton (1981), phenomenological investigation seeks to describe how the world looks without having learned how to see it, whereas a phenomenographic investigation seeks to describe the world through the subject's conception rather than through the researcher's view of how the subject sees it. This highlights the most important distinction between the two research traditions in the role played by the researcher. A phenomenological investigation takes a first-order perspective in that it is impossible to separate that which is experienced from the experience itself (Marton 1981). Phenomenography takes a second-order perspective where the experience is separate from the object of the experience. In this present study, the object of the experience is the professionalism of financial planners which will be experienced in a qualitatively limited number of ways by the research groups.

In phenomenology, the essence is an internal, conceptual, structure of a phenomenon, whereas with phenomenography the essence is the actual, empirical, variation of conceptions of the phenomenon (Uljens 1996). Phenomenographic essence of a phenomenon is therefore the total variation of conceptions represented by the categories of description and their underlying structure (Uljens 1996). Marton (1981) also suggests that the notion of "essence" is central to phenomenology as the common, intersubjective meaning of the aspect of reality under investigation. In this sense, "essence" refers to a single core meaning. With phenomenography, aspects of reality are experienced not as one core meaning, but rather as a relatively limited number of qualitatively different ways of experiencing (Marton 1981). This is captured by Marton and Booth (1997, p. 116):

> *Philosophers engage in investigating their own experience. Phenomenographers ... adopt an empirical orientation: they study the experience of others.*

Larsson and Holmström (2007), who argued that phenomenography had been misunderstood when applied to studies on anaesthesiologists' work, defined

---

2   Edmund Gustav Albrecht Husserl was a German philosopher and mathematician who is deemed the founder of phenomenology.

phenomenology as the pre-reflective meaning of work experiences, thereby giving a better understanding of what it is to be an anaesthesiologist. In contrast, the authors contend that with phenomenography we study how anaesthesiologists, on a more cognitive level, make sense of their work. Applied to this current study, phenomenology would provide us with a better understanding of what it is to be a professional financial planner and phenomenography would provide us with how CFP® professionals make sense of their work in relation to the professionalism of financial planners (or how they experience this phenomenon). What it is to be a professional financial planner and how this phenomenon is experienced are two different things. This present study is interested in the latter.

In phenomenography, the different categories described in a categorisation are treated as the final description and not part of the whole or essential description of the phenomenon (Sjöström and Dahlgren 2002). The next section will consider conceptions and research positing a structure of awareness or consciousness which do not carry the same meaning as in other fields (Marton and Booth 1997).

4.3.3 CONCEPTIONS AND STRUCTURE OF AWARENESS

Phenomenography is based on the epistemological foundation that people conceive or think of various events or phenomena around them in different ways. This is encapsulated in the following:

> *in order to make sense of how people handle problems, situations, the world, we have to understand the way in which they experience the problems, the situations, the world that they are handling or in relation to which they are acting. Accordingly, a capability for acting in a certain way reflects a capability experiencing something in a certain way (Marton and Booth 1997, p. 111).*

The basic unit of description in phenomenographic research is called a *conception*. Conceptions have has been called various names, such as "ways of conceptualising", "ways of experiencing", "ways of seeing", "ways of apprehending" and "ways of understanding" (Marton and Pong 2005).

Marton and Booth (1997) have put forward a view that a way of experiencing something comprises a "what" aspect and a "how" aspect which is related to how a person constructs awareness. This was explained by Marton (1988) in terms of gestalt theory. Gestalt theory says that when we experience or see something, we discern a whole figure distinct from its surrounding. According to Wagner-Moore (2004) the person's actual experience is not determined by the raw pieces of data but by the gestalt (the whole).

> *The way in which multiple data are shaped is based on the individual's needs, appetites, and impulses (Wagner-Moore 2004, p. 181).*

This whole figure (or gestalt) has structure composed of various items or aspects which relate to each other. Marton (1988) said that awareness also has structure as defined by a theme. This theme is conceived in a certain way by the subject as a result of how it is "delimited from, and related to a context and in the way its component parts are delimited from, and related to each other and the whole" (Marton 1988, p. 10). An experience has two objects – the obvious direct object being the content of the experience (for example,

This is the *act* of the *experience* which comprises two aspects:

Experience: professionalism of financial planners

HOW

This is the *act* of the *experience* which comprises two aspects:

WHAT

This is the *direct object* of the *experience*; i.e. a conception of the professionalism of financial planners

Act

The way in which the act of experiencing the professionalism of financial planners is carried out. For example a financial planner might comply with the relevant law and follow the code of ethics and rules of professional conduct incumbent upon being a CFP® professional.

Indirect object

This is the intention behind the act. For example the intent of a financial planner might be to ensure that he/she is complying with the law or to protect the professional association from loss of reputation.

Figure 4.2   The "how" and "what" aspects of the experience of the professionalism of financial planners

Source: Adapted from Marton and Booth (1997, p. 85).

a conception of the professionalism of financial planners) and this is referred to as the "what" of the experience. But there is another indirect object of the experience which refers to the quality of the act of the experience or what the act of the experience is aimed at (Marton and Booth 1997). The "how" aspect of how a phenomenon is experienced can itself be broken down into "what" and "how" aspects. The "what" aspect is the indirect object, and is the intention behind the act. For example the intent of a financial planner might be to ensure that he/she is complying with the law or to protect the professional association from loss of reputation. The "how" aspect is the way in which the act of experiencing the professionalism of financial planners is carried out. For example a financial planner might comply with the relevant law and follow the code of ethics and rules of professional conduct incumbent upon being a CFP® professional. The "what" and "how" aspects of professionalism of financial planners are illustrated in Figure 4.2.

Not only does a conception have "what" and "how" aspects, a conception also has two dialectically intertwined aspects: a *referential* aspect which is the meaning as defined by a subject; and a *structural* aspect which is the combination of features that are discerned by a subject (Marton and Pong 2005). Marton and Booth (1997, p. 87) illustrate this distinction in the following:

> *to experience something in a particular way, not only do we have to discern it from its context, as a deer in the woods, but we also have to discern its parts, the way they relate to each other,*

and the way they relate to the whole. Therefore, on seeing the deer in the woods, in seeing its contours we also see parts of its body, its head, its antlers, its forequarters, and so on, and their relationships in terms of stance. The structural aspect of a way of experiencing something is thus twofold: discernment of the whole from the context on the one hand and discernment of the parts and their relationships within the whole on the other. Moreover, intimately intertwined with the structural aspect of the experience is the referential aspect, the meaning. In seeing the parts and the whole of the deer and the relationships between them we even see its stance – relaxed and unaware of our presence or alert to some sound unheard by us – and we thus discern further degrees of meaning.

Experiencing something in a certain way therefore has a *structural* and *referential* aspect. The *structural* and *referential* aspects apply to both *what* is experienced and *how* it is experienced as illustrated in Figure 4.3. In the content of this present study, the structural aspect of the professionalism of financial planners is twofold: discernment of the whole (that is, professionalism of financial planners) from the context (that is, the profession of financial planning or the practice of financial planning) and discernment of the parts (for instance, education, experience and ethical requirements) and their relationships within the whole (Marton and Booth 1997). The structural aspect cannot be experienced in isolation of the referential aspect or the meaning of the experience. The structural aspect of what is experienced is the direct object of the experience which is the professionalism of financial planners. The referential aspect of how the direct object is experienced is the indirect object of the experience, which in the present study might be that a financial planner ensures that he/she is complying with the law or to protect the professional association from loss of reputation.

The relationship between the different aspects of concepts as they relate to the phenomenon of the *professionalism of financial planners* is illustrated in Figure 4.3 and is adapted from Marton and Booth (1997, p. 91). Experience, awareness or conceptions

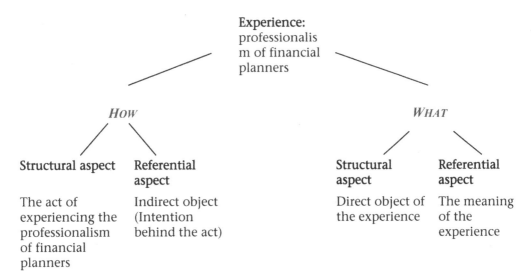

Figure 4.3   Aspects of the experience professionalism of financial planners
Source: Adapted from Marton and Booth (1997, pp. 88 and 91).

have both a "what" and "how" aspect. There is also a "structural" aspect and "referential" aspect of an experience. The "structural" aspect relates to the context of the experience which is the direct object of the experience – the professionalism of financial planners. The direct object has both an internal and external horizon. The actual act of experiencing the phenomenon of *professionalism* is the "how" aspect.

Marton and Booth (1997) also contend that the structural aspect can be described in terms of an external and internal horizon. The internal horizon consists of the aspects of the phenomenon which form a theme of awareness, the relationships between these aspects and between the aspects and the phenomenon as a whole; whereas the external horizon consists of all aspects that are part of awareness but is not part of the main theme of the awareness of the phenomenon. In other words the external horizon forms the context in which a theme of awareness sits. This is illustrated by a continuation of the deer in the forest example used by Marton and Booth (1997, p. 87):

> *the external horizon of coming on the deer in the woods extends from the immediate boundary of the experience – the dark forest against which the deer is discerned – through all other contexts in which related occurrences have been experienced (e.g. walks in the forest, deer in the zoo, nursery tales, reports of hunting incidents, etc.). The internal horizon comprises the deer itself, its parts, its stance, its structural presence.*

Marton and Booth (1997) use the distinction posited by Gurwitsch (1964) between the object of focal awareness called the *theme*, and those objects related to and embedded in the theme called the *thematic field*. The thematic field(s) and the margin belong to the external horizon. The thematic theme and margin are indefinite in space and time.

Svensson and Theman (1983) contend that there are two sides to a conception – what the conception is and what the conception is about. What the conception is about is the direct object of the experience. There is no general relationship between these two sides as can be illustrated by differences between individuals in their conceptions of the same part of the surrounding world (Svensson and Theman 1983). Svensson and Theman (1983) explain that they see a parallel between conceptualisation and describing conceptions. In describing conceptions, the researcher is conceptualising a conception of another person and, given the constructive nature of this process, cannot result in an exact reproduction.

The literature reveals two frameworks that have been used by phenomenographers to analyse conceptions (Harris 2011a). The first framework distinguishes between the "what" and "how" aspects which are broken down to the "act" itself, the "direct object" of the experience and the "indirect object" of the experience. The second framework distinguishes between structural and referential aspects of the experience which are further broken down into the internal and external horizons (Harris 2011a). Researchers such as Marton and Booth (1997) who have used the phenomenographic approach have variously used either framework or the two frameworks as one, as they are not mutually exclusive. An analysis of studies using phenomenography reveals differences in how these terms are defined and how they are used (Harris 2011a).

For the purpose of this proposed study, the "what" aspect of an experience is the direct object of experiencing the professionalism of financial planners; the "how" aspect is the act of experiencing the phenomenon as well as an indirect object. The "structural" aspect comprises an "internal horizon" which consists of the aspects of the phenomenon which forms a theme of awareness, the relationships between these aspects and between the aspects and the phenomenon as a whole; and the "external horizon" which consists of all aspects that are part of awareness. The "referential" aspect is the intrinsic meaning attributed to the professionalism of financial planners. Therefore the internal horizon of the structural aspect of how professionalism is experienced is the way in which the act of experiencing the professionalism of financial planners is carried out. For example a CFP® professional might follow all the rules and requirements to attain certification against the CFP® mark. The internal horizon of the structural aspect of what is experienced about the professionalism of financial planners is the intention behind the act. For example, for the CFP® professional, the intent might be to ensure that he/she is doing their job correctly or to protect the professional body from loss of reputation.

4.3.4 CATEGORIES OF DESCRIPTION AND VARIATION THEORY

The object of phenomenography is to capture the variation in the ways of experiencing phenomena (Marton and Booth 1997). This is important because phenomenography is interested in variation captured in qualitatively distinct categories and in this sense it doesn't matter whether this variation is within individuals or between individuals. Marton and Booth (1997, p. 124) explain this as:

> *a description of a way of experiencing might apply in some sense across a group, or ... might apply to some aspect of an individual ... the extent that the group represents the variation of individuals in a wider population ... the categories of description can also be said to apply to that wider population. Variation is the key and that variation can result from one person's way of experiencing a phenomenon or it could be found collectively across a group.*

The results of a phenomenographic inquiry are the categories of description which correspond to the different understandings and relationships that can be established between them (Marton and Booth 1997). Categories of description describe the different ways the phenomenon can be understood at a collective level. They are the researcher's abstractions of the different ways of understanding, which have been identified and are often based on ways of understanding expressed by more than one participant (Larsson and Holmström 2007). Therefore an individual category of description represents one way of experiencing the phenomenon (Cope 2004). "The differences between categories are distinct ones with regard to the possible ways the phenomenon can be experienced" (Cope 2004, p. 6). Phenomenographic research aims to investigate the qualitatively different ways in which people understand the aspects of the world around them and these different ways are represented in the form of categories of description (Marton and Pong 2005). The categories of description represent the qualitatively different ways of experiencing a phenomenon which form a hierarchy of complexity of experience (Marton and Booth 1997). Categories of description are usually placed in a hierarchy, and it is argued that learning occurs when a person becomes aware of a phenomenon in a different way (Tan 2009). In other words, when there is variation in the experience.

Categories of description are not individual or attributed to individuals, but refer to the collective level (Marton and Booth 1997). The ways of experiencing something and the categories of description are inextricably intertwined, so "the description is never the whole of what it describes, just as a way of experiencing is never more than part

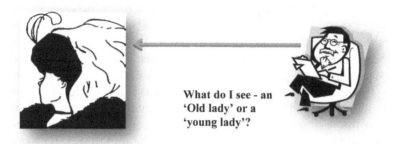

Figure 4.4 "Old lady" and "young lady"
Source: Available at: http://www.askix.com/avav/zoi_wife_and_mother_in_law.htm [accessed 19 November 2010].

of the phenomenon experienced" (Marton and Booth 1997, p. 128). In the structural component of each category, the awareness structure is usually delimited in terms of internal and external horizons where the internal horizon represents the focus of the participants' awareness, while the external horizon represents essentially the perceptual boundary associated with participants' ways of seeing (Bruce et al. 2004).

According to Marton (1988), categories of description share the following four primary characteristics:

- *they are relational as they deal with conceptions comprising a relation between the subject and the object;*
- *they are experiential as they are derived from the experience of participants in the study;*
- *they are content-oriented as they are focused on the meaning of the phenomenon under investigation;*
- *they are qualitative or descriptive as they are based on the meaningful description provided by research participants (p. 181).*

Variation theory is based on the concept that people become aware of a phenomenon through the way that it varies from its environment (external horizon) or the way in which its internal parts vary in relation to one another (internal horizon) (Marton and Booth 1997). Utilising knowledge of the variations of a phenomenon in the context of its external and internal environment enables focus on those aspects that build understanding (Suhonen et al. 2008). Variations help in identifying a phenomenon such as with the old lady/young lady phenomenon in Figure 4.4. In phenomenography, variations in the ways in which people are aware of a phenomenon are used to develop *categories of description*.

People experience a phenomenon in different ways. The same object will be seen differently by different people. This phenomenon can be illustrated very readily by observing the picture in Figure 4.4. This picture represents a black and white image composed of shaded sections (in black) and numerous curved lines which highlight sections of white. People who observe this picture see two qualitatively different images – one is of a young lady and the other is that of an old lady. Many people will see both images and can swap between the two images. Yet the subject is one and doesn't have to be changed or amended in order for people to see the two images. Many people can see both images by switching one image to the other. To see each of the images requires the observer to concentrate on different aspects of the image. The aspects that are focussed upon are the internal horizon which contrasts against the other aspects which form the background as the external horizon.

Variation theory signals a shift in the phenomenographic project from its descriptive orientation to more theoretical concerns (Åkerlind 2005a). Pang (2003) describes this shift in terms of "two faces of variation". The first face of variation, depicting the prior orientation of phenomenography, deals with a descriptive variation of experiencing phenomena and the second face of variation represents a shift from methodological concerns to more theoretical concerns investigating the dimensions of variation as experienced by the "experiencer" (Pang 2003). This present study will deal with the first face of variation by focussing on the descriptive variation of the phenomenon of professionalism as experienced by CFP® professionals.

4.3.5 OUTCOME SPACE

The outcome space depicts the different ways of experiencing a phenomenon by the subjects as categorised by description. The outcome space is an interpretation of a phenomenon, through the collective experience of the participant group as gathered through whatever data collection method is used, for example, interview. The outcome space is comprised of the complex of categories of description capturing the different ways of experiencing the phenomenon (Marton and Booth 1997, p. 125). According to Bruce et al. (2004), the outcome space depicts the manner in which the individual ways of experiencing are related to form a whole picture representing all participants interviewed. In this sense, it is an interpretation of the phenomenon from the collective experience of the participants of a particular group. For this current study, these participants are represented by three groups – CFP® professionals from Australia, Hong Kong and the United States.

Part of this complex of categories, and as a further step after identifying the categories of description, is an investigation of the internal relations between the categories (Larsson and Holmström 2007). The logical relationships between the categories then form the outcome space. These relationships are normally hierarchical (Bruce 1997; Marton and Booth 1997) or developmental (Bruce 1997). As a hierarchical relationship it is defined in terms of layers of increasing complexity (Marton and Booth 1997).

4.3.6 THE APPROACH TAKEN IN THIS STUDY

For the purpose of this study, the framework which distinguishes between the "what" and "how" aspects has been applied. The "what" aspect of the experience is the direct object of experiencing the professionalism of financial planners; the "how" aspect is the act of experiencing the phenomenon. The indirect object that is the intention behind the act is not the focus of this study. This present study will adopt terminology used by Cope (2004) and refer to how/what as a framework. When these terms are used and discussed individually they will be referred to as aspects – what aspect and how aspect. This adopts terminology which Harris (2011a) has found to be commonly used within phenomenographic research.

The *how/what* framework (see Figure 4.5) has been applied in this study instead of the *referential/structural* framework because the nature of how the interviews of participants were structured and carried out didn't allow for deeper probing of conceptions. Many of the interviews were held within a limited period of time, such as in the United States during the FPA Annual Conference and in Hong Kong, where there was a variation in the participants' proficiency in English. In Australia, where most of the interviews were held in the participant's workplace, there were generally time constraints due to work commitments. The *referential/structural* framework requires more in-depth interviews to uncover the various layers of understanding. The *how/what* framework does not require the same level of in-depth interview to uncover the deeper layers of understanding as required in the *referential/structural* framework. Given the nature of the study being transnational in scope and with an interest in uncovering the differences in the variations in the ways CFP® professionals experience *professionalism* from Australia, Hong Kong and the United States – the *what/how* framework provided a more appropriate phenomenographic basis for the study.

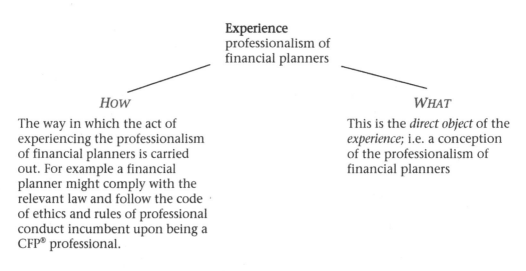

Experience
professionalism of
financial planners

How

The way in which the act of experiencing the professionalism of financial planners is carried out. For example a financial planner might comply with the relevant law and follow the code of ethics and rules of professional conduct incumbent upon being a CFP® professional.

What

This is the *direct object* of the *experience*; i.e. a conception of the professionalism of financial planners

Figure 4.5   Approach taken in this study: The "how" and "what" aspects of the experience of the professionalism of financial planners

Source: Adapted from Marton and Booth (1997, p. 85).

5 *Phenomenographic Analysis*

5.1   What this Chapter is About

The aim of this chapter is to outline the process followed when undertaking phenomenographic analysis and how that process has been applied to the present study. Care has to be taken with phenomenographic analysis to ensure that it is conducted in a way that will capture accurately the conceptions of the research participants.

Phenomenographers take a non-dualist perspective (Bowden 2005) in that there is only one world. Qualitative researchers using other methods take a dualist view such as with individual constructivism or social constructivism where the focus is on an inner or outer world with each being an explanation for the other. With phenomenography, there is only one world, the world which is experienced (Marton and Booth 1997). Phenomenographic studies also differ from other qualitative methods as the focus is on the collective understandings of groups, not individuals (Harris 2011b). Phenomenography has a focus on gathering evidence to illustrate the range of conceptions within a given population involved in the study. In this present study, there is one group – CFP® professionals – but across three countries. The approach chosen in this study is to treat CFP® professionals as three discrete groups because one of the most useful outputs of this study is to identify differences in how the same professional groups from three different countries experience the one phenomenon. Essentially the study comprises three separate phenomenographic studies.

The chapter outlines the research plan, including a discussion on how data was gathered and who provided the data as research participants. The case for interview as the predominant phenomenographic method for gathering data is presented. Undertaking phenomenographic interviews is not a simple process and it is useful to carry out pilot interviews to allow the researcher as interviewer to hone his or her skills. Pilot interviews were conducted in Australia to provide the researcher with an opportunity to reflect on the experience and make any necessary adjustments, and this process is outlined in the chapter. This is followed by a description of how the interviews are analysed to identify the categories of description and outcome space. The importance of bracketing the researcher's own background is discussed, including how this was dealt with in the present study. Ensuring the validity and reliability of phenomenographic results is an important consideration and the chapter explains how these have been addressed in this present study, including the use of member checking.

5.2   Data Collection: Interview

It has been established that there are a limited number of qualitatively different ways of experiencing a phenomenon (Marton 1981). This brings us to a discussion on how data is collected under phenomenography. The unit of phenomenographic research is a way of experiencing a phenomenon (Marton and Booth 1997), which is also known as a conception. The way of experiencing a phenomenon constitutes a relationship between the subject (as the experience) and the experienced (which we know has both a "what" aspect and a "how" aspect). With phenomenography, the researcher is interested in collecting data about the relationship between the subject and the experience.

The dominant method of collecting data within phenomenographic research is the interview (Marton 1986, 1994). However, Marton (1994) points out that there are many different ways a person can express how something is experienced, including group interviews, observations, drawings, written responses and historical documents. Data collection in phenomenographic research aims to capture the utterances of the participants (Richardson 1999). Interview will be the method of collecting data for this current study.

Marton and Booth (1997) contend that the participant group for phenomenographic research should be a small number chosen from a particular population. Given the nature of phenomenography as a qualitative research approach, the number of participants only needs to be sufficiently large enough to gather the qualitatively limited number of ways of experiencing a phenomenon. Collecting data from an exceptionally large group of participants will not add any more understanding about the ways in which particular cohorts experience a phenomenon. Marton (1986) and Marton and Booth (1997) argue that phenomenographic research supports the assumption that there are a limited number of qualitatively different ways that people view a particular phenomenon. Moreover, a single person may not articulate every part of a conception (Marton and Booth 1997).

What then is an ideal number of research participants? Marton (1988) recommends a research group of between 15 and 30 participants to best achieve the aims of phenomenographic enquiry. Experiences from a large number of phenomenographic studies have shown that data from 20 informants is usually enough to discover all the different ways of understanding the phenomenon in question (Larsson and Holmström 2007). In this present study, 15 research participants were interviewed in Australia, 16 in Hong Kong and 17 in the United States. The researcher found that, based on the analysis of the interviews, these numbers were sufficient and that given the nature of the phenomenon being investigated and the homogenous nature of the group, 10–15 participants may have been sufficient to discover the qualitatively limited number of conceptions.

According to Larsson and Holmström (2007) the preferred phenomenographic method of data collection is the open-ended interview. This encourages participants to be open and respond freely and also operates as a check on the researcher who might inadvertently influence the response by steering or leading the participant in a certain way. Lankshear and Knobel (2004) posit that interviews are semi-structured to encourage elaboration of important themes raised during the interview. This is designed to facilitate an open and free-ranging exchange between participant and researcher, to fully explore how participants understand their world. It seems that Larsson and Holmström (2007) and Lankshear and Knobel (2004) are referring to the same attributes of phenomenographic interviews. Open-ended or semi-structured interviews are appropriate given the nature of a phenomenographic enquiry as empirical research, where the researcher as the interviewer is studying the participant's awareness of a phenomenon. A phenomenographic interview therefore should not have too many questions made up in advance, or too many predetermined details (Marton 1994). The point of the interview is to establish the phenomenon as experienced and its different aspects are explored jointly and as fully as possible as a dialogue between the researcher and participant (Marton 1994).

Interviews are generally tape or digitally recorded and then transcribed verbatim. This is a time-consuming and laborious part of the research, but very important as the transcribed interviews form the basis of the categories of description.

The purpose of the interview is not to understand the phenomenon itself, nor is it to test the participant's understanding against the interviewer's beliefs (Bowden 2005), but to immerse oneself in the individual understanding of the "life world" (Ashworth and Lucas 1998) of the interview participant. The aim is to understand the phenomenon as the participant understands it. The purpose of a phenomenographic interview is to find out the different ways that a group sees a particular phenomenon (Bowden 2005). This requires a certain amount of discipline from the interviewer so as not to introduce any new content when making the interviewee feel comfortable at the beginning of the interview (Bowden 2005).

Phenomenographic interviews attempt to elicit underlying meanings and intentional attitudes towards the phenomenon under investigation (Åkerlind 2005b), in this present study – the professionalism of financial planners. There is a difference between "what" questions and "why" questions. In this present study an example of a "what" question might be "what did you do to act in a professional way"? An example of a "why" question would be as a follow-up to the "what" question in the previous example – "why did you do it that way"? This distinction between "what" and "why" questions can counter the criticism that phenomenographic interviews do not elicit what actually happens in practice (Åkerlind 2005b). This criticism is valid if only "what" questions are asked, but the real purpose of phenomenographic interviews is to elicit awareness or understandings of a phenomenon. This notion is captured by Åkerlind (2005b, p. 66):

> *What is important in a phenomenographic interview is not the examples of practice per se, but the way the interviewee thinks about those examples.*

Doing a phenomenographic interview is not easy and requires some practice to acquire the necessary skills. Conducting mock or pilot interviews is essential and they should be used as a basis of analysing the researcher's interview technique (Åkerlind 2005b). Learning how to ask follow-up questions after the participant responds to the primary question in order to elicit deeper meaning is very important (Åkerlind 2005b).

As empirical research, phenomenography has as its interest the experience of reality of the subjects, not the researcher, and this influences the nature of how the interview is conducted. The interview has to be carried out as a dialogue to facilitate the thematisation of aspects of the subject's experience and, hence, these understandings are jointly constituted by interviewer and interviewee (Marton 1994).

Theman (1979) cautions about the importance of applying appropriate protocols in conducting interviews. She has raised several issues, such as how respondents may give a different report of their experience of phenomenon in a contrived interview situation than they would in a more realistic setting. It is important that the researcher (interviewer) is aware of this and tries to overcome it. Another area of concern is the tendency to miss utterances through anticipating the utterance only to be surprised to find that transcript of the interview does not record any such utterance. Respondents may become dependent upon the interviewer during the interview, particularly during times where they may feel uncertain or insecure. This can occur during the early part of the interview. The interviewer has to be mindful not to provide too much support to the respondent so that the utterances will not reflect those of the respondent but what the respondent thinks the interviewer wants to hear. Another problem is one of ignorance in the sense that the respondent utters that he or she does not know any more. The interviewer has to be able to tease this out somewhat to establish whether the respondent can't in fact add anything more, or if they are simply tired or not confident in responding. Theman (1979) also stresses the importance of establishing a social context for the interview. Interviews cannot run to a formula as no two interviews situations will be identical. The interviewer has to demonstrate sincerity around a desire to know the subject's conception of the phenomenon in question. The interviewer also has to allow for a respondent's irrelevant feelings or inappropriate responses (Theman 1979).

Data collection in phenomenographic studies must be taken with great care. This is because the researcher's own relation to the phenomenon and to the subjects must be controlled so as not to distort the results (Bowden 2005). The object of a phenomenographic study is the relation between the subjects and the phenomenon, not the phenomenon itself (Marton and Booth 1997); nor is it the relationship between the researcher and the subjects, or the researcher and the phenomenon (see Figure 5.1).

The most important control that the researcher should implement during the interview process is to always use an identical opening scenario within any one phenomenographic study (Bowden 2005). The researcher should avoid introducing any new information during the interview or getting into a conversation with the subject.

The idea in phenomenographic interviewing is to limit the inputs by the researcher to planned sequences that are primarily designed to introduce the phenomenon to the interviewee whose relation to it is being investigated (Bowden 2005, p. 14).

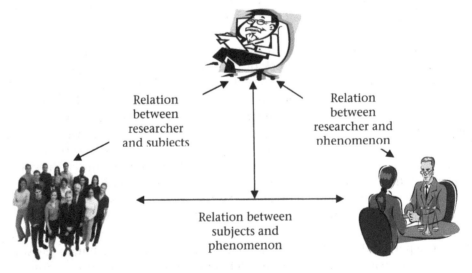

Figure 5.1   Relation between subjects and phenomenon

Table 5.1 Examples of interview participant's responses to researcher's questions

Australia	Can you tell me about an occasion in your role when you acted professionally? Like a little story about a particular thing that happened or you did, and you thought "I was really being professional".
	I would like to think we always act professionally – I think it depends on where you are. We have – our main mantra here is client first. So we always thinking about whatever we do for product development or discussions or communications. And on that front – an example of that in terms of how we put investments together there have been periods of time over the last little bit where it has been pretty tough with investment markets. I think people lost a lot of money and part of that was around some poor investment decisions – but also part not being – certainly some advisors weren't strong enough to make some pretty hard calls. An example when I think it really hit home that we were acting with the clients' interest and very professionally was that we actually took quite a bit of money off the table. Now that meant that we didn't get a fee [Interview M1:02].
Hong Kong	The first question, can you tell me about an occasion when you acted professionally. I know you act professionally all the time, but just a little story about something in your work that you think – "yeah that demonstrates me being professional".
	I think in some client conversations first I need to gather some client data and show, show, show them I have the qualification and then I gather some information I need to tell her what his, what his responsibility or some rights or obligations and after I get some information – when I do some analyse and I should be confidential and privacy. And other, when I hold the meeting for the solution presentation, maybe I need to perform, first I need to perform some analyse for her, for him and then show him what my solution, why my solution perform to him and tell her the evidence or some findings about her situation and after conversation or the meetings I need to perform some after sales service and I need to perform some review – half year or ever year. I think the professionalism is that [Interview HK6:06].
United States	Can you tell me about an occasion when you acted professionally? So I know you act professionally all the time, but just a little story or something you did with a client or colleague or which would demonstrate your professionalism.
	I was working with a female client and she owned a business – some gentlemen wanted to buy a piece of the business and I thought the valuation was very low and I went to her and said – the reason why they want to do this is because they wanted a new revenue stream at minimum capital – and you valued the business at this and so if they want this piece they should be paying you considerably more than they offered. I got no compensation for it but the fact that she was an investment client of mine and a business owner and she was getting very bad advice with respect to what her business was worth. Ultimately when she presented my findings to these investors they concurred and significantly increased the offer for a smaller percentage of her business [Interview US15:02].

In this present phenomenographic study, the opening interview question used for all interviewees in each of the three studies in Australia, Hong Kong and the United States was:

Tell me about an occasion when you acted professionally.

This opening question was designed to be an open-ended question providing scope for the interviewees to respond with an example of something they did which they considered professional. However in most cases when I asked this opening question I added the following or similar words:

> *I know you act professionally all the time, but what I am looking for is a little story or scenario which would illustrate your professionalism.*

I felt obliged to add these words as it occurred to me that the question might suggest an inference by the interviewee that I wasn't convinced they acted professionally. Table 5.1, on the previous page, provides an example of how interviewees responded to this question from each of the three countries.

5.3   Pilot Interviews

Undertaking phenomenographic interviews is a skill which requires some practice. In this present study, the researcher interviewed CFP® professionals who in some cases were known to the researcher. In this situation, the temptation was to make comments or sometimes debate things said by the interviewee. This is what occurred during the pilot interviews which were held in Australia. It was also important to undertake pilot interviews in Australia before interviewing CFP® professionals in the United States and Hong Kong. It was relatively easy to source additional research participants in Australia, but because of the cost, time and logistics, the interviews conducted in the United States and Hong Kong had to be of sufficient quality to enable analysis and contribute to this research study.

It is also important to test whether the planned inputs through the questions actually elicit comment on the intended topic (Bowden 2005), in this study being the professionalism of financial planners.

> *Pilot interviews are always essential to ensure that the topic the interviewees are encouraged by the planned inputs to discuss is the topic that is the subject of the research (Bowden 2005, p. 19).*

Pilot interviews are important for allowing a researcher to hone their (phenomenographic) interview skill. Novice interviewers often find themselves making comment and sometimes discussing or debating something said by the interviewee (Bowden 2005). This was the experience of the researcher in this present study with the researcher as interviewer providing commentary and offering views on aspects of the questions as asked.

In this present study it was decided to conduct pilot interviews in Australia. Four pilot interviews were conducted and pilot interview questions were constructed, as shown in Table 5.2 opposite.

At this stage of the research project, it was envisaged by the researcher that interview questions would be constructed to reflect the regulatory and practice environment of the country where CFP® professionals were being interviewed. The pilot interview questions used in Australia show questions 4, 5 and 7 being constructed in the context of the Australian regulatory and practice environment. The acronym "AFSL" stands for "Australian Financial Services Licensee" and is the regulatory term to describe the

Table 5.2   Pilot interview questions

Pilot Interview Questions
1. What does it mean to you to be a professional CFP® professional?
2. What does it mean to be an unprofessional CFP® professional?
3. How do you know you are professional?
4. How does your AFSL or clients know you are professionals?
5. Do you think there is higher standard of professionalism required of a CFP® professional than simply someone who has RG 146?
6. Is professionalism important for financial planners?
7. What has the greatest influence on your professionalism – your own understanding of what it is to be professional; your licensee; ASIC compliance; consumer expectations?

individual who holds the licence issued by the regulator. The Corporations Act 2001 requires people who run a business providing financial services to hold an AFS licence.

As the object of a phenomenographic study is the relationship between the interviewee and the phenomenon, it is important the transcripts reflect this relationship at the time of the interview (Bowden 2005). It is therefore important to limit the inputs by the interviewer and to ensure that the same issues or questions are raised in each interview (Bowden 2005). This was not the case during the pilot interviews of this present study. The interviewer engaged in a two-way dialogue with the interviewees, which was different during each interview. This experience was important in honing how the research interviews that were later carried out as collecting the data for analysis were to be conducted.

On reviewing the digital interview recordings of the pilot interviews, it was determined that the interview questions to be used in the study for CFP® professionals in each of the three countries should be the same. This would allow for a common base of studying the phenomenon and differences in the regulatory and practice environment would emerge from the data rather than being imposed on the data as predetermined or structured questions.

5.4   Interview Participants

Phenomenographic research investigates the limited number of qualitatively different ways a particular group experiences a phenomenon. The scope of the current research study has defined *financial planner* as those individuals who have been certified against the CERTIFIED FINANCIAL PLANNER/CFP® marks (referred to as CFP® professionals). The CFP® mark is an international mark owned outside the United States by the Financial Planning Standards Board (FPSB). FPSB has 24 affiliate member organisations who certify individuals in their country or territory who demonstrate competence against the four Es – education, examination, experience and ethics. The CFP® mark and the CFP® certification process were explained in detail in Chapter 2 as background to this research.

Given the international nature of the CFP® mark, participants were chosen from two FPSB affiliate member organisations – Australia and Hong Kong – and the FPA (USA) as members certified by the CFP Board of Standards in the United States. When phenomenography is used as a research approach, the aim is to understand collectively the qualitatively different ways of experiencing a phenomenon, not individual ways of experiencing a phenomenon. In this present study, participants from the three countries were chosen as this will hold more interest and relevance to each of these member organisations, FPSB and the CFP Board of Standards. The results of the analysis will present an outcome space for each of the three countries which will facilitate a discussion on the similarities and differences in how *professionalism* is experienced.

The selection of participants represents a convenience sample where participants have been sourced from affiliate member organisations of FPSB – Australia and Hong Kong – and the FPA in the United States as a body whose members hold CFP® certification with the CFP Board of Standards in the United States. Financial planners have been chosen from each of the three countries on the basis that they have completed the respective CFP® certification programme and have met the requirements for the CFP® credential within the past five years. This will ensure that financial planner participants have not been "grandfathered" the CFP® credential.[1] Cope (2004) argues that where convenience samples are used, the characteristics of the participants should be stated clearly. This is done not only for transparency purposes but also to provide background for other studies applying the results in a different context.

5.4.1   INTERVIEW PARTICIPANTS: AUSTRALIA

In Australia, interview participants were sourced from the Financial Planning Association of Australia's website section *"Find a Planner"*. This provided the researcher with contact details. The researcher then made initial contact by telephone or by email. The majority of CFP® professionals contacted were willing interview participants. Appointments were made, which in most cases were in the office of the interview participant. Participants were provided with a "Participant Information Sheet" and a "Consent Form". Agreement was reached to allow an hour for the interview. Of the 15 participant interviews, 8 were from Melbourne (3 female, 5 male); 6 from Sydney (3 female and 3 male); and 1 male participant from Queensland. The average number of years of experience of the group was 10.4.

5.4.2   INTERVIEW PARTICIPANTS: HONG KONG

Interview participants in Hong Kong were sourced by the Institute of Financial Planners of Hong Kong (IFPHK). The IFPHK sourced participants who had the CFP® designation had a reasonable command of English and a range of experience levels. Meetings were arranged either in the IFPHK office or in the office of the interview participant. Of the 16 participant interviews, 2 were female and the average number of years of experience of the group was 5.5. All interviews were conducted during the second half of 2011.

---

1   A grandfather clause is a situation in which an old rule continues to apply to some existing situations, while a new rule will apply to all future situations. As applied to CFP certification, non-grandfathered CFP professionals will have completed all the prescribed education, examination, experience and ethical requirements.

5.4.3   INTERVIEW PARTICIPANTS: UNITED STATES

The interviews for the US participants were conducted during the FPA's 2011 Annual Conference in San Diego. Interview participants were sourced by the FPA, which introduced the researcher via email contact with willing participants. The FPA also arranged for a meeting room in a hotel adjoining the convention centre in San Diego. Of the 18 interviews conducted over three days, only eight participants arrived at the scheduled time. In most cases this was due to communication problems and difficulty in contacting the researcher to cancel or arrange an alternative time. In order to ensure a minimum of 15 CFP® professionals were interviewed, the researcher had to mingle with the conference participants and source volunteers. Ten additional participants were sourced in this way, although one of these could not be included in the analysis as the person was a Japanese CFP® professional, not an American CFP® professional. Of the 17 participant interviews, 8 were female and the average number of years of experience of the group was 13.

5.5   How the Interviews were Conducted

As explained in the previous section, the selection of interview participants represents a convenience sample. The common characteristic of all research participants across all three countries was that they were CFP® professionals having met the relevant criteria for certification in their particular country. In Australia, the certifying body is the Financial Planning Association of Australia; in Hong Kong, the Institute of Financial Planners of Hong Kong; and in the United States, the CFP Board of Standards. The controlling body for Australia and Hong Kong is the Financial Planning Standards Board (see Chapter 4).

As a counter to the criticism that interviewees may embellish their description of what they do, Åkerlind (2005b) contends that what is important with phenomenographic interviews is not the examples of practice, but the way the interviewee thinks about the examples. Therefore it is not whether interview participants sanitised, exaggerated or embellished their experience of professionalism, but rather how they thought about this experience.

5.5.1   INTERVIEWS: AUSTRALIA

The interviews for each country were conducted under different conditions. The majority of CFP® professionals contacted were willing interview participants. Appointments were made which in most cases were in the office of the interview participant. Although for most interviews, agreement was reached to allow an hour for the interview, some of the participants were obviously under time constraints and in some cases interruptions occurred during the interview. This wasn't seen by the researcher as affecting the quality of the interview and sufficient material was gathered to facilitate an analysis applying the "what"/"how" framework. The 15 interviews averaged 31 minutes in length and included over 31,000 words of transcript collected as data.

Table 5.3   Profile of interview participants

Australia			Hong Kong			United States		
Interview participant	Male/female	Years' experience as CFP®	Interview participant	Male/female	Years' experience as CFP®	Interview participant	Male/female	Years' experience as CFP®
A1	M	14	HK1	M	6	US1	M	3
A2	F	2	HK2	M	8	US2	M	7
A3	F	10	HK3	F	10	US3	F	6
A4	M	11	HK4	M	2.5	US4	F	6
A5	F	8	HK5	M	11	US5	F	5
A6	M	20	HK6	M	5	US6	M	13
A7	M	10	HK7	M	8	US7	Not included*	
A8	M	19	HK8	M	1	US8	M	15
A9	F	10	HK9	M	6	US9	F	21
A10	F	9	HK10	M	4	US10	M	20
A11	M	12	HK11	M	11	US11	F	30
A12	M	14	HK12	M	2	US12	M	1
A13	F	1	HK13	M	6	US13	F	17
A14	M	8	HK14	M	4	US14	M	1.5
A15	M	8	HK15	M	2	US15	M	15
			HK16	F	2	US16	M	21
						US17	F	22
						US18	M	17

Note: * US7 was later assessed as being a Japanese CFP® professional and not included in the study.

5.5.2   INTERVIEWS: HONG KONG

In Hong Kong, interviews were either held in the office of the Institute of Financial Planners of Hong Kong or in the office of the interview participant. All interview participants spoke English, although there was some variation in the degree of fluency in English. Some interviews required some restatement and paraphrasing by the researcher. It was agreed between the researcher and interviewer to allow an hour for the interview. In general the Hong Kong participants were comfortable in discussing their conceptions of professionalism. The 16 interviews averaged 26 minutes in length and included over 28,000 words of transcript collected as data.

5.5.3   INTERVIEWS: UNITED STATES

The interviews for the United States participants were conducted during the FPA's 2011 Annual Conference in San Diego. Eight interviews were scheduled in a meeting room and the remainder were conducted outside the session break-out rooms or in the conference lunch room. This provided a broad mix of interview participants ranging from leaders in the profession to average CFP® professionals plying their profession in the United States. The 17 interviews averaged 21 minutes in length and included over 27,000 words of transcript collected as data.

The researcher asked each participant all of the six structured questions (see Table 5.4). This would ensure the discussion of the comparison of the conceptions was based

Table 5.4   Interview questions

Interview questions	Purpose of question
1. Tell me about an occasion when you acted professionally?	This question is designed to encourage the participant to reflect on their professional behaviour. The question provided an opening for the researcher to seek clarification or further information.
2. Why do you think you were acting professionally?	The question is designed as natural follow-up to the first question. Many participants responded to this question without the need for it to be asked.
3. What specific behaviours or actions do you exhibit or undertake to ensure you are professional?	This question probes deeper than the first two questions to seek examples of behaviours and actions which demonstrate professionalism.
4. What specific behaviours or actions have you observed in CFP® professionals who are unprofessional?	This question is aimed at seeking further clarification of professional behaviour by taking the flipside to question 3.
5. What factors or influences determine the professionalism of a CFP® professional?	This question is designed to probe influences the professional behaviour of the participant. The question is designed to seek an opening to explore where a sense of professionalism comes from.
6. What does it mean to you to be a professional CFP® professional?	This final question is designed to be a capstone question. It is asked to provide interview participants with the opportunity to reflect on what they have said and to add further insights into their experience of the phenomenon.

on reliable data. This approach limited the number of unstructured questions which are usually used in phenomenographic interviews to provide deeper understanding of the awareness of a phenomenon. However the researcher does not believe this has detracted from the quality of the data collected and resultant analysis. Interview participants generally provided sufficient depth of understanding in response to the structured questions, requiring little need for clarification or additional insight.

5.6   Bracketing the Researcher's Background

In phenomenographic studies, researchers focus on the experiences of other people whilst bracketing preconceptions based upon their own experiences of the field in question (Marton 1994; Uljens 1996; Marton and Booth 1997). Marton (1994) contends that when interviews have been transcribed verbatim, the researcher is supposed to bracket preconceived ideas instead of judging to what extent the responses reflect an understanding of the phenomenon in question which is similar to their own. The researcher's task is to focus on similarities and differences between the ways in which the phenomenon appears to the participants, to look for variation in the way participants experience the phenomenon.

> *Phenomenographers do not claim to study 'what is there' in the world (reality) but they do claim to study 'what is there' in people's conceptions of the world ... this retains at the second level ... view of the pristine nature of perception and the ability of the researcher to 'bracket' his or her own socially and historically contaminated conceptual apparatus (Webb 1997).*

Bracketing is important in applying a second-order perspective required of phenomenography (Harris 2011b).

Uljens (1996) stresses that phenomenological bracketing as used in phenomenography sometimes is taken to mean that the researcher must approach both the interview and the empirical data to be analysed very open-mindedly, without any kind of preconceived ideas of the problem at hand. Uljens (1996) argues that it is impossible to achieve total bracketing in any empirical science because of the guiding role of prior theory in empirical research and the knowledge interest of the researcher of a specific study. He doesn't see this as a problem as researchers have the ability to suspend their own knowledge and understanding in order to understand someone else's.

An important aspect of phenomenographic research is that the researcher, in identifying the phenomenon to be investigated and why it is to be investigated, needs to be cognisant that the research participant's meaning of the phenomenon may vary significantly from the researcher's meaning of the phenomenon (Ashworth and Lucas 1998). This process is referred to in phenomenology as "bracketing". Uljens (1996) points out an important part of the process of undertaking phenomenographic research in that the researcher carries out a phenomenological reduction by delimiting his or her own understanding of the phenomenon. My own role in this field of inquiry also has to be accounted for. This research study has been influenced by my former role as a senior education manager for the Financial Planning Association of Australia and my current role as an associate professor teaching in the discipline of financial planning. This has been addressed in the research by applying Cope's (2004) validity strategies of providing a full and open account of a phenomenographic research study (see Table 5.6 on page 85).

It has been acknowledged that the object of a study is never completely separated from the researcher (Bowden 2005). It is impossible to assert that the research outcomes are completely independent of the researcher. Bowden (2005) says they are relational. However the procedures that are applied with phenomenographic analysis are designed to maximise the research subject's influence on research outcomes and to minimise the researcher's influence (Bowden 2005).

5.7   Data Analysis

Phenomenography is a research method designed to discover and describe the qualitatively different ways in which phenomena are experienced, conceptualised or understood. In a study carried out by Carlsson et al. (2001) the researchers collected all the statements concerning understanding from each interview and compared statements between and within interviews. This approach to data analysis as used in phenomenography is a form of iterative content analysis which is applied in many qualitative inquiries (Cope 2004) and is comparative involving the continual sorting and resorting of data and comparisons between data as categories of description emerge, as well as the relationships which emerge between the categories themselves (Åkerlind 2005a).

Larsson and Holmström (2007) contend that phenomenographic analysis can be carried out in different ways, but the structural and referential aspects of the phenomenon are essential. That is, when the research participants talk about a phenomenon in response to the researcher's questions, what do they talk about and how do they talk about it?

The emphasis is on how things appear to people in their world and the way in which people explain to themselves and others what goes on around them and how these explanations change (Barnard et al. 1999, p. 214).

Marton and Pong (2005) in their study[2] describe a two-stage process of data analysis. The first stage focused on identifying and describing the conceptions in terms of their overall meanings – the referential aspect; and the second stage focused on identifying the structural aspect of the ways of experiencing from the participants. The units, which were denoted by the various overall meanings, were then studied in detail to identify within each unit the elements of the phenomenon that were focused upon, and to develop a description of each conception's structural aspect. This was done by paying attention to the clear variations that the student brought in as they focused on a particular element (Marton and Pong 2005).

Marton (1994) explains that after the relevant quotes have been grouped, the focus should then shift the relationship between the groups. This is the process followed to develop the set of categories of description in a way which can identify the variation in how certain phenomena are understood. Logical hierarchical relationships will be

---

2   Forty Canadian high school students, aged between 16 and 19, were individually interviewed about two economic themes: price and trade. Marton and Pong refer to a "conception" as the basic unit of description in phenomenographic research, which they note has been called various names, such as "ways of conceptualising", "ways of experiencing", "ways of seeing", "ways of apprehending", "ways of understanding".

identified in the categories of description and these will form the outcome space (Marton 1994). Uljens (1996) stresses the importance of the way the researcher analyses the empirical data by comparing, evaluating and summarising, focussing on a reasonable descriptive variation that reflects the content as well as possible in relation to the research questions presented.

According to Gurwitsch (1964) the total field of consciousness consists of three domains which helps during the analysis stage in determining what is important from the participants' utterances:

> The first domain is the theme that which engrosses the mind of the experiencing subject, or as it is often expressed, which stands in the 'focus of his attention'. Second is the thematic field, defined as the totality of those data, co-present with the theme, which are experienced as materially relevant or pertinent to the theme and form the background or horizon out of which the theme emerges as the center. The third includes data which, though co-present with, have no relevancy to, the theme and comprise in their totality what we propose to call the margin (Gurwitsch 1964, p. 4).

The temporal aspect and the consciousness plays an important role in the assessment phase, where the focus can oscillate so that aspects from the thematic field can be the theme and so on. The historical aspect of the conceptions is represented by the experience. These internal historical conditions are established in the individual's past. It is important to emphasise that Gurwitsch (1964) has a phenomenological perspective and that there are similarities between this and the phenomenographic perspective.

One of the challenges of phenomenographic research is the amount of data collected through the interviews that has to be analysed. It is important to make this data manageable. Svensson and Theman (1983) suggest discarding irrelevant or unhelpful transcript segments to enable focus on those excerpts which do reflect meanings from the larger interview transcript. The need to manage the interview transcripts is obvious and has been handled differently by different researchers, with the most common approach being an emphasis on an iterative process looking at the data from different perspectives and at different times (Trigwell 2000). A reasonable restriction on the number of interviews is also recommended as a data management strategy (Trigwell 2000).

The analysis is an iterative process which requires several readings of the transcripts. Some phenomenographers believe that 5, 10 or even 15 versions of the categories of description are necessary (Bowden 2005). In this present study, given that it involved three phenomenographic studies, albeit on the same object (*professionalism of financial planners*) and the same subjects (*CFP® professionals*) from different countries, five iterations were necessary to settle the categories of description. A well conducted interview should elicit awareness from the interviewee that they themselves were previously unaware (Bowden 2005).

Some phenomenographers (Bowden 2005) argue that there is a temptation in the early part of the analysis to focus on the differences. Researchers can be overwhelmed by the variation and the potential categories. Bowden (2005) says that phenomenographers should be focussed on holistic meanings. Bowden (2005, p. 26) explains this as follows:

> The presence of a highly populated urban centre along with industrial complexes and location on a river or the seaboard might indicate a state capital. A smaller urbanised area, perhaps on

a river that connects to the state capital with some industrial activity around, but significant farming land as well, might indicate a regional centre ... Both kinds of analysis are accurate, but the second provides greater insights ... You can get a sense of the whole from the analysis for holistic meaning.

Sjöström and Dahlgren (2002) recommend basing judgments on three indicators:

1. How often an idea is articulated, referred to as *frequency*.
2. Where statements are positioned; and often the most significant elements are found in the introductory parts of an answer, referred to as *position*.
3. Where participants explicitly emphasise that certain aspects are more important than others, referred to as *pregnancy*.

The digital voice recordings were transcribed into Word format. During the process of transcription the researcher concentrated primarily on completing the task. However where conceptions of the phenomenon of the professionalism of financial planners were obvious in the transcript, the researcher used bold text to highlight this for later analysis. The researcher then read all 48 transcripts to ensure that they were complete and that there were no obvious omissions or errors. In order to stay immersed and familiar with the data, the researcher chose not to use software such as NVivo as a tool of analysis.

The next step involved a slower and more detailed reading of the transcripts and highlighting with a coloured highlighter pen passages of text which potentially contain data relating to conceptions. At this point, no attempt was made to distinguish between "what" aspects and "how" aspects. These highlighted passages were all recorded separately in a Word document. This process was repeated to capture any utterances which may have been overlooked in the first reading.

The extracted relevant utterances were then read again and assigned as being either a "what" aspect or a "how" aspect. The "what" aspect related to how CFP® professionals described what *professionalism* means to them. The "how" aspect relates to how CFP® professionals behaved professionally. Table 5.5 provides an example of how research participants' utterances were classified as either "what" or "how" aspects. Interview transcripts were coded by using a code representing the country identifier, interview participant identifier and dialogue sequence in the interview (that is, interview turn where each time the researcher asks a question and each time the interviewee responds being classed as one interview turn and each numbered consecutively). For example [A4:09] means the ninth interview turn from interview participant 4 of Australia.

The quotations were then compared and contrasted to identify commonalities and differences. As variation is the key with phenomenography, the researcher's efforts were on ensuring that conceptions could be individually identified. There was no attempt to quantify the conceptions or instances of variations as conceptions, as ways of understanding are not an individual quality, but rather as *categories of description* they can be attributed to the group as explained by Marton (1981). Once the categories of description are defined and labelled, they remain absolutely reliable and stable even though individual CFP® professionals in this study move from one category to another (Marton 1981).

The outcomes of phenomenographic analysis can be reported as an outcome space with the focus on the key areas of variation which represent the qualitatively limited ways

Table 5.5   Classification of utterances as "what" or "how"

Utterance	Classification as "what" or "how" aspects
… our main mantra here is client first … [A3:02].	This utterance was classified as a "what" aspect because this is how A3 described the meaning of professionalism. "Client mantra" also provided an apt label which represented the collective conception from the group.
I think the number one thing is consistency. You have to be consistent in your dealings – with all stakeholders – whether it's clients or people you work with [A11:06].	This utterance was classified as a "how" aspect because it is describes how the interview participant acts (professionally) and that is by being consistent.
They [clients] will tell how professional you are by measuring the length of the designation – 3, 4, 5 or 6, 7, 8, 9, 10 characters in total, must be more professional than the other one [HK2:22].	This utterance was classified as a "what" aspect because this Hong Kong CFP® professional understands professionalism through the client's eyes as being the number of letters on a business card.
… when I show my card I say I have the CFP® status and I explain what CFP® means [HK15:22].	This utterance was classified as a "how" aspect because this interview participant demonstrates or acts professionally by showing his business card with his CFP® designation and explains to clients what this means.
It's about service – providing a service and the service is helping people make good financial decisions for their families [US18:14].	Professionalism to this US interview participant means "providing service" – "it's all about service". This was classified as a "what" aspect.
So for my way of thinking – what I do to be professional – is how do I help people accumulate assets, how to help them protect those assets, through insurance or what not – and then how do I them distribute that either in the form of a legacy or some sort of tax efficient fashion they can use in retirement [US15:16].	How professionalism is experienced by this interview participant is expressed as a list of things or actions carried out to be professional. The actual action is not described but it doesn't need to be to clearly categorise this as a "how" aspect.

the phenomenon is experienced or it can be in the form of common themes with marked aspects of similarity and difference between the categories (Åkerlind 2005). The next step therefore involved organising the categories of description in a tabular form delineating between the "what" aspect and "how" aspect of the conceptions. The labels given to the categories emerged from the data and the professional judgment of the researcher.

Phenomenographic findings represent collective variations of the phenomenon as conceptions rather than the conceptions of individuals (Marton 1994). In reporting of the results, quotes from the interviews are used to illustrate the variation in experiencing the phenomenon rather than as an example of a conception from one individual.

5.8   Validity and Reliability

Qualitative researchers are still subjected to issues of validity and reliability of their research. Due to the nature of qualitative research, the usual ways in which criteria are applied to evaluate quantitative research rigour may not be appropriately applied to evaluate qualitative research (Sin 2010).

The principle of defensibility in design applies to the internal consistency of the research question(s), the nature of the knowledge of the object of study, the data, and the method(s) of analysis (Sin 2010). Cope (2004) contends that the rigour of phenomenographic studies is a contentious issue with no clear resolution, and references Sandberg (1997) in support of this contention. The lack of resolution to this issue has resulted in the difficulty of getting phenomenographic studies published (Cope 2004).

The core of this problem is aptly captured by Morse (2006):

> in qualitative inquiry, we are concerned not with measurement but with description and meaning; hence, reliability and validity take on a different role (p. 5).

Qualitative researchers need to bring a different critical mind in assessing the rigour of qualitative enquiry. The categories of description and the outcome space are the main results of a phenomenographic study and once they have been identified they should be able to be reapplied to the original interview transcripts (Marton 1994). This is an area of potential unreliability in phenomenographic research as the researcher uses his or her judgment in deciding when a conception emerges from the data and the label that it is given.

Traditionally, phenomenographers have established the reliability of their research by inter-judge reliability (Sandberg 1997), also referred to as inter-rater reliability. Inter-judge reliability requires one or more researchers to judge the categories of description devised by the original researcher to determine the percentage of agreement (Sandberg 1997). Sandberg (1997) argues that inter-judge reliability is an unreliable way of establishing the reliability of phenomenographic results because it firstly ignores the researcher's procedures for achieving accurate descriptions of an individual's descriptions of their world; and secondly that the concept of inter-judge reliability as an objective epistemology is inconsistent with phenomenography as a qualitative and interpretative approach based on phenomenological epistemology. Sandberg (1997) addresses this problem by contending that reliability in researching conceptions can be the researcher's *interpretative awareness* (Sandberg 1994). Interpretative awareness means that the researcher acknowledges his or her subjectivity and deals with it during the research process. Sandberg (1994) proposes adopting phenomenology reduction or bracketing so that the researcher withholds certain theories and prejudices when interpreting the individual's conceptions. The importance of bracketing was discussed in Section 5.7.

Entwistle (1997) regards some of the criticisms of phenomenographic research as cautions rather than aimed at undermining the validity of the phenomenographic approach altogether, including the following:

1. Interview questions must be framed in the participant's terms of reference and not imposed by the interviewer.
2. Categories of description must be sufficiently detailed to define the meaning of the category fully.
3. Care must be taken in formulating the categories of description and this process will be aided by collegial input.
4. Analysis of the categories of description should logically account for the variation among categories in order to identify their relationships – hierarchical or otherwise.

Sjöström and Dahlgren (2002) in a study applying phenomenography to nursing argue that the core question of credibility in a phenomenographic study is about the relationship between the empirical data and the categories for describing ways of experiencing a certain phenomenon. They claim this may be achieved by providing excerpts from the interviews to support the relevance of the categories which enable the reader to consider the relevance of the categories. Qualitative research is also subject to the question of whether a different researcher would come up with the same results. In phenomenographic studies would another researcher come up with the same categories of description and outcome space? Marton (1988) considered this question and argued that replicability is not justified or even desirable but, rather, the actual identification and description of the categories constitute the discovery of the study and discoveries do not have to be replicable. Although, having identified the categories of description, Marton (1988) argued that it must be possible to reach a high degree of intersubjective agreement concerning the presence or absence of categories if other researchers are to be able to use them.

Cope (2004) argues that the task of ensuring validity and reliability in phenomenographic research is more straightforward if all aspects of the research have been underpinned with a structure of awareness. Cope (2004) refers to the work of Gurwitsch (1964) who suggested that awareness was made up of three overlapping areas: the margin, the thematic field and the theme.

The next section will discuss the issues around validity and reliability and how these are addressed in this present study.

5.8.1   VALIDITY

Research validity basically means the internal consistency of the object of study, data and findings (Sin 2010).

Trigwell (2000) says there are two types of validity – communicative and pragmatic validity. Communicative validity refers to the extent that the participants understood the questions that were put to them during the interviews. Pragmatic validity refers to the extent to which the research outcomes are useful (Sandberg 1994; Trigwell 2000) and the extent to which they are meaningful to their intended audience (Uljens 1996). Trigwell, it appears, uses the term *validity* in the sense of the results being reliable which is discussed in the next section.

Several researchers (Creswell and Miller 2000; Morse 2006) have addressed the issue of quality in qualitative inquiry. Creswell and Miller (2000) position themselves by using several validity procedures within a qualitative lens (researcher, participants and reviewers/readers) and applying post-positivist, constructivist and critical being paradigms. Sin (2010) provides suggestions for addressing the quality of phenomenographic research at each stage of the process. Cope (2004) discusses the different views on the validity of phenomenographic studies such as Booth (1992) who argues that validity is based on a researcher's justification for presenting the outcome space, and claims based on those results, as credible and trustworthy. Morse et al. (2002) argues that verification strategies should be incorporated into a study's method that identify and correct problems with processes and interpretations and these should be reported as part of the method description and as a means of demonstrating a researcher's responsibility for ensuring rigour. Cope (2004, pp. 8–9) provides a list of validity strategies (see Table 5.6) that he argues would

Table 5.6 Validity strategies

Validation strategy	How applied
1. The researcher's background is acknowledged. Describing the researcher's scholarly knowledge of a phenomenon is a means of illuminating both to the researcher themselves, and to readers of the study, the context within which analysis took place. Related to this is the strategy of "reflexivity". Reflexivity is when a researcher identifies his or her own preconceptions that are being brought into the research at the outset and then systematically questions at each stage of the research process how to minimise the effects and whether the effects have been sufficiently dealt with (Sin 2010). *Because qualitative inquiry is verified in the process of data collection and analysis, good qualitative inquiry must be verified reflexively in each step of the analysis. This means that it is self-correcting – inadequate or poorly supported constructions are not supported and "fall out" of the analysis. In this way, qualitative inquiry, properly conducted, is self-correcting and rigorous, and the results are strong (Morse 2006, p. 6).*	The researcher was employed as the senior manager, Education & Certification of the Financial Planning Association of Australia from September 1995 to March 2004. During this period, the researcher served on several International CFP Council committees and was a member of a Standards Australia committee on developing a financial planning standard and was at the same time a member of the ISO Full Committee on TC22222 Personal Financial Planning.
2. The means by which an unbiased sample was chosen is reported. In cases where convenience samples are used the characteristics of the participants should be clearly stated, providing a background for any attempt at applying the results in other contexts.	This study uses a convenience sample and the characteristics of the research participants were stated and described in this chapter.
3. The design of interview questions is justified.	The design of the interview questions was based on the information gathered during the literature review on financial planning and on phenomenographic research methods. The interview questions used were also honed by the use of pilot interview questions.
4. The strategies taken to collect unbiased data are included.	The researcher ensured that all six structured questions were asked of all interview participants. The researcher was also mindful not to participate in a dialogue with the participant that would offer opinions or otherwise lead the participant along a particular path. Irrelevant dialogue was deleted from the transcripts to make the data and analysis more manageable.

Table 5.6 Continued

	Validation strategy	How applied
5.	Strategies used to approach data analysis with an open mind rather than imposing an existing structure are acknowledged.	The researcher used the approach proposed by Sjöström and Dahlgren (2002) of looking at *frequency, position* and *pregnancy* of ideas expressed in the participant utterances. *Frequency:* how often an idea was articulated. *Position:* where the statement was situated (often the most significant elements were found in an answer's beginning). *Pregnancy:* when participants explicitly emphasised that certain aspects were more important than others (Sjöström and Dahlgren 2002).
6.	The data analysis method is detailed.	The data analysis method has been described in detail in this chapter.
7.	The researcher accounts for the processes used to control and check interpretations made throughout analysis.	The iterative process of phenomenographic research was applied in this study. This involved several readings of the transcripts. The researcher was the interviewer; the researcher transcribes the digital recordings to Word documents; and the researcher read these transcripts several times as described in this chapter.
8.	The results are presented in a manner which permits informed scrutiny. Categories of description are fully described and adequately illustrated with quotes.	Categories of description and outcome space are fully detailed in Chapters 6, 7 and 8 for each of the three countries. The categories have been presented as "what" and "how" aspects with the relationship between the categories fully explained.

seem reasonable in providing a full and open account of a phenomenographic research study. This approach has been applied in a phenomenographic study on Internet usage for information-sharing on construction projects which involved interview participants in Australia, the United Kingdom and the United States (Magub 2006). This approach has been applied to this study and Table 5.6 provides comments on how this has been used to establish an acceptable level of validity.

5.8.2 RELIABILITY

Reliability in qualitative research in general and phenomenographic studies in particular is not considered to have the same sense as reliability in quantitative research (Cope 2004). In a phenomenographic study, the aim of a researcher is to be able to defend their interpretation of the data to the "outside world" (Collier-Reed et al. 2009).

Morse (2006, p. 6) argues that "we must not and cannot borrow rules from quantitative inquiry for the conduct of inquiry, assessing ethical risks, or ascertaining rigor". Morse's (2006) framework considers direct, semi-direct and indirect data to provide qualitative insight, qualitative inference, qualitative evidence and appropriate verification as creating a new discipline in phenomenographic research.

Qualitative researchers use a variety of techniques to increase the trustworthiness of the research they conduct (Carlson 2010).

Other common terms used interchangeably with trustworthiness include authenticity, goodness, plausibility, and credibility (Carlson 2010, p. 1103).

A widely accepted definition for reliability is the extent to which the findings of a study can be replicated (Sin 2010).

Marton (1981) regarded the different ways in which a phenomenon can be experienced as a process of discovery that does not have to be replicated but the outcome space should be communicated in such a way that another researcher should be able to judge what categories of description apply to each individual case in the material in which the categories of description were found. Where agreement is reached between the two researchers in two-thirds of the cases (Marton 1981) the results are considered reliable.

Sandberg (1997) argues that inter-judge reliability is not an appropriate verification method for phenomenographic findings as it overlooks researcher procedures. For instance, Sandberg (1997) argues that individual statements may be difficult to locate in a category of description by co-judges who lack the same degree of familiarity as the original researcher. Interpretative awareness has been proposed by Sandberg (1997) as an alternative to inter-judge reliability. The researcher's interpretative awareness is when the researcher acknowledges and explicitly deals with his or her own preconceptions throughout the research process (Sin 2010). Researchers should document and explain clearly how they have practised interpretative awareness so that the reader can make a judgment about the research process and assess the reliability of the findings (Sin 2010).

Collier-Reed et al. (2009) posit that the trustworthiness of phenomenographic research comes from the internal horizon and external horizon of trustworthiness. The internal horizon in this context refers to the research project itself leading to the outcome space. The external horizon refers to the context of the project itself and brings in notions of the results being accepted by other researchers and considered useful by external users and readers of the research.

5.8.3   MEMBER CHECKING

Member checking provides an opportunity for members, that is, research participants, to check aspects of the interpretation of the data (interviews) they provided. Basically, with member checking, the validity procedure shifts from the researcher to the participants who provide the data (Creswell and Miller 2000).

Essentially member checking involves taking the data and interpretations back to the participants for their confirmation of its credibility (Creswell and Miller 2000). A popular strategy for member checking is to convene a focus group to review the findings (Creswell and Miller 2000). An alternative to this is to provide participants with the interview transcriptions and any field notes and ask them to verify their accuracy (Creswell and Miller 2000). In this present study, a summary of the categories were provided to research participants as it was impractical to carry out focus groups given the geographical spread of the interviewees. Communication was via email.

Some writers (Bowden 2005; Harris 2008) argue against member checking because it may not make sense to an individual interviewee if one or more of the categories do not fit their experience of the phenomenon. However, if the interviews have been carried out well, the feedback will be positive. This was the outcome for this present study which is discussed in Chapters 6 and 7. Given the geographical spread of the study's research participants, the researcher considered the use of member checking to be a valid and useful reliability method.

Member checking can be utilised in various ways that may be chosen intentionally, naively or haphazardly (Carlson 2010). Given the geographical spread of the interview participants in this study, not only across the three countries, but geographically spread within each country – especially for Australia and the United States – it is not feasible to conduct focus group meetings. A modified form of member checking will be implemented in this study to test the reliability (communicability) of the research findings. Four interview participants from each of the three countries were sent a draft of the relevant outcome space, including some background material to explain theory of categories of description, outcome space and what is meant by the "what" and "how" aspects of the conceptions. Interview participants were asked to comment on the categories and outcome space with the primary objective of assessing whether it makes sense to them. This is discussed in Chapters 6, 7 and 8 in the context of how member checking was applied to each group of interview participants in Australia, Hong Kong and the United States.

6 Conceptions of Professionalism: Australia

6.1 What this Chapter is About

The aim of this chapter is to show the results of the analysis of the phenomenographic interviews of CFP® professionals in Australia. This present study attempts to capture how CFP® professionals in these three countries experience the phenomenon of the professionalism of financial planners. Fifteen CFP® professionals were interviewed in Australia (not including four interviewed as part of the pilot interview process). These phenomenographic interviews were designed to capture the range of experience of the whole population of CFP® professionals in each of the countries. Phenomenography is the study of the qualitatively limited number of ways that phenomena in the world around us are experienced, conceptualised, understood, perceived and apprehended (Marton 1994). This present study's analysis applies the "what"/"how" framework for analysing the experience of the professionalism of financial planners.

This section provides an analysis of the research outcomes of the phenomenographic interviews carried out on CFP® professionals in Australia. Following the process of phenomenographic analysis described in Chapter 5, this section will include analysis of the following areas:

- outcome space;
- "what" aspect categories;
- "how" aspect categories;
- discussion on the "what" aspects, "how" aspects and outcome space;
- validity and reliability of the outcomes.

6.2 Outcome Space

The outcome space is comprised of the complex of categories of description capturing the different ways of experiencing the phenomenon (Marton and Booth 1997). According to Bruce et al. (2004) the outcome space depicts the manner in which the individual ways of experiencing are related to form a whole picture representing all participants interviewed.

Table 6.1 shows the outcome space resulting from the interviews of CFP® professionals in Australia. The outcome space is divided between the conceptions relating to the "what" aspect and those relating to the "how" aspect. This study found five categories relating to CFP® professionals' awareness of the "what" aspect of professionalism and four relating to the "how" aspect of the ways CFP® professionals conceptualised being professional or acting professionally. Descriptions of these categories and their relationship to each

Table 6.1 Outcome space – Australia

	What aspect		How aspect		
Conception	**Description**	**Example**	**Conception**	**Description**	**Example**
Client first mantra	Putting the client's interests first or acting in the client's best interest.	... you haven't tried to sell me anything, all you have done is tried to help me, you have tried to find out what I'm trying to do and give me advice on how I might be able to achieve that ... [A1:08] ... our main mantra here is client first ... [A3:02]	**Acting in the client's best interest.**	Providing advice and recommendations on strategies and products that are in the client's best interests; and doing so with integrity.	... we were acting with the client's interest and very professionally ...[A3:02] So for me its best interests for clients – is this course of action I'm suggesting in the best interests of the client ... [A11:06] ... try and be fair and courteous to the people ... [A4:10] I think the number one thing is consistency. You have to be consistent in your dealings – with all stakeholders – whether its clients or people you work with. [A11:06]
Integrity	Integrity is used here as a catch-all term to cover acting ethically, honestly, fairly and consistently.	So it's something in you to know to act with integrity and sort of be fair in your dealings and those sorts of things ... [A2:14] I guess you have to have a certain level of personal integrity – because without that then I don't think the rules are really going to – you're really going to follow the rules at heart ... [A9:22] Acting in the client's best interest, absolute integrity and the remuneration process by which I get rewarded is irrelevant – that's being professional. All the rest of it is quite frankly crap. [A15:10]			
Financial "doctor"	The analogy here is to a medical doctor, but also relates to the more general usage of being an expert (or knowledgeable) and being thorough.	I see myself like a financial doctor – I explain to the customer that way. [A10:06] ... protecting a person and/or family or business in advising them on their wealth accumulation and how to build and develop financial security ... [A5:34]	**Expert**	Acting as a financial expert in much the same way as a medical doctor would act as an expert.	... it's also being able to back it up with knowing the answers, being well read, not pretending to be something you are not. [A3:12] So we actually did a lot of homework – got all the policies – studied the terms and conditions ... [A5:08]

Table 6.1   Continued

	"*What*" aspect			"*How*" aspect	
Conception	**Description**	**Example**	**Conception**	**Description**	**Example**
Being a project manager	Being a project manager by managing a client's financial affairs which also incorporates the notion of following a process.	… we actually project manage and clients come to me to discuss how to arrange their financial affairs or to better arrange their financial affairs. [A6:04] … you are in an office you do this every day, you go through the same procedure – so it's a sort of template – you tell them what's going to happen next. [A9:08]	**Managing**	Managing the financial affairs of clients in an organised and planned way by following a process.	You need to manage them so that they are completing documents in a timely manner to achieve what you want. [A6:04] We try and coordinate where we have a lot of different professionals to work on particular clients … [A8:11]
Holding to a higher standard than government regulation	Regulations set minimum standards which are built on by dealer group compliance systems and FPA standards.	I think it means you are part of a group of people who have been willing to study to set themselves apart. They haven't just gone and done RG 146 in 6 or 1 week somewhere. So I think there is part of that. And I think its nice to be in a group which is a little bit more special. [A4:36] … the FPA and the regulators give you a framework … [A12:28]	**Complying with government regulations and FPA standards**	Comply with regulation (ASIC), standards set by FPA Australia and those set by dealers (AFSL holders).	So I won't use it because it's in breach of FPA rules for that sort of inducement to be there. [A4:12] … our overarching internal policies around doing the right thing by the client … is much more robust than what any external body impose on us. [A3:26]

other are shown in Table 6.1. The outcome space has been ordered to show the ways of experiencing professionalism from the most complex to the least complex. In this present study, *frequency* and *pregnancy* of ideas expressed in the participant utterances (Sjöström and Dahlgren 2002) was relied upon in ordering categories. The "what" aspect of *client first mantra* is shown first as being the most important and complex conception emerging from the interviews as it was more frequently articulated and indicated as being more important than other aspects. The *client first mantra* was expressed as a complex all-encompassing experience of what professionalism means. *Integrity, financial "doctor", being a project manager* and *holding to a higher standard than government regulation* were expressed as subsets of the *client first mantra*. *Holding to a higher standard than government regulation* was expressed as the least complex experience of professionalism because it is the experience of meeting minimum government regulation but with awareness that CFP® professionals are held to a higher standard by holding the highest professional membership of the FPA. The outcome space has also been ordered to show the relationship between the "what" and "how" aspects. For example the "what" aspects of *client first mantra* and *integrity* have been grouped as they relate to the "how" aspect of acting in the *client's best interest*.

The remainder of the chapter will discuss the categories with reference to the data collected highlighting the similarities and differences between them.

6.3   "What" Aspect Categories

Marton and Booth (1997) have espoused that a way of experiencing something comprises a "what" aspect and a "how" aspect which is related to how a person constructs awareness. In this particular section, the focus is on the "what" aspect of the conceptions of the professioanlism of financial planners. Applying Marton's (1988) definition of the "what" aspect, which in the context of learning is stated simply as *what is learned*, the "what" aspect for this present study is what professionalism means.

The following discussion looks at each of the five "what" aspect categories of the conception of the professionalism of financial planners. These are illustrated in Table 6.2.

Table 6.2   "What" aspects – Australia

Category	Description
1. Client first mantra.	Putting the client's interests first or acting in the client's best interest.
2. Integrity.	Integrity is used here as a catch-all term to cover acting ethically, honestly, fairly and consistently.
3. Financial doctor.	The analogy here is to a medical doctor, but also relates to the ore general usage of being an expert (or knowledgeable).
4. Being a project manager.	Being a project manager by managing a client's financial affairs which also incorporates the notion of following a process.
5. Holding to a higher standard than government regulation.	Regulations set minimum standards which are built on by dealer group compliance systems and FPA standards.

6.3.1   CATEGORY 1: CLIENT FIRST MANTRA

This category shows that CFP® professionals in Australia experience professionalism as putting the client's interests first. The label attached to this "what" conception – *client first mantra* – has been taken directly from participant A3's utterance as an apt depiction of its meaning:

> *I would like to think we always act professionally – I think it depends on where you are. We have – our main mantra here is client first. [A3:02]*

Putting the client's interests first or acting in the client's best interest is the description for this category as depicted in Figure 6.1. Putting the client's interests first or acting in the client's best interest is evidenced by the utterances of Australian CFP® professionals. There are several characteristics which depict this category. Professionalism is conceived in the form of a self-check by questioning whether the course of action being recommended is in the best interest of the client. This has the qualifier of the action also being a win-win for the CFP® professional as well, which means there must also be a benefit to the CFP® professional. Although this is contrary to the traditional notions of professionalism as discussed in Chapter 2 where a professional is someone who finds intrinsic enjoyment out of the act of providing service (Schaefer 1984) without necessarily the need to receive compensation; this reflects the realities of contemporary professionalism where remuneration is standard and an accepted part of being a professional.

> *I can remember once instance when one person was very shocked – was one of the financial review – financial journos came in, was referred in by another one and at the end of the meeting she was quite obviously shocked and said this was not what I was expecting at all – you haven't tried to sell me anything, all you have done is tried to help me, you have tried to find out what I'm trying to do and give me advice on how I might be able to achieve that – and I said that's what we do. And so there was clearly a misconception from her as to what goes on and I think the problem ... [A1: 08]*

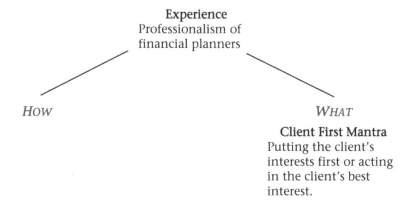

Figure 6.1   "What" category 1 – client first mantra

Professionalism is also experienced as the advice given to financial planning staff that the primary reason they are here is for their clients, and secondly for themselves. This supports the *client first mantra* which is the basis of this category.

> *We really focus on our client's objectives and needs. You know sometimes words are said around that but we actually say to our staff that the reason why we are here is for our clients and secondly for each other. [A8:02]*

Another characteristic of the *client first mantra* is the conflict of interest that financial planners experience – the conflict of self-benefit against client benefit. Professionalism is not being influenced in the decision-making process by the commission that is on offer. This category is clearly about being focused on the client's best interest ahead of every other interest.

> *Because to me professionalism is sitting in front of a client knowing full well that you could earn 10 per cent commission on one product and earn 3 per cent on another product but still not having that thought process in the back of your mind influence your decision. [A15:08]*

> *Well I think you are actually – you are acknowledging the interests of the client ahead of your own – basically – and the moment you do that – then that's a pretty good guiding principle for the behaviour … [A12:08]*

6.3.2   CATEGORY 2: INTEGRITY

Integrity is another way CFP® professionals in Australia experience professionalism. *Integrity* is closely related to the *client first mantra* conception but sufficiently different to suggest a variation in the awareness of professionalism. *Integrity* is used here to cover acting ethically, honestly, fairly and consistently as depicted in Figure 6.2.

This variation in experiencing professionalism is dealing or treating clients in a way that the CFP® professional expects to be dealt with or treated. Acting with *integrity* is

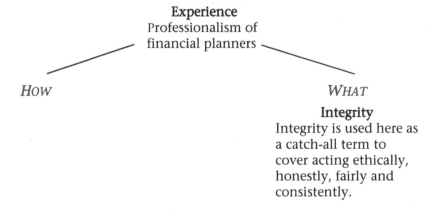

Figure 6.2   "What" category 2 – integrity

experienced as something that is known innately and the experience of *integrity* also suggests fairness. This innateness is where professionalism actually comes from a mindset, not just from acting in a certain way. The variation suggested here is that the mindset is formed with a notion that motivation is to give something (that is, to give advice) and not to get something for yourself (that is, receive self-benefit).

> *... dealing with your clients in a way you expect to be dealt with by other professionals. So it's something in you to know to act with integrity and sort of be fair in your dealings and those sorts of things. [A2:14]*

> *It comes from a mindset, it doesn't come from just acting in a certain way – it is in my view essential that you start with the idea that you are not trying to get something for yourself, but rather you are trying to give something – you are trying to give advice. You see selling is getting something for you in my view. So a professional has the mindset that I'm going to try and give something ... [A1:12]*

Another characteristic of this variation of experiencing professionalism as *integrity* relates to the "rules". The "rules" means those rules set by regulators and financial planning bodies and form a set of formal rules and standards that financial planners are obliged to follow. The "rules" by themselves are not sufficient to ensure financial planners act professionally because personal integrity is necessary in addition to "rules" to ensure compliance.

> *I guess you have to have a certain level of personal integrity – because without that then I don't think the rules are really going to – you're really going to follow the rules at heart – I guess. You might follow the rules generally but I don't think you really take it on board. So you do need to have a level of personal integrity. [A9:22]*

6.3.3   CATEGORY 3: FINANCIAL "DOCTOR"

The conception of *financial doctor* has been adopted from the terminology used by interview participant A10 in providing an analogy. However this conception is wider than simply the experience of professionalism as a *financial doctor*. It also covers experience of being considered an expert and to be regarded as being knowledgeable and is described as analogous to a medical doctor, but also relates to the more general usage of being an expert (or knowledgeable) as depicted in Figure 6.3.

The relevant context of interview participant A10's utterance is included to understand the basis on which the *financial doctor* analogy is experienced. While financial planners may have an expectation that clients are expecting to be sold a financial product, they are aware of the need to convey to clients that they are there to look at a client's overall situation and to provide a solution if a solution is required. In this sense CFP® professionals experience professionalism as being a *financial doctor*.

> *I see myself as professional because I'm not seeing myself as a salesperson. I think in other people's eyes they always think that when they come to see a financial planner ... they think that you are trying to sell them something. So in that sense before they come in they were not positioned the right ... I need to position myself as professional. Look you are coming here to*

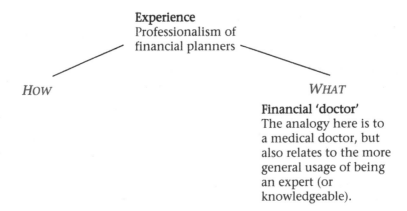

Experience
Professionalism of
financial planners

HOW

WHAT

Financial 'doctor'
The analogy here is to
a medical doctor, but
also relates to the more
general usage of being
an expert (or
knowledgeable).

Figure 6.3   "What" category 3 – financial "doctor"

see me because I need to look at your overall situation and then provide you a solution. Maybe you don't need to do anything – maybe you are doing very well already – I couldn't actually give you any more input – I see myself like a financial doctor – I explain to the customers that way. [A10:06]

Other examples of this conception can be seen as relating to having superior technical knowledge, being thorough and providing quality advice in the same way as lawyers, accountants and doctors.

So I just decided to give up on it and not even try to be a salesperson but rather try to make sure that I knew more than anybody else technically and to be able to give really great advice and then it really became clear to me as I matured that was really the only way to do business anyway – and that was in fact professional behaviour. [A3:20]

It is so important to be retentively thorough in your job. To be professional I expect that when I walk into a client, knowing the client as much as possible even before my first meeting ... but we still make sure for instance if I was reviewing a client's portfolio, I will still make sure I know everything else – his insurance, his debt and so forth because I think they all intertwine and if you don't you give advice which is relevant to that scope of his life but it can be it could be undone because I didn't delve further into detail about his whole life. [A5:12]

I think if we remember that we are here for our clients and I think an overarching view of mine is that all advice providers – think of lawyers, accountants, doctors – they all provide advice and they do that with a tool belt full of tricks – if you like – but ultimately it is what they say and how they communicate it to the client. [A11:10]

6.3.4   CATEGORY 4: BEING A PROJECT MANAGER

Another variation in how Australian CFP® professionals experience professionalism is being a *project manager*. The label for this conception has been borrowed from interview

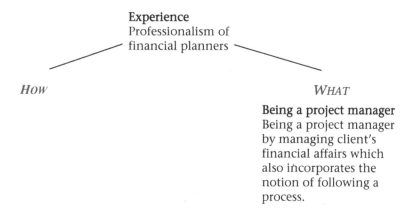

Figure 6.4   "What" category 4 – being a project manager

participant A6's experience of professionalism as "we actually project manage". The emphasis here relates to the implementation phase where clients have to be managed so that they are completing documents in a timely manner.

> *One of the advantages we offer is that we actually project manage and clients come to me to discuss how to arrange their financial affairs or to better arrange their financial affairs. It's not to say there is always a better mousetrap – sometimes they are doing the best thing and you need to tell them that. But when you are actually going through that process you need to make sure they are not being caught out by the implementation. You need to manage them so that they are completing documents in a timely manner to achieve what you want. It's also staying abreast of what the client is doing. [A6:04]*

This conception is described as being a *project manager* by managing a client's financial affairs which also incorporates the notion of following a process as depicted in Figure 6.4. This experience of professionalism as a *project manager* brings in the notion of financial planning being a process comprising steps which are iterative. The steps or the process or the way a client is project managed is the same for every client, although the advice will obviously vary. This notion of "process" is important for CFP® professionals as it defines the methodology of how planners manage clients from the initial client discovery meeting to the Statement of Advice.

> *I guess it's the steps you go through which are repeated. You have documentation and you do the same steps for each client essentially. Your advice might be different, but how would you get to those things you gather as much information as you can, you do research, you confirm it and then you put something together for the client. [A9:10]*

> *So we have a pretty robust process that we go through – everybody knows what that is. If a client comes in for the first time – we get all their tax information – tax statements etc. – we actually request that before they come in and then we go through that and we have a discovery meeting as I mentioned – work out what is important to them, we set expectations up front. [A8:04]*

6.3.5   CATEGORY 5: HOLDING TO A HIGHER STANDARD THAN GOVERNMENT REGULATION

Australian CFP® professionals' experience of professionalism is influenced by government regulation. Regulation is an important part of the Australian financial planning operating environment. Regulation in Australia is sourced principally through corporations law and administered by the Australian Securities and Investments Commission. Government regulation sets a minimum or base standard which is augmented by internal company compliance systems. Dealer groups play a role in filtering the compliance requirements for financial planners in Australia. Dealer groups also develop templates and other tools which help their advisors comply with the law. Compliance is an important conception of professionalism which relates to the corporations law requirements of financial planners such as providing an FSG (Financial Services Guide) to clients.

CFP® professionals conceive of regulation as setting minimum standards or a professional framework for financial planners. In this sense it is analogous to the role played by regulators and professional bodies as the go-guards of a 10-pin bowling alley. Regulators and professional bodies provide the rules and standards of the game – by setting the boundaries which should not be broken. These boundaries in 10-pin bowling are the go-guards which keep the ball in check and from going out into the gutters.

CFP® professionals however understand that they are held to a higher standard than minimum standards set by regulation. Regulation provides a framework on which CFP® professionals build their professionalism. The FPA arguably provides higher standards through its professional and practice standards required of CFP® professionals.

I'm thinking 10-pin actually – I'm thinking of my kids when they go bowling and they've got the go-guards – I actually think that's what regulators and the FPA provide us – it stops us from – you know – having a poor game if you like. We necessarily have to be held within certain parameters otherwise the industry is a bit like it was when I was 20 – and we wouldn't want to go back to that. So I sort of draw a parallel with 10-pin bowling and say these things are a necessary evil – because until you have learnt it you are going to hit the gutters – but I would hope that after a certain amount of years you wouldn't need those guards there – but ultimately … [A11:16]

I think it means you are part of a group of people who have been willing to study to set themselves apart. They haven't just gone and done RG 146 in 6 or 1 week somewhere. So I think there is part of that. And I think it's nice to be in a group which is a little bit more special. [A4:36]

And now we follow this compliance system way – and everything we say to a customer, everything we do we write it in a file note and actually help me because – when I go back – especially now getting bigger. I can go back and refer to it. So the compliance systems and also that is developed by the company which helps me. We are so strong in this country because of compliance. [A10:16]

I think the ASIC – the regulatory stuff comes back down to you through a dealer group. So for us, because the dealer groups says you have got to use standard templates of <Proprietary Name> that does all the disclosure stuff – so you don't even think about it and you don't look at ASIC. [A4:26]

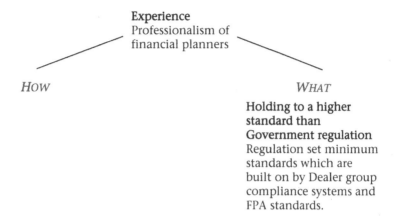

Figure 6.5 "What" category 5 – holding to a higher standard than government regulation

There is a legislatory requirement to make sure you provide an FSG and go through all the parameters in that and the things you can advise on and can't advise on. [A7:06]

This conception of professionalism as *holding to a higher standard than government regulation* is depicted in Figure 6.5.

6.4 "How" Aspect Categories

Marton and Booth (1997) have espoused that a way of experiencing something comprises a "what" aspect and a "how" aspect which is related to how a person constructs awareness. In this particular section, the focus is on the *how* aspect of the conceptions of the professionalism of financial planners. Applying Marton's (1988) definition of the "how" aspect which in the context of learning is stated simply as, *how is it learned* – the "how" aspect for this present study is *how do CFP® professionals act professionally.*

The following discussion looks at each of the four "how" aspect categories of the conception of the professionalism of financial planners. These are illustrated in Table 6.3.

Table 6.3 "How" aspect categories – Australia

Category	Description
1. Acting in the client's best interest.	Providing advice and recommendations on strategies and products that are in the client's best interests.
2. Manage.	Managing the financial affairs of clients in an organised and planned way.
3. Expert.	Acting as a financial expert in much the same way as a medical doctor would act as an expert.
4. Complying with government regulations and FPA standards.	Comply with regulation (ASIC), standards set by FPA Australia and those set by dealers (AFSL holders).

6.4.1 CATEGORY 1: ACTING IN THE CLIENT'S BEST INTEREST

CFP® professionals in Australia experience professionalism as putting the client's interest first and there are many examples of how they do this. CFP® professionals also act professionally by acting with *integrity*. This conception is described as providing advice and recommendations on strategies and products that are in the client's best interests; and doing so with integrity as depicted in Figure 6.6. Acting with *integrity* is both a "what" conception and a "how" conception. As a "how" conception, the researcher has grouped it with "acting in the client's best interest" as clearly acting with the client's interest first also assumes or predisposes acting with *integrity*. The interview participant's utterances provide a range of examples of the "how" conception of acting in the client's best interest.

CFP® professionals in Australia experience a conflict between selling and putting the client's interest first. Commissions are part of an ongoing debate in Australia about whether they are bad or not.

> *I don't think a professional tries to sell things to a client – and in fact selling and putting the client first – I think there is a real conflict in there – but a lot of people don't agree with me. [A1:06]*

The issue around commissions is in the forefront of how financial planners in Australia conceive of acting professionally. Commissions are a powerful motivator of decision-making behaviour in the form of advice given to clients and financial planners deal with this by blocking out their self-interest when recommending products to clients.

> *Because to me professionalism is sitting in front of a client knowing full well that you could earn 10 per cent commission on one product and earn 3 per cent on another product but still not having that thought process in the back of your mind influence your decision. [A15:08]*

Financial planners experience a "disconnect" in professionalism when money is the key. This disconnect is addressed by asking the question of whether the course of action being suggested is in the best interests of the client, as a kind of self-checking mechanism as to whether he or she is acting professionally. This is added with the proviso of being

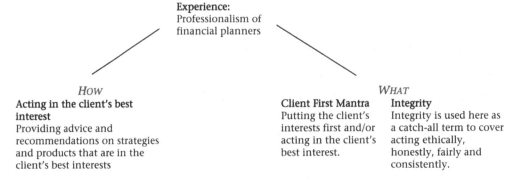

Figure 6.6 "How" category 1 – acting in the client's best interest – and related "what" categories 1 and 2 – client first mantra and integrity

a win-win situation in that he or she is compensated for the course of action being recommended to the client.

> *I think there is a disconnect in professionalism when money is the key to everything. So for me its best interests for clients – is this course of action I'm suggesting in the best interests of the client – and is there a win-win for me too which is obviously part of being professional. But at all times can you stare yourself in the mirror at the end of the day and say you have done a great job. [A11:06]*

Awareness of the numerous rewards on offer to a financial planner is part of acting in the client's best interest.

> *There are lots and lots of choices where we can say this or say that and sometimes there are rewards one way – they're not even rewards its maybe that I am going to make my life simpler this way or that way. It's a case of being aware of those things when they crop up and it's really easy to be aware of that if you have started with personal commitment to put the client first. [A1:24]*

How CFP® professionals act in the client's best interest is also achieved by asking a self-question of whether this course of action is in the best interests of the client. It comes back to the *client first mantra* and then choosing a course of action which is in the client's best interest. Acting professionally might also be to recommend someone else if they are able to better help a client.

> *The one issue is the fact that it would nice to capture the funds where I would have an ongoing trial commission for a long time or whatever. So is that in the best interests of the client? Or is the client well served with what they are used too. Is the asset allocation any different to what I might have recommended anyway? In which case why go through the process of disturbing the client by introducing them to something different which may not work quite as good for the client and may even be more expensive. [A7:04]*

> *If I can't help someone or they can be helped better by someone else then I have no hesitation in actually recommending that they talk to someone else – or you are actually saying I'm not the best person to assist you. I don't have the skill set. So that's probably a tangible example of that happening. [A12:06]*

How CFP® professionals envision acting in the client's best interest also includes acting in a fair and courteous manner to clients. Trying to avoid difficult situations and being exposed to a conflicted position by acting for example for both wife and husband who are separating.

> *... try and be fair and courteous to the people, try and avoid difficult situations where the real estate agent is acting for buyer and seller – we try and avoid that sort of thing as much as possible. When a couple splits up – one of the other guys in the office has to take the file ... [A4:10]*

CFP® professionals envision being completely honest in all their dealings with clients and other stakeholders. This conception of acting honestly also relates to admitting a lack of knowledge rather than fudging the truth with clients.

I believe I try to sort of act with the utmost of integrity. To be totally – in all my dealings – not just with clients – but with anyone I come into contact with – be it other staff members of other people in the community – to be completely honest and all those sorts of things. [A2:28]

You certainly have to be honest with a client and I think you need to say – I don't know – if you don't know – don't just tell them something. [A9:16]

There have been cases where I have given pro bono advice because people have needed advice but haven't been able to afford it and I think it is the responsibility of the industry to be able to effectively cover that cost yourself and still be able to give something back to people and I'm not sure enough of that really goes on. There have been a number of occasions where I have given advice and I have taken clients through what they need to do and not charged them for it. [A1:06]

I mean you do the right thing by the client – we had a case where a client's wife had in our conversation with him we found out that she was sick and we delve further into it and found that she had a policy by another advisor and she was really entitled to a claim that was three years ago. She had some major illness and nobody did anything about it and she still wasn't a client of ours, just that she was the wife of a firm that we manage ... we managed to successfully appeal for her at least three years after and she got nearly $300,000 trauma claim. [A5:08]

I did read one article on ethics which did stick in my mind because it said if you were doing something or about to do something that you would prefer the public at large didn't know about, then you need to stop and think. Often that means it's not exactly as it should be – even though you might justify it in your own mind. So part of it is the ethical sense and part of it is just how you prefer to be treated yourself. I try to put myself in the client's shoes. [A14:10]

6.4.2   CATEGORY 2: MANAGE

CFP® professionals in Australia conceive of professionalism as the act of being a *project manager* by managing clients' financial affairs, which also incorporates the notion of following a process. How they do this is to manage the financial affairs of clients in an organised and planned way by following a process. In this case, the "what" and "how" conceptions are difficult to distinguish from each other. What professionalism means to CFP® professionals is that it is *a process of managing* and how this is done is by *managing*. Several examples of the interview participant's utterances illuminate this.

To manage also includes managing clients so that they are completing documents in a timely way. Managing also embraces the idea of following a process (which is the six-step financial planning process) and this process provides the robustness for managing clients.

You need to manage them so that they are completing documents in a timely manner to achieve what you want. [A6:04]

So we have a pretty robust process that we go through – everybody knows what that is. If a client comes in for the first time – we get all their tax information – tax statements etc. – we actually request that before they come in and then we go through that and we have a discovery meeting as I mentioned – work out what is important to them, we set expectations up front. [A8:04]

I guess it's the steps you go through which are repeated. You have documentation and you do the same steps for each client essentially. Your advice might be different, but how would you get to those things you gather as much information as you can, you do research, you confirm it and then you put something together for the client. [A11:10]

... so when going through the process of a financial plan – the financial planning process we have in the organisation it's not coming across too complicated and that's what I find clients do really appreciate. It's going back to the bare basics if that's what they need and explaining to then the process and the pros and cons to it all and making it extremely transparent. [A13:08]

So try and make the process as easy as possible and look my style is fairly conversational rather ask them a lot of questions. I'll have a chat about what's important to them, how they are feeling about work – try to put them at ease – because the more you can do that – the more they will tell you about themselves and the more in the back of your mind you can start to construct the strategy. [A14:06]

The "how" category of *manage* is depicted in Figure 6.7.

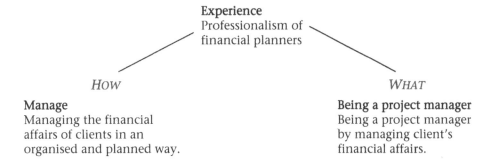

Experience
Professionalism of
financial planners

HOW

Manage
Managing the financial
affairs of clients in an
organised and planned way.

WHAT

Being a project manager
Being a project manager
by managing client's
financial affairs.

Figure 6.7   "How" category 2 – manage – and related "what" category 2 – being a project manager

6.4.3   CATEGORY 3: EXPERT

This category is described as acting as a financial expert in much the same way as a medical doctor would act as an expert as depicted in Figure 6.8. CFP® professionals not only act in the same sense as a general practitioner medical doctor, but they also act as a specialist medical doctor would act. Financial planning is an activity that an individual can perform themselves. Much of the activity of financial planning is around the implementation of transactions. In this simplified view of financial planning, the financial planner may simply be performing a role of facilitating the purchase of financial products. Australian CFP® professionals have an awareness of professionalism which

Experience
Professionalism of
financial planners

HOW

WHAT

Expert
Acting as a financial expert in
much the same way as a
medical doctor would act as
an expert.

Financial 'doctor'
The analogy here is to a medical
doctor, also relates to the
more general usage of being an
expert (or knowledgeable).

Figure 6.8 **"How" category 3 – expert – and related "what" category – financial "doctor"**

goes beyond simply facilitating financial transactions. They see themselves as adding value, adding expertise and providing a depth of analysis that individuals would not be expected to perform themselves.

The "how" conception of acting as an *expert* is illustrated with the following examples of the interview participant's utterances.

So professionalism in the visual sense I think is important but it's also being able to back it up with knowing the answers, being well read, not pretending to be something you are not. [A3:12]

I had some people that were not particularly well and they had a son and a daughter and we thought – OK they are going to go in aged care and so it will cost them a lot of money. And this is quite some years ago and I said to them you have got to get around this problem of having to pay too much. So we actually went to a solicitor and had the title changed from joint tenants to tenants in common and only one of the elderly couple had competency and was able to make a will. But he was able to will away his half of the property to his children. And he – it was a toss-up of who would die first – he died first and actually saved the surviving spouse thousands of dollars a year in fees and charges – and kept her on the Age Pension because her assets were diminished by the half of the property going through the estate rather than going through – because you couldn't gift it away, that would cause problems. [A4:06]

So be very, very thorough – be extremely comprehensive in our research – on products, on rules and regulations. [A5:12]

Being able to make a difference for clients – that's what we are here for. It's about making a difference. We have a few elderly clients who are able to sleep well at night because they know we are looking after them. [A8:24]

I think I need to know the technical areas. The client doesn't need to know the technical areas. I think it's my – certainly it's my advice – I think you should do this – certainly have more questions about it or whatever ... [A9:18]

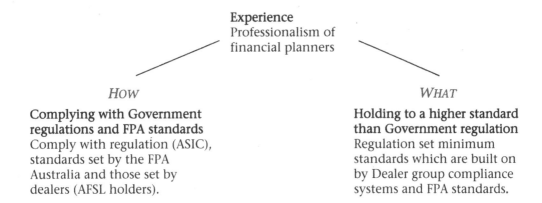

Figure 6.9   **"How" category 4 – complying with government regulations and FPA standards – and related "what" category 5 – holding to a higher standard than government regulation**

6.4.4   CATEGORY 4: COMPLYING WITH GOVERNMENT REGULATIONS AND FPA STANDARDS

Professionalism to Australian CFP® professionals means operating in an environment regulated by corporations law and administered by the Australian Securities and Investments Commission (ASIC). ASIC regulates the activities of CFP® professionals as "authorised representatives" of Australian Financial Services Licensees (also referred to as "dealers"). It also means operating in an environment of professional practice and ethical standards set by the FPA. This category is described as to comply with regulation and standards set by FPA Australia and those set by dealers as depicted in Figure 6.9.

Australian CFP® professionals act professionally by complying with minimum regulatory standards but to a higher standard that is morally and ethically appropriate. Australian Financial Services Licence Holders don't necessarily communicate regulatory standards or the higher morally and ethically desirable standards to their advisors. The FPA however does provide a professional framework which leads to a more rigorous standard than government regulation.

The regulators and professional body are designed to keep people who operate at the fringes or outside the fringes motivated in the right way – they are not designed for people who have got the right motivation – so you accept that they need to exist because there are lots of people who don't exhibit the right sort of values and professional ethics and standards. [A12:28]

... it's fair to say that our overarching internal policies around doing the right thing by the client and ensuring there is no mishaps or errors or fraud – God forbid – that is much more robust than what any external body impose on us. I think particularly because we have – one of our parents is <NAME> their level of scrutiny around standards and policies that lead to professionalism are much more than an Australian body has in place. [A3:26]

I think ASIC makes it even harder because it involves so much written compliance that you have to do step by step. It's almost as if your professional notion is disregarded to do a checklist of things to keep you in line. [A7:16]

From the continuing education point of view – there are various sections of Corps Law which says you should operate in your clients best interests and the FPA has similar rules saying what you should and shouldn't do. I must admit I will sort of take note of it but it doesn't drive me heavily. Probably the only thing is does do when you are doing your file notes and things like that – if there is a risk area you will make sure you file note that in a correct matter so that if you ever needed to defend the advice, but I don't know if it really changes my – how I approach the job. [A14:14]

... and that's where I think codes of conduct and professional practice actually assist because here's a scenario, he's never experienced it before – you've got some innate values that sort may mean you actually go the right direction, but here's some codes, practices that you can actually relate to or assist you for something that is new that you have never experienced – I think that's where those things help ... [A12:22]

But a professional says – I mightn't agree with it, but that's what the law is and so I comply with the law. So those things are – I mean they are part of being professional because you operate in an environment – someone sets the rules, you mightn't agree with them – but you actually fundamentally comply with things that you don't even agree and don't necessarily think they add any value to the client – which I don't. [A12:28]

6.5 Analysing the Conceptions

Understanding the qualitatively limited number of ways CFP® professionals in Australia experience *professionalism* is a collective understanding rather than an individual understanding as is the second-order perspective of phenomenographic enquiry. The interviews were approached by the researcher with a view to understanding how the research participants understand or experience *professionalism*. The interest in this study is twofold: firstly "what" professionalism means to the research participants and secondly "how" they think about acting professionally. The preceding analysis shows that there is a fine distinction between "what" is experienced and "how" it is experienced with the phenomenon of *professionalism*.

Australian CFP® professionals experience *professionalism* as putting the *client's interest first* and *acting with integrity*. They do this by providing advice and recommendation on products and strategies which are in the client's best interest. This understanding of professionalism is consistent with a financial planner's fiduciary responsibilities. Australian corporations law (Corporations Act 2001)[1] requires financial advisors to have a reasonable basis on giving advice to clients which is covered under section 945A corporations law.[2] Corporations law also requires financial advisors to have sufficient understandings of the products they recommend to ensure their suitability to the

---

1   An Act to make provision in relation to corporations and financial products and services, and for other purposes.

2   Available at: http://www.austlii.edu.au/au/legis/cth/consol_act/ca2001172/s945a.html [accessed 30 March 2012].

client, known as the "know your product" rule. These principles are also embedded in the FPA's Code of Ethics and Practice Standards with Rules of Professional Conduct (FPA Australia 2011).

CFP® professionals in Australia also experience *professionalism* as being an *expert* or *knowledgeable* and thorough in what they do. They see themselves as acting as an expert in much the same way as a medical doctor. CFP® professionals in Australia now have more stringent initial education requirements than was the case when the CFP® designation first came to Australia in 1992. Candidates must now hold a bachelor's degree as a minimum requirement before completing the five units of the FPA's CFP® certification programme. CFP® professionals also experience *professionalism* as being a *project manager* and their conception of doing this is by *managing*. This conception of *managing* is really about financial planners following a process, and this process is influenced by the six-step process which is core to the CFP® certification education curriculum and which is also reinforced through ASIC's Regulatory Guide 146 (ASIC 2008). ASIC's Regulatory Guide 146 builds on the six-step process by listing nine steps as part of the skill requirements for financial advisors.

Corporations law sets a regulatory framework for how CFP® professionals should behave, but *professionalism* as experienced means holding out to a higher standard than regulation. These higher standards are sourced not only through standards set by the FPA, but also by a sense that CFP® professionals ought to hold themselves to a higher standard. Regulators such as ASIC can glean from this which professional bodies, such as the FPA, have a legitimate role and the capacity to build on the regulatory framework in developing the professionalism of their members.

Many of the ways CFP® professionals in Australia experience *professionalism* can be related back to earlier notions of professionalism. Of Weber's (1968) distinguishing characteristics of a *profession* the notions of *rational training, vocational qualifications* and *specialisation*, relate to being a *financial doctor* and acting as an *expert*. The *client first mantra* and *acting in the client's best interest* can also be related to Weber's (1968) notion of having *clients*. Further support of how Australian CFP® professionals experience *professionalism* can be seen by other writers such as Millerson (1964) and Roddenberry (1953) with such notions as the *use of skills based on theoretical knowledge, education and training in these skills, examinations that ensure the competence of professionals* and a *code of conduct to ensure professional integrity* (Millerson 1964). Similarly the characteristics of an occupational group as identified by Roddenberry (1953) can also be related to the way CFP® professionals in Australia experience *professionalism* with such notions as *a duty to prepare as fully as possible before practising, a duty to continually improve skills and to freely communicate the knowledge gained from these skills,* and a *duty to set high standards of entry to the profession and to upgrade peers solely on merit and to protect society from substandard or unethical practice.*

Analysis against the list of attributes of *profession* and *professionalism* derived from the literature in Section 2.2 shows similarities in the conceptions of professionalism held by Australian CFP® professionals (see Table 6.4). *Client first mantra* matches the attribute of *having clients* and *a relationship with clients based on trust*. Experiencing professionalism as a *financial "doctor"* and the related "how" conception of *expert*, matches the attribute of *a specialised (and common) body of knowledge. Holding to a higher standard than government regulation*, which means meeting more than minimum government licensing standards, to include higher standards expected of a CFP® professional from the FPA suggests a match

Table 6.4   Conceptions of professionalism compared to theories of professionalism – Australia

Attributes of profession and professionalism (derived from the literature)	What professionalism means	How professionalism is acted upon
Vocational qualifications.	Financial "doctor".	Expert.
A specialised (and common) body of knowledge.	Financial "doctor".	Expert.
Having clientele.	Client first mantra.	Acting in the client's best interest.
A relationship with clients based on trust (fiduciary).	Client first mantra.	Acting in the client's best interest.
Professional responsibilities (acting in the public interest).		
Membership of a professional association.		
Adherence to a code of ethical behaviour.	Integrity.	Acting in the client's best interest.

with the attribute of *professional responsibilities (acting in the public interest).* The attribute of *adherence to a code of ethical behaviour* matches the conception of *integrity* which is used as a catch-all awareness of professionalism covering acting ethically, honestly, fairly and consistently.

The attributes of *vocational qualifications* and *membership of a professional association* are not as clearly matched to the conceptions of Australian CFP® professionals. However this doesn't mean these attributes are not important or not thought of as important but rather assumed by virtue of CFP® professionals requiring vocational qualifications and membership to the FPA in order to hold the CFP® designation. So for this reason they are matched to the conceptions of financial "doctor" and expert. The awareness of being a *project manager*, experienced by CFP® professionals as managing a client's financial affairs and which also incorporates the notion of following a process is not clearly represented in the list of attributes derived from the literature. This can be explained in that the list of attributes derived from the literature are generic in nature, whereas to be a project manager is conceived specifically in relation to the vocation of financial planning.

6.6   Validity and Reliability of the Outcomes

The importance and challenges of validating phenomenographic research methods and ensuring the reliability of outcomes was discussed in Chapter 5. The following section discusses issues of validity and member checking as they relate specifically to the data collection (interviews) and analysis in identifying the collective way CFP® professionals in Australia experience *professionalism.*

6.6.1   VALIDITY

The validity of research refers to the internal consistency of the object of the study, the data and the findings (Sin 2010). In Chapter 5 the issues of validating phenomenographic research were discussed. For this research study, validity strategies proposed by (Cope 2004) have been applied, and this application is detailed in Chapter 5.

6.6.2   MEMBER CHECKING

Given the nature of this present research study representing the study of conceptions of financial planners (all certified against standards of the global CFP® mark), the researcher considered the use of member checking as the most acceptable method of assessing the reliability of the findings. In applying member checking, the researcher is testing the communicability of the categories and resultant outcome space.

The researcher selected four of the 15 interview participants and presented them with a preliminary list of the categories and outcome space with examples of quotes from the interviews, similar to that shown in Table 6.1. The prime test applied was done so in order to establish if the categories accurately labelled the descriptions attached to them, and if the outcome space made sense to the interview participant. Secondly, did the quotations used as examples support the labelling of the categories? This process resulted in an exchange of (mostly) email communication between the researcher and interview participants to clarify certain issues and descriptions. The outcome of this process resulted in some revision to the descriptions applied to the conceptions which indicated the communicability and hence reliability of the results to an acceptable level.

An example of how members' feedback resulted in revisions to the categories is now discussed.

The original "what" category 5 label of "10-pin bowling" attracted feedback because of the unusual label given to the conception. The label was drawn from an analogy one of the original interview participants used to describe the role played by regulation. The researcher adopted the analogy as a label because it seemed to capture very well how CFP® professionals in Australia experienced professionalism in a way that took cognisance of the role played by regulation. The activities of financial planners in Australia are regulated by corporations law and administered by ASIC and this has a strong influence on how CFP® professionals experience professionalism in Australia.

Although one of the members found the analogy to be "quite good", two of the members struggled with the analogy. One of the members commented that, "I see what they are saying however there is an awful lot of lane to move around on before on hits the gutters". Another commented, "I struggle with this one a little i.e. going into the gutter until you learn to do better. Being a CFP® would suggest that you're already learnt the ropes and don't go down gutters at this point of your career". The researcher considered a review of the category by revising the label to *holding to a higher standard than government regulation*. This label retains the conception of regulation setting boundaries or limits to professional behaviour, but brings to the fore the conception that CFP® professionals understand that regulation is a minimum standard and they hold themselves out to a higher standard.

7 Conceptions of Professionalism: Hong Kong

7.1 What this Chapter is About

This chapter provides an analysis of the research outcomes of the phenomenographic interviews carried out on CFP® professionals in Hong Kong. Following the process of phenomenographic analysis described in Chapter 5, this chapter will include analysis of the following areas:

- outcome space;
- "what" aspect categories;
- "how" aspect categories;
- discussion on the "what" aspects, "how" aspects and outcome space;
- validity and reliability of the outcomes.

7.2 Outcome Space

The outcome space is divided between the conceptions relating to the "what" aspect and those relating to the "how" aspect. This study found five categories relating to the "what" aspect of CFP® professionals' awareness of professionalism and three relating to the "how" aspect of CFP® professionals' conceptualisation of being or acting professionally. Descriptions of these categories and their relationship to each other are shown in Table 7.1. The outcome space has been ordered to show the ways of experiencing professionalism from the most complex to the least complex. In this present study, *frequency* and *pregnancy* of ideas expressed in the participant utterances (Sjöström and Dahlgren 2002) was relied upon in ordering categories. The "what" aspect of *feeling finding* is shown first as being the most complex conception emerging from the interviews as it was more frequently articulated and indicated as being more important than other aspects. The experience of *feeling finding* is closely related to being a *professional salesman*. Here, the experience of professionalism is very much about selling financial products, but with awareness that these products must meet the client's needs so that that client's interest is put first. *Being knowledgeable*, *being credentialed* and *requiring a process* are expressed as subsets of *feeling finding* and are a less complex way of experiencing professionalism. The outcome space has also been ordered to show the relationship between the "what" and "how" aspects. For example the "what" aspects of *feeling finding* and *professional salesman* have been

Table 7.1   Outcome space – Hong Kong

	What aspect		How aspect		
Conception	Description	Example	Conception	Description	Example
"Feeling finding"	This denotes finding out what the client wants, showing empathy and caring to the client; and putting the client's interest first.	… is what the client really needs and what they currently has or have in their financial lives … [HK13:06] … special advisor who care their feelings or care their situation – don't only want to sell product – they want to caring … [HK6:14]		Act with empathy and caring towards the client and find out what the client needs; acting in a professional way by managing the inherent conflict in client benefit and advisor/organisation benefit.	… what kind of product fits to what kind of a client and what situation, or any situation or circumstances that a client would fit into this kind of product. [HK1:02] For me, the very first thing to understand the widest area of the client's financial situation. But during the process of the understanding you have to know his or her financial fact – like their family, their personal needs … [HK13:04] I still have to remind myself to get a good balance between my interest of earning commission and the interest of the client. [HK4:06]
Professional salesman	This acknowledges that financial planning in Hong Kong ultimately involves selling a product but this can still be done ethically by managing conflicts of interest.	… as a CFP® professional in Hong Kong actually we carry products and actually we are salesmen as well … And there are occasions to show professionalism but will not all the time to show CFP® professionalism which is something different. [HK2:02] Eventually I did not offer any insurance products to her because she has already had the insurance agent, but I still get some information about her insurance products – to tell her what I think if her insurance coverage is good enough. [HK4:02]	Balance client benefit with self/organisation benefit		

Table 7.1 Continued

What aspect			How aspect		
Conception	Description	Example	Conception	Description	Example
Being knowledgeable	Being knowledgeable on technical matters, products and the current economic and regulatory environment.	So we try to back [up] our requirements on professionalism or knowledge you know with all the promotion requirement of our sales team. [HK1:10] … of course highly educated should be very knowledgeable …. I think – Asian culture read ethics into it which I think is a mistake, a misconception. [HK3:52]			
Being credentialed	Being qualified (education) and credentialed (CFP®) as signs of professionalism and ethics to clients.	They [clients] will tell how professional you are by measuring the length of the designation – 3, 4, 5 or 6, 7, 8, 9, 10 characters in total, must be more professional than the other one. [HK2:22] I always contact the stranger the people I don't know them. I will need to show my name card and I will introduce the CFP® – what does it mean – professional. [HK16:08]	**Education and credentials**	Acquiring education and professional credentials.	… when I show my card I say I have the CFP® status and I explain what CFP® mean. [HK15:22] So I read lots of reports and attend different courses just to upgrade myself even though I have a Master degree in Finance … [HK14:06]
Requiring a process	Requiring a process which refers to the CFP Board of Standards' six-step process.	Every day I meet my client and then I need the six steps- six steps. [HK9:08] I think it is a process to me. [HK10:10]	**Following the financial planning process**	By following the six-step financial planning process (which is espoused by the CFP Board and FPSB)	… I think that's the key issue because you have to let the client understand the whole financial planning process … [HK10:12] I tried to go through the financial planning process to get more information from her say for example to ask her experience before – why her thing was not up to her standard. [HK4:02]

grouped as they relate to the "how" aspect of *balance client interest with self/organisation benefits*. Awareness of professionalism as *being knowledgeable, being credentialed* are acted by acquiring education and professionalism credentials. Awareness of professionalism as *requiring a process* is acted by following the six-step financial planning process.

The remainder of the chapter will discuss the categories with reference to the data collected highlighting the similarities and differences between them.

7.3 "What" Aspect Categories

In this section, the focus is on the "what" aspect of the conceptions of the professioanlism of financial planners. Applying Marton's (1988) definition of the "what" aspect which in the context of learning is stated simply as *what is learned* – the "what" aspect for this present study is *what professionalism means*.

The following discussion looks at each of the five "what" aspect categories of the conception of the professionalism of financial planners. These are illustrated in Table 7.2.

Table 7.2   "What" aspect categories – Hong Kong

Category	Description
1. Feeling finding.	This denotes finding out what the client wants, showing empathy and caring to the client; and putting the client's interest first.
2. Professional salesman.	This acknowledges that financial planning in Hong Kong ultimately involves selling a product but this can still be done ethically by managing conflicts of interest.
3. Being knowledgeable.	Being knowledgeable on technical matters, products and the current economic and regulatory environment.
4. Being credentialed.	Being qualified (education) and credentialed (CFP® certification) as signs of professionalism and ethics to clients.
5. Requiring a process.	Requiring a process which refers to the CFP Board of Standards' six-step process.

7.3.1   CATEGORY 1: "FEELING FINDING"

CFP® professionals in Hong Kong experience professionalism as *the feeling finding*. This label has been taken from the utterance of interview participant HK13 which the researcher felt was a suitable descriptor of the conception. This conception denotes finding out what the client wants, showing empathy and caring to the client, and putting the client's interest first as depicted in Figure 7.1.

This conception is about understanding what the client really needs and not what the financial planner thinks they need. In this sense, there is an aspect of putting the client's interest first although CFP® professionals do not articulate their experience of professionalism exactly in this way. The *feeling finding* also includes a sense of *caring* or *care for their situation*. CFP® professionals in Hong Kong experience professionalism as being aware that their clients are looking for caring.

Professionalism relates to understanding that clients want a *special advisor*, which means an advisor who will care for them and not just simply sell them a product. The *feeling finding*

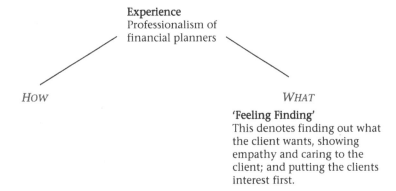

Figure 7.1 "What" category 1 – "feeling finding"

is also experienced as a way of understanding the client which acknowledges that clients have different needs and different attitudes towards their wealth. Good communication is stressed as being important in order to understand clients. Treating clients as a boss is another aspect of the *feeling finding* ensuring that the financial planner will understand what clients need and to take the time and show caring in order to please the *boss*.

The following examples of interview participants' utterances illustrate this "what" aspect conception of the *feeling finding*.

And therefore the very first thing I think is the feeling finding. The feeling finding means to understand what they really needs and what they are currently has or have in their financial lives. [HK13:06]

I think most likely wants some advisor, special advisor who care their feelings or care their situation – don't only want to sell product – they want the caring … [HK6:14]

I think the first thing is you have to understand the client. Because different clients have different needs. And also the same situation clients they have different behaviour than their wealth. So I think you have to have good communication with them and understand what is their attitude behind and also what is the planning. [HK10:04]

And if someone asks me what you mean by professionalism – I would say professionalism is very simply – I just treat each client as my boss. So as long as I'm doing that my professionalism will come out naturally, because if my client is my boss I know what I should do to keep my boss happy and not I happy … [HK14:04]

… to be a professional financial planner, I need to put my client's interest first – that's number one. [HK14:12]

I always place the client's interest top of my mind – that's very important. [HK11:26]

… it's not just about credentials and it's not just about making money. It's actually about helping clients to build their dreams – their financial goals or even life goals. [HK5:26]

So that would be a case where I try to act in a professional way in terms of trying to put the client's interest first as the most important consideration in terms of advising a certain – proposing a solution. [HK8:08]

7.3.2 CATEGORY 2: PROFESSIONAL SALESMAN

Financial planning in Hong Kong is very much about selling investment and insurance products. Although this is also true of financial planning in Australia and the United States, the practice of providing advice independent or distinct from selling financial products is not as widespread in the Hong Kong financial planning environment. This category is described as acknowledging that financial planning in Hong Kong ultimately involves selling a product but this can still be done professionally by managing conflicts of interest as depicted in Figure 7.2. The label for this category – *professional salesman* – has been taken directly from interview participant HK4 and the researcher considers this an appropriate label for this way of experiencing professionalism.

... my employer of course requires me to be professionally selling things so from that perspective, I am a professional salesperson. [HK2:04]

CFP® professionals in Hong Kong experience professionalism in terms of selling investment or insurance products. This conception is captured in the utterance of interview participant HK1 below.

I believe investment planning and insurance planning that CFP® professionals do the most in HK, but in taxation planning, in estate duties planning it probably goes to a trust company or tax professional. [HK1:22]

CFP® professionals in Hong Kong sell financial products. Hong Kong CFP® professionals experience professionalism as balancing the inherent conflict of interest in selling products and showing *feeling finding* towards clients. This pressure to sell products is captured by the utterance of interview participant HK7 where insurance companies are espousing the *financial planning concept* merely as a *cosmetic just to sell products*. CFP® professionals in Hong Kong as part of their day-to-day jobs are required to sell products and there are occasions when they do not always show CFP® professionalism. Showing

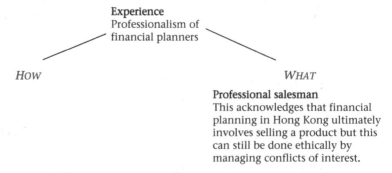

Figure 7.2   "What" category 2 – professional salesman

CFP® professionalism in Hong Kong is very much around following all of the steps of the six-step financial planning process. An inherent conflict arises where financial planners are only remunerated by commission and there is a temptation for unprofessional CFP® professionals, who maybe have a cash flow problem, to sell financial products that are more in their interest and not in the client's interest.

... because since I joined this industry, I joined a very big insurance company and they attract my – I joined the financial planning industry because of the financial planning concept – but when I joined them, they told me it was just a package or a cosmetic just to sell products – so that make me feel really disappointed. [HK7:28]

... as a CFP® professional in HK actually we carry products and actually we are salesmen as well. So that day-to-day operation of us is to sell something to people. And there are occasions to show professionalism but will not all the time to show CFP® professionalism which is something different. [HK2:02]

... in HK our jobs involve selling and most of us working in the industry do not have a fixed income so for those who are maybe have some kind of cash flow problem – say for example – they are very easy to fall into a situation to sacrifice clients' interest in order to maximise as their only interest – so I think that is one way of doing so. [HK14:08]

I share many times with this case in many different occasions because I really think it demonstrates a certain level of professionalism and on the other hand I really enjoy the case being the whole process. The first time I call her she regret me and eventually we become good client relationship and also good friends. [HK4:02]

For me, the very first thing to understand the widest area of the client's financial situation. But during the process of the understanding you have to know his or her financial fact – like their family, their personal needs ... [HK13:04]

7.3.3   CATEGORY 3: BEING KNOWLEDGEABLE

CFP® professionals in Hong Kong experience professionalism as *being knowledgeable* on technical matters and on products as depicted in Figure 7.3. Knowledge is experienced as having the *hardware*, where the *hardware* is the knowledge. Having the *hardware* is

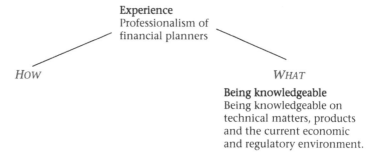

Figure 7.3   "What" category 3 – being knowledgeable

important, but having the *software*, which means communication skills, is more important than knowledge. Being equipped with enough knowledge in different areas is experienced as being able to provide the best advice to the clients. Knowledge in the context of the Hong Kong financial planning environment generally refers to knowledge of different insurance and investment products, including their features and benefits and being able to match these to the needs of clients. It is important for the CFP® professional to have more product knowledge than the clients they are advising. Clients have an expectation that if they seek advice from a CFP® professional, the CFP® professional will have more knowledge and understanding of the different insurance and investment products.

The following examples of the utterances of Hong Kong CFP® professionals illustrate the "what" aspect conception of *being knowledgeable*.

> *... to be a professional financial planner there are two ways – one is hardware and one is software. Hardware is the knowledge, the wordings and software is the communication – your presentation is very important. And for me, if I rate hardware and software I rate software even more – about 7 to 3. Because I really understand, really feels what the client's needs today. [HK13:22]*

> *... advising clients in the best interests of the client and having the knowledge and the background. Perhaps not much background but the knowledge to advise the client in terms of different aspects. I think it is very important to be equipped in terms of enough knowledge in different areas, to be able to give the best advice to the clients ... [HK8:32]*

> *... so that they can't sell certain type of product because we said that you know you should possess better knowledge when selling that product to the client. Also, in terms of promotions now apart from being, you have your quota done, but apart from that you have to have relevant licences before you move up, before you recruit. So we try to back (up) our requirements on professionalism or knowledge you know with all the promotion requirement of our sales team. [HK1:10]*

> *One is the knowledge of the product is very important and often – if you have a sales professional talk to you and sell you a lot of things, you expect him to understand the product from head to tail. And I think the salesman in whatever company they don't know exactly what it is. So very difficult to understand completely. So product knowledge is one thing ... [HK2:14]*

> *So as a new – being new to this industry – you know – it – the downside to it is that I don't have enough knowledge – expertise or experience to be able to be professional. [HK5:06]*

> *... to be a professional I think we need to be knowledgeable for our industry and in the simplest way of describing our industry, our job involve mainly – mainly the two "I's" insurance and investment. Investment has been changing quite a lot on a daily basis – we need to be well informed of what is going on before we our advice to our client to protect their interest and that's what I do on a daily basis. [HK14:06]*

7.3.4   CATEGORY 4: BEING CREDENTIALED

Another way that CFP® professionals in Hong Kong experience professionalism is by being credentialed. This is related closely to the "what" category of *being knowledgeable*, but the researcher determined that there was sufficient variation in this way of experiencing

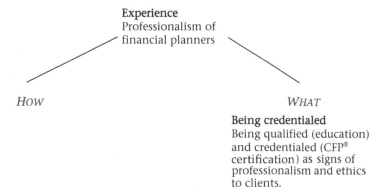

Figure 7.4 "What" category 4 – being credentialed

professionalism to justify a separate category. This is because, in the Hong Kong context, being credentialed is understood and valued by itself, quite apart from the technical knowledge a CFP® professional possesses. This category is described as being qualified (that is, having education) and credentialed (that is, having the CFP® designation) as signs of professionalism and ethics to clients as depicted in Figure 7.4.

Obtaining the CFP® designation and *being credentialed* is important for providing a professional guidance to practice in Hong Kong. Having the CFP® credential means being a professional. It is evidence to colleagues and clients that an individual has professional status. Hong Kong CFP® professionals ensure that their clients are aware that they are a CFP® professional. The CFP® credential and professionalism are synonymous.

> *Then I come to realise that the CFP® in HK and I knew I had to get the designation … I had done so because it really turns out to be a professional guideline to my practice in HK to now. [HK1:24]*

> *… always I meet the client – new client or old client I will talk to him or I will tell him I'm a CFP® professional. I have the CFP®. [HK9:22]*

To earn the respect and acceptance of clients as a professional financial planner, having credentials as evidence of knowledge and expertise is what professionalism means. Having credentials as a symbol of professionalism is experienced as acknowledging the value placed on the length of the designation on a name card. In the Hong Kong culture, the number of credentials on a name or business card is an important indicator to clients of the professionalism of a person.

> *You know in our industry the name card tells a lot of things. But the client won't tell the difference between different designations. They will tell how professional you are by measuring the length of the designation – 3, 4, 5 or 6, 7, 8, 9, 10 characters in total, must be more professional than the other one. They don't need to explore, how professional are each designation. They will just say how professional are you before they make business with you. [HK2:22]*

> *And the training in insurance company – if you want to be professional and need some education in financial industry – maybe CFP®. [HK16:04]*

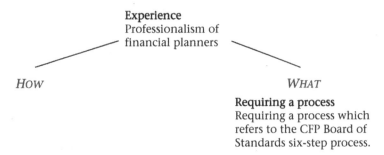

Experience
Professionalism of
financial planners

HOW

WHAT

Requiring a process
Requiring a process which
refers to the CFP Board of
Standards six-step process.

Figure 7.5 "What" category 5 – requiring a process

7.3.5 CATEGORY 5: REQUIRING A PROCESS

CFP® professionals in Hong Kong experience professionalism as *a process* as depicted in Figure 7.5. This process is the CFP® six-step process which is promoted by the international CFP® professional community. Professionalism is experienced as applying the six-step process every day when meeting with clients.

Professionalism is a process, but a process which is modified in practice because not all clients require all six steps of the process all the time. However the six-step process provides a guide to the CFP® professional in ensuring that all areas of advice and the CFP®–client relationship are being covered. There is an aspect of this experience of professionalism where a CFP® professional has gained a formal or structured knowledge on what the six-step process is and how is it applied in the process of providing advice to clients.

> *Every day I meet my client and then I need the six steps – six steps – every day I meet the client. [HK9:08]*

> *I think it is a process to me – of course I know something before I start my career in financial planning but after studying of course I got the formal or rules of how to run the business, but you still have to modify in your daily works because you can't just tell everybody step one step two and then you get because it won't be that easy. [HK10:10]*

> *And throughout the so-called 6-steps of the financial planning, the first thing I think as a financial planner – as a professional planner you did a good job in the very first step and then the second to sixth step you feel very comfortable. [HK13:06]*

7.4 "How" Aspect Categories

Applying Marton's (1988) definition of the "how" aspect which in the context of learning is stated simply as *how is it learned* – the "how" aspect for this present study is *how do CFP® professionals act professional*.

The following discussion examines each of the three "how" aspect categories of the conception of the professionalism of financial planners. These are illustrated in Table 7.3.

Table 7.3 "How" aspect categories – Hong Kong

Category	Description
1. Balance client benefit with self/organisation benefit.	Act with empathy and caring towards the client and find out what the client needs; acting in a professional way by managing the inherent conflict in client benefit and advisor/organisation benefit.
2. Education and credentials.	Acquiring education and professional credentials.
3. Following the financial planning process.	By following the six-step financial planning process (which is espoused by the CFP Board and FPSB).

7.4.1 BALANCE CLIENT BENEFIT WITH SELF/ORGANISATION BENEFIT

This category is related to the "what" aspects of *feeling finding* and *professional salesman*. CFP® professionals in Hong Kong have to balance client benefit with their own benefit and/or the benefit to their organisation. In other words, in order to act professionally, CFP® professionals have to manage this inherent conflict of interest in how financial planning is practised in Hong Kong. This category is described as acting with empathy and caring towards the client and find out what the client needs; and acting in a professional way by managing the inherent conflict in client benefit and advisor/organisation benefit as depicted in Figure 7.6.

The following interview participant's utterances are provided as examples of the "how" conception of to *balance client benefit with self/organisation benefit.*

I think client's interest has to come first. And also because they are representing the company to deal with the clients – I think – also they have duties to their employers – to us – because they are representing the company – they should not do something that jeopardise the reputation – financial interest of the company. [HK11:02]

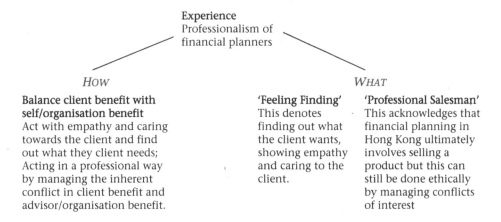

Figure 7.6 "How" category 1 – balance client benefit with self/organisation benefit – and related "what" categories 1 and 2 – "feeing finding" and professional salesman

I have to meet a target. Sometime I meet the target and the company has competition. But I know I need to act on behalf of the client and at the same time I need to fulfil the company's requirement and so some of the conflict will be happening here. The most important thing for the balance is the client comes first. [HK15:16]

Firstly, now you've got to be non-biased ... we receive commission from the product provider, but apart from that, now, being absolutely unbiased, we structure all our commission with the same kind of product at the same level regardless you know when the product provider gives us more or less commission. [HK1:08]

I still have to remind myself to get a good balance between my interest of earning commission and the interest of the client. Why is it that I have to get a balance because if we do not consider anything about our self – is not good – also not how – because we may not survive in our company or this industry then on the other hand we will lose the responsibility of our client because need us to serve them to take care of their financial planning to sign the contract – so on the other hand we have to make sure we can survive in this industry to serve them. [HK4:06]

Can I say this so I can paraphrase or clarify what you are saying ... even though your role requires you to sell financial products, but, but you do that in a professional way in the sense that you can answer questions the clients might have on other aspects that aren't directly to do with financial products – might be tax and some of the other things you mentioned. [Researcher – HK2:07]

Yes, well I think if you expect a salesman to do a professional sales, you wouldn't expect them to answer anything like estate duty or retirement planning – you just expect the salespeople to tell you exactly what the product is. [HK2:08]

... what kind of product fits to what kind of a client and what situation, or any situation or circumstances that a client would fit into this kind of product. [HK1:02]

You have to have this ability to understand, to step into his shoes of your client ... so you have to have a set of skills such as god listening skills, questioning skills, you have to have empathy, and you have to be empathetic – keep in mind that empathy and sympathy are two different things. [HK5:12]

... and so sometimes I will phone them to chat with them or chat with some other things, other than financial – the caring and I think behaviour should be – when I have some advisor crisis or some situation that effect their portfolio you should contact them to tell them what the result of the – what the view you have. I should tell them and other thing I feel that caring is most important. [HK6:14]

If the client for example – I come across someone who is less experienced and is just looking for something straight – straight advice, then I will just recommend a solution that would be best for him or her. If I come across a client – for example I just mentioned who knows some ideas about what he wants to do, he wasn't sure what options he had. I would tell him a couple of solutions he could go for and the pros and cons of each solution and I would always advise the client not to rush into things until he had all the facts considered before making a decision. [HK8:12]

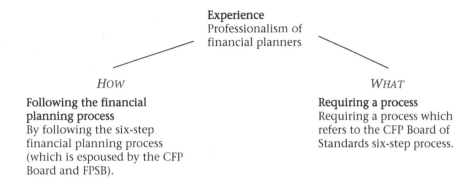

Figure 7.7 "How" category 2 – education and credentials – and related "what" categories 3 and 4 – being knowledgeable and being credentialed

7.4.2 EDUCATION AND CREDENTIALS

The analysis of what CFP® professionals in Hong Kong experience as being professional revealed two related categories but demonstrating sufficient variation to be separate conceptions of professionalism – *being knowledgeable* and *having credentials*. "How" CFP® professionals experience this conception is described as acquiring *education* and professional *credentials* as depicted in Figure 7.7.

Obtaining *education* and *credentials* is an important step towards being and acting professionally. This is considered an important aspect of acting professionally as credentials are a strong indicator of professionalism for the general public. Hong Kong CFP® professionals act professionally by showing clients they have qualifications and this is achieved by showing a business card to clients as evidence of CFP® certification status. This also provides an opportunity to explain to clients what the CFP® mark means. Credentials are highly valued and respected by the general public in Hong Kong as a symbol of knowledge, qualifications and professionalism. Therefore CFP® professionals in Hong Kong act professionally by showing their business card to clients.

The following interview participant utterances provide examples of this "how" conception of *education and credentials*.

Credential is the first step. I mean, first of all the general public has already accepted CFP® as – you know – a profession in financial planning – and that – umm so they would tend to trust a CFP® more than someone who doesn't have any credentials at all. Although that there are many other elements trust to build rapport – but again credential is the first step. [HK5:10]

I think in some client conversations first I need to gather some client data and show, show, show them I have the qualification and then I gather some information I need to tell her what his, what his responsibility or some rights or obligations and after I get some information – when I do some analyse and I should be confidential and privacy. [HK6:06]

… when I show my card I say I have the CFP® status and I explain what CFP® mean. [HK15:22]

I will need to show my name card and I will introduce the CFP® –what does it mean – professional. Actually every advice, every consultation is a benefit. The clients will say – you speak different because my colleagues don't have CFP®. Well I really enjoy to show my name card. [HK16:08]

So I read lots of reports and attend different courses just to upgrade myself even though I have a Master degree in Finance ... [HK14:06]

7.4.3   FOLLOWING THE FINANCIAL PLANNING PROCESS

One conception of professionalism for CFP® professionals in Hong Kong is as a *process*. This conception is described as following the six-step financial planning process (which is espoused by the CFP Board and FPSB) as depicted in Figure 7.8.

The focus of this section is *how* they experience professionalism as a process. In this conception the "what" and the "how" are closely related and only subtly distinguished from each other. Hong Kong CFP® professionals act professionally by educating clients about the whole financial planning process. Even though clients may want to talk about certain aspects of the advice or products they are interested in, a CFP® professional will bring the client back to the process. The importance of following a process is made clear to clients who may only want to know one thing or receive advice on one thing in the absence of the following all the steps of the financial planning process. Following financial planning process enables the CFP® professional to gather more information about the client which enhances the quality of the advice in ensuring the insurance or investment products recommended match the client's needs.

... some people they will talk about one things – they will be interested to know one thing before and you are stuck on that at that time and then you go back to go through the whole process. I think that's the key issue because you have to let the client understand the whole financial planning process ... [HK10:12]

And then I met with her at our office. I tried to go through the financial planning process to get more information from her say for example to ask her experience before – why her thing was not up to her standard. [HK4:02]

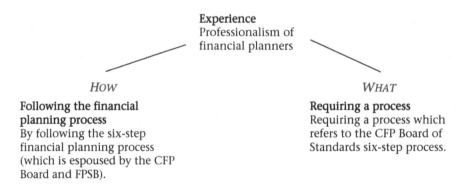

Figure 7.8   "How" category 4 – following the financial planning process – and related "what" category 5 – a process

The six-step process is also used every day as a way of keeping or maintaining professionalism. Applying the six-step process provides a disciplined and structured approach to framing advice and recommendations given to clients. Part of this conception of acting professionally is to explain to clients how they can locate CFP® professionals who follow the six-step process as this six-step process is a way of distinguishing themselves from those financial planners who don't follow the six-step process.

Many of my clients the six steps most important because measure the result usually the six step – OK and then everyday do this to keep my professional and then all the time I meet the new client, a new prospect – OK – I will teach him or teach her what is the CFP®, how you can do this – how you can find CFP® – you can use Internet, you can use to find what is the CFP® – how to be professional … [HK9:08]

I have to do the financial needs analysis first before engaging in any business. OK and therefore after doing this kind of needs analysis I may need to know more about their future – their future needs and their future planning and overall the picture I conclude as a comprehensive financial plan and then present it to the clients … [HK13:14]

7.5   Analysing the Conceptions

CFP® professionals in Hong Kong have five conceptions of "what" professionalism means to them. They experience what has been labelled as the *feeling finding*. This is about finding out what the client wants and showing empathy towards them. This is in contrast to simply telling the clients what they need and selling an investment or insurance product to them which may or may not suit their needs. This concept of *feeling finding* is accompanied by the experience of being a *professional salesman*. Hong Kong CFP® professionals think about acting professionally by balancing the client benefit with their own benefit or the benefit accruing to their organisation if they sell a financial product to the client.

Being *knowledgeable* and *credentialed* also means being professional to Hong Kong CFP® professionals. They think about doing this by acquiring the necessary education and professional credentials. CFP® candidates in Hong Kong must complete a comprehensive education programme from one of the approved education providers, sit the CFP® certification examinations and satisfy experience and ethics requirements. In Hong Kong, being able to show a client a business card which attests to these credentials is highly regarded. The CFP® certification six-step process provides CFP® professionals in Hong Kong with a measure of professionalism. Professionalism means applying this process and this is one point of differentiation from non-professional financial planners.

Acquiring *education* and professional *credentials* is how CFP® professionals act professionally and this accords with Weber's (1968) distinguishing characteristics of a *profession* with notions of *rational training, vocational qualifications,* and *specialisation*. What professionalism means is *being knowledgeable* on technical matters and on products and being qualified and credentialed as this signals *professionalism* and *ethics* to clients. This accords with Millerson's (1964) and Roddenberry's (1953) notions of *the use of skills based on theoretical knowledge, education and training in these skills, examinations ensure the competence of professionals* and a *code of conduct to ensure professional integrity* (Millerson 1964).

Table 7.4   Conceptions of professionalism compared to theories of professionalism – Hong Kong

Attributes of profession and professionalism (derived from the literature)	What professionalism means	How professionalism is acted upon
• Vocational qualifications.	Being knowledgeable	Education and credentials
• A specialised (and common) body of knowledge.	Being credentialed	Education and credentials
• Having clientele.	"Feeling finding"	Balance client benefit with self/organisation benefit
• A relationship with clients based on trust (fiduciary).		
• Professional responsibilities (acting in the public interest).		
• Membership of a professional association.	Being credentialed	Education and credentials
• Adherence to a code of ethical behaviour.	Being credentialed	Education and credentials

While not the focus of this present study, an analysis of conceptions against the list of attributes of *profession* and *professionalism* derived from the literature in Section 2.2 provides useful contextual information (see Table 7.4). The present study reveals that CFP® professionals in Hong Kong conceive of professionalism in many of the areas that the literature suggests are attributes of *profession* and *professionalism*.

Professionalism means *being knowledgeable* and *being credentialed* to Hong Kong CFP® professionals and they act on this by *acquiring education and professional credentials*. These conceptions relate to the following attributes of professionalism derived from the literature – *vocational qualifications, a specialised (and common) body of knowledge, membership of a professional association* and *adherence to a code of ethical behaviour*. Experiencing professionalism as *"feeling finding"* can be matched with *having clientele* as derived from the literature. However the related "how" conception of *balance client benefit with self/organisation benefit* has a weaker connection to *having clientele* as it conveys notions of self and organisation in at least equal weighting to that of clients. This would make the attributes of *a relationship with clients based on trust (fiduciary)* and *professional responsibilities (acting in the public interest)* tenuous.

The results of the present study also reveal that the notion of following the six-step financial planning process is not clearly represented in the list of attributes derived from the literature. As with the conception of project manager for Australian CFP® professionals, this can be explained by the fact that this conception is experienced specifically in relation to the vocation of financial planning.

7.6   Validity and Reliability of the Outcomes

The importance and challenges of validating phenomenographic research methods and ensuring the reliability of outcomes was discussed in Chapter 5. The following section discusses issues of validity and member checking as they relate specifically to the data collection (interviews) and analysis in identifying the collective way CFP® professionals in Hong Kong experience professionalism.

7.6.1 VALIDITY

The validity of research refers to the internal consistency of the object of the study, the data and the findings (Sin 2010). In Chapter 5 the issues of validating phenomenographic research were discussed. For this research study, validity strategies proposed by Cope (2004) have been applied. The following section discusses how these strategies have been applied for this current research study as they relate to the conceptions of professionalism of CFP® professionals in Hong Kong.

7.6.2 MEMBER CHECKING

The researcher selected four of the interview participants and presented them with a draft list of the categories and outcome space with examples of quotes from the interviews. None of the participants responded. The researcher then sought the assistance of the IFPHK and received two participants' responses. The IFPHK responded that they thought the feedback forms were too complicated for the participants to be able to complete. The researcher sent out simplified feedback forms and one further response was received.

The prime test applied was did the categories accurately label the descriptions attached to them, and did the outcome space make sense to the interview participant? Secondly, did the quotations used as examples support the labelling of the categories? This process resulted in an exchange of (mostly) email communication between the researcher and interview participants to clarify certain issues and descriptions. The outcome of this process was some minor revision to the descriptions applied to the conceptions which indicated the communicability and hence reliability of the results to an acceptable level.

An example of how members' feedback resulted in revisions to the categories is now discussed.

The "what" category of *being knowledgeable* was extended to include being knowledgeable on the current economic and regulatory environment. The description of the conception was therefore changed to read: *Being knowledgeable on technical matters, products and the current economic and regulatory environment.* The label remained unchanged as *being knowledgeable*. Another feedback item related to the "what" conception – *professional salesman*. The feedback was that *professional salesman* may have a negative connotation as the planner should not focus on selling. An alternative label of *ethical product provider* was provided. The researcher decided not to use this label as it suggested that only ethical products were being provided whereas the cohort of CFP® professionals were expressing an experience which was more in line with being a *professional salesman* rather than the more specific descriptor of *ethical product provider*. The participant also suggested that the description of the conception be modified to include: ... *ethically by managing conflicts of interest.* The feedback was that the word *ethically* should be replaced with the word *professionally*. The researcher made this change as it was still consistent with the label *professional salesman*.

8 Conceptions of Professionalism: United States

8.1   What this Chapter is About

This section provides an analysis of the research outcomes of the phenomenographic interviews carried out on CFP® professionals in the United States. Following the process of phenomenographic analysis described in Chapter 5, this section will include analysis of the following areas:

- outcome space;
- "what" aspect categories;
- "how" aspect categories;
- discussion on the "what" aspects, "how" aspects and outcome space;
- validity and reliability of the outcomes.

8.2   Outcome Space

Table 8.1 shows the outcome space resulting from the interviews of CFP® professionals in the United States. The outcome space is divided between the conceptions relating to the "what" aspect and those relating to the "how" aspect. This study found five categories relating to CFP® professionals' awareness of professionalism – the "what" aspect; and three relating to how CFP® professionals conceptualised being or acting professionally – the "how" aspect.

The outcome space has been ordered to show the ways of experiencing professionalism from the most complex to the least complex. In this present study, *frequency* and *pregnancy* of ideas expressed in the participant utterances (Sjöström and Dahlgren 2002) were relied upon in ordering categories. The "what" aspect of *serving the client* is shown first as being the most complex conception emerging from the interviews as it was more frequently articulated and indicated as being more important than other aspects. In the same way as *client first mantra* (Australia) and *feeling finding* (Hong Kong), *serving the client* is an all-encompassing experience of professionalism. *Listening, having standards, having technical competence* and *a planning process* represent less complex awareness of professionalism but as a subset of *serving the client*.

Table 8.1 Outcome space – United States

	What aspect		**How aspect**		
Conception	**Description**	**Example**	**Conception**	**Description**	**Example**
Serving the client	Being motivated by serving the client well, showing the client respect and acting in their best interest.	It comes first from my spontaneous desire to serve individuals well. [US16:12] It's about service – providing a service and the service is helping people make good financial decisions for their families. [US18:14]			
Listening	Being a listener, not a talker to clients; having good communication.	… we have a diagram (two ears and one mouth) … and say we have one of these and two of these and we use them proportionately. [US5:08] I think that they [unprofessional CFP® professionals] talk a lot more than they listen which is an important part of the communication. [US3:24]	**Acting in the client's best interest**	Showing empathy and caring; listening to clients, being motivated by providing advice and not motivated by selling a financial product which may or may not be appropriate.	But I can tell when someone is getting concerned and my goal is that this is not supposed to be a bad experience – this is supposed to be a good experience. So that's my concern. [US4:06] So for my way of thinking – what I do to be professional – is how do I help people accumulate assets, how to help them protect those assets, through insurance or what not – and then how do I them distribute that either in the form of a legacy or some sort of tax efficient fashion they can use in retirement. [US15:16]
Having standards	Not selling financial products that are not appropriate for a client; having standards.	Where if you think about the beginnings of the medical profession … and how they had to build kind of a professional reputation by getting rid of – the term that is often used – is snake oil salesmen. [US2:16] … snake oil salesmen – but they can sell anything, but I wouldn't consider them professional. [US3:18]	**Education and certification**	Relates to "having standards" and "having technical competence" (over page).	

Table 8.1   Continued

	What aspect			How aspect		
Conception	**Description**	**Example**	**Conception**	**Description**	**Example**	
Having technical competence	Being knowledgeable and competent on technical matters gained through initial and ongoing education.	The education programme can give you a high level of competence. [US2:12] … try and stay ahead of my peers and technology and knowledge. I spend several hours each night just researching … what's going on in the industry. [US9:10]	**Education and certification**	Completing prescribed and non-prescribed education courses.	… and I think I believe there are a lot of CFP® professionals even who have not educated themselves well enough to be giving the type of advice they give. [US17:10] … continuing education, I think is another key thing – it keeps people on their toes – keeps them involved in the field. [US12:24]	
A planning process	Following a process which refers to the six-step process.	I … see CFP® professionals as … I see them as professional, but I see more of a link to a planning process than to a professional standard. [US1:42] But I was always striving for a process … asset allocation was a process that I implemented; financial planning was a process I implemented. [US13:10]	**Following a planning process**	By following the six-step financial planning process (which is espoused by the CFP Board).	I think that the influence the CFP Board has is in delineating specific parts of each of the steps of the process – practice standards for instance. That alone is not enough but it does give a framework from which to outline your activities. [US18:10] I've seen in some instances CFP professionals who have promised financial planning – it's a very compelling promise – and then not follow through and then take short cuts that serve their business – collect revenue from client's assets and never return to the financial planning process for example. [US16:10]	

The outcome space has also been ordered to show the relationship between the "what" and "how" aspects. For example the "what" aspects of *serving the client, listening* and *having standards* have been grouped as they relate to the "how" aspect of acting in the *client's best interest*. The experience of professionalism as *having technical competence* is acted by completing prescribed and non-prescribed education courses to obtain and maintain CFP certification. Professionalism experienced as *a planning process* is acted by following the six-step financial planning process.

The remainder of the chapter will discuss the categories with reference to the data collected highlighting the similarities and differences between them.

8.3 "What" Aspect Categories

The following discussion looks at each of the five "what" aspect categories of the conceptions of the professionalism of financial planners experienced by American CFP® professionals. These are illustrated in Table 8.2.

Table 8.2 "What" aspect categories – United States

Category	Description
1. Serving the client.	Being motivated by serving the client well, showing the client respect and acting in their best interest.
2. Listening.	Being a listener, not a talker to clients; having good communication.
3. Having standards.	Not selling financial products that are not appropriate for a client; having standards.
4. Having technical competence.	Being knowledgeable and competent on technical matters gained through initial and ongoing education.
5. A planning process.	Following a process which refers to the six-step process.

8.3.1 CATEGORY 1: SERVING THE CLIENT

CFP® professionals in the US experience professionalism as being motivated by *serving the client well*, showing the client respect and acting in their best interest as depicted in Figure 8.1.

The label given to this "what" conception has been taken from the utterance of US16 shown below. *Serving the client* well is putting the client's interests first.

It comes first from my spontaneous desire to serve individuals well. [US16:12]

What it means to me is that I need to take a look at my clients and put their interests first. [US2:20]

A common characteristic of this conception is the notion of *respect* for other people. This is also experienced as *treating people with respect* and not being tainted by any conflict of

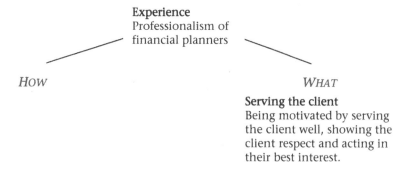

Figure 8.1 "What" category 1 – serving the client

interest as well as having a moral obligation to do the right thing by clients at all times. To American CFP® professionals, professionalism means doing the right thing by clients and being able to make a difference to their lives, both professionally and personally. There is a strong sense of doing the right thing by clients, acting in the client's best interests and serving the client well. Professionalism is experienced as working for the clients, by providing service and not simply choosing and selling financial products. This reflects the relatively mature stage of the profession of financial planning in the United States – particularly those holding the CFP® credential – which has moved on from the evolutionary stage of the profession characterised by an emphasis on selling financial products.

The following utterances of interview participants in the United States are provided as examples of the "what" conception of *serving the client*.

... professionalism is a basic respect for other people. [US4:26]

Treat people with respect and make sure that you are not tainted by any kind of conflict of interest or anything like that. [US6:06]

I have a moral obligation to do what's right for my clients at all times. [US9:16]

To do the right thing by the client. To make a difference in their lives professionally and personally. [US11:22]

It means I work for the clients. It's not choosing financial products and making investment decisions, insurance decisions – it's not a game. It's not a numbers game. It's about service – providing a service and the service is helping people make good financial decisions for their families. [US18:14]

What it means to me is that I need to take a look at my clients and put their interests first. [US2:20]

I just try and put myself in their shoes. If it was me I would want everything to be fair and people that were assisting me to be not on either side but to be fair as well. [US14:04]

Figure 8.2   "What" category 2 – listening

8.3.2   CATEGORY 2: LISTENING

The label for this conception has been taken directly from an utterance of US5, which the researcher determined provided an appropriate description of what professionalism means to CFP® professionals in the United States. The quote of *two ears and one mouth* was only used by one interview participant but it does pick up the notion of the importance of good communication. This category is described as being a listener, not a talker, to clients; and having good communication as depicted in Figure 8.2.

> *Right and we have a diagram – two ears and one mouth – and I show other planners and say we have one of these and two of these and we use them proportionately. [US5:08]*

This conception is expressed as behaviour exhibited by unprofessional CFP® professionals in that they talk more than they listen. Professionalism means listening to clients, showing humility and a lack of narcissism to clients. But it also extends to being a good collaborator, being an effective discussion leader, and walking in the client's shoes. Having emotional intelligence is arguably the contemporary listening skill.

> *I think that they [unprofessional CFP® professionals] talk a lot more than they listen which is an important part of the communication. They say, I almost think there is a sense of narcissism there. And it is very self-oriented of how smart and intelligent and how much they bring to the table, instead of what do you as a client need and how can I best help you and what can I best do. There is a lack of humility maybe. [US3:24]*

> *... being very precise in your communication to clients and following religiously a well thought out process to evaluate their situation – evaluate products – evaluate alternatives. [US18:06]*

> *They talk one – I think that they talk a lot more than they listen which is an important part of the communication. [US3:24]*

> *Well – being very careful to extract my own opinions and attitudes – personal opinions and attitudes or at least be aware of those circumstances under which I have an opinion or hold a cultural value or social value that is different to my clients and its very important for me to be aware of that. Primarily so that I can give advice which is not biased by my personal background or opinions or social norms. [US16:06]*

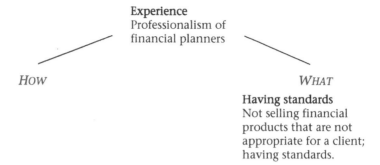

Figure 8.3   "What" category 3 – having standards

8.3.3   CATEGORY 3: HAVING STANDARDS

This conception is experienced by CFP® professionals in the United States in a negative sense of labelling the behaviour of unprofessional financial planners. Unprofessional financial planners are able to sell financial products that are not appropriate for a client; they don't have standards or principles but are driven by self-motivation and their actions are self-serving, rather than serving the interests of the client. These unprofessional financial planners are referred to as *snake-oil salesmen*. This conception highlights the problem of participants reporting socially desirable responses rather than reporting acting in an unprofessional way. As discussed in Chapter 5, phenomenographic interviews are criticised because they do not elicit what actually happens in practice. However phenomenography attempts to elicit awareness and understandings of a phenomenon and therefore the way the participant thinks about acting is more important than what is practised (Åkerlind 2005b). This conception is described as *having standards* as depicted in Figure 8.3.

Professionalism means upholding standards. This is expressed in the context that a lot of hard work has gone into establishing standards which frame the reputation of the CFP® brand and that this reputation should not be jeopardised but improved. Professionalism is envisioned as being a CFP® certificant and with the knowledge that that sends a message of having standards. Financial planners can be professional without the CFP® credential, but having the CFP® credential places the planner in an environment where there is accountability for maintaining those standards. When a financial planner has the CFP® credential, professionalism is not about *having* the CFP® credential, it's about *being* a CFP® professional.

American CFP® professionals' awareness of professionalism is expressed by comparing financial planning with other professions such as the medical profession and how that profession was built by getting rid of the snake-oil salesmen.

The following interview participant utterances provide examples to illustrate the "how" aspect conception of *having standards*.

It means upholding the standards – there's been a lot of CFP® professionals that come before me – will be after – so I wouldn't want to do anything to jeopardise that – so a lot of colleagues and a lot of hard work go into building the reputation and so I wouldn't want to damage that. You know I would want to uphold all the standards and improve them if possible. [US14:20]

... I am a CFP® certificant and we have standards. [US8:22]

Yes there is – I don't think anyone should do financial planning without having a CFP®. You can be just as professional without it but once you have it you are in a community that's all about professionalism and I think there is accountability for it. [US17:22]

... because it's a being it's not a having. I wrote an article 100 years ago in the last midst of all this professionalism and I got to put in that article – when you are truly a financial planner as a CFP® – you don't have a CFP®, you are a CFP®. [US17:18]

I think it means that having – at least my clients having the confidence to be able to come to me for any kind of a financial issue and know that I will be able to give them an unbiased educated experienced opinion on whatever their financial question might be. [US6:14]

We are the ones that if we are practising at our best – we are the ones that help people educate their children, care for their ageing parents, provide for a comfortable retirement, remove the financial anxieties that damage and destroy so many families – wielding incredible powers – we have to be mindful of that – and yes we are blessed to this – it's a very interesting thing to do, it can compensate one very well – but we must always be mindful of the fact that we have deeper responsibilities – that this is not something to be taken lightly. [US16:18]

Where if you think about the beginnings of the medical profession ... and how they had to build kind of a professional reputation by getting rid of – the term that is often used – is snake oil salesmen. [US2:16]

... snake oil salesmen – but they can sell anything, but I wouldn't consider them professional. [US3:18]

8.3.4 CATEGORY 4: HAVING TECHNICAL COMPETENCE

CFP® professionals in the United States experience professionalism as meaning *having technical competence*. This conception is described as being knowledgeable and competent on technical matters gained through initial and ongoing education as depicted in Figure 8.4.

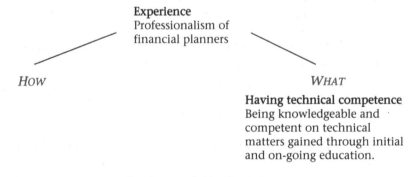

Figure 8.4 "What" category 4 – having technical competence

Professionalism has, at its core, competence or the knowledge that a CFP® professional brings to the table. Professionalism is personal reputation and the acknowledgement that the CFP® professional has the knowledge. This technical knowledge and competence is delivered through the CFP® education programme which provides a framework for being professional. This is evidenced by the following examples of the utterances of CFP® professionals in the United States.

When I think of the professional I think competence has to be a core piece of it. So the knowledge of what you bring onto the table … [US3:20]

… personal reputation and the acknowledgement that I have the knowledge … [US4:32]

I think the nature of the CFP® that programme and the educational content you receive gives you a pretty good basis for being a financial planner, for being a professional. [US2:10]

I think it means that having – at least my clients having the confidence to be able to come to me for any kind of a financial issue and know that I will be able to give them an unbiased educated experienced opinion on whatever their financial question might be – and I said my specialty was investment management, but if they have an insurance question or a mortgage question or whatever it might be and they can come to me and get a solid opinion without subject to some kind of bias. [US6:14]

I would say the skills involved – the ability to identify the key issues and the key drivers that are in play, be able to identify the financial implications of the various choices they face – and then be able to engage in a form of synthesis where we take into account both the financial implications and the key drivers that we have identified and what we know about the client as a human being. [US16:04]

8.3.5   CATEGORY 5: USING THE FINANCIAL PLANNING PROCESS

This conception is described as following a process which refers to the six-step process as depicted in Figure 8.5. The six-step financial planning process is one of the fundamental areas which are taught in the CFP® curriculum, as discussed in Chapter 4, and is a defining characteristic of the CFP® mark.

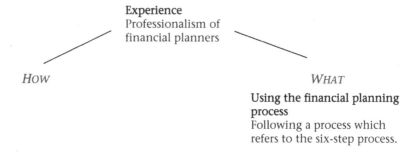

Figure 8.5   "What" category 5 – using the financial planning process

The financial planning process provides a framework for the professional activities of a CFP® professional. American CFP® professionals experience professionalism as following the six-step process. The financial planning process is experienced as a powerful process which provides a rigorous approach to providing advice to clients. The financial planning process is covered in detail in the registered CFP® education programmes and is applied in practice. Following a process allows CFP® professionals to have a similar pattern woven into many different techniques. It can be referred to in academia as theory, in that a theory guides the process of the research, even though it is applied in many ways and settings.

The following utterances of CFP® professionals in the United States as interview participants provide examples of professionalism being experienced as *using the planning process*.

... the influence the CFP Board has is in delineating specific parts of each of the steps of the process – practice standards for instance. That alone is not enough but it does give a framework from which to outline your activities. [US18:10]

... but I see more of a link to a planning process than to a professional standard ... They really have identified the planning process really well – pretty good rigour. I follow that when I train, we learned on that process even though I wasn't a CFP® – so I really admire it and I follow it – we do everything on that process. [US1:42]

... what it means to me to be a CFP® professional is to operate in a realm where I am mindful of the fact that I am yielding great and powerful forces – that I am using this incredibly powerful process to help people achieve better lives. [US16:18]

I think that the influence the CFP Board has is in delineating specific parts of each of the steps of the process – practice standards for instance. That alone is not enough but it does give a framework from which to outline your activities. [US18:10]

I always believe that things should have a process because when I first got in the business I had inherited a lot of clients' accounts and things were helter skelter and things didn't make any sense ... But I was always striving for a process – certainly asset allocation was a process that I implemented, financial planning was a process I implemented. [US13:10]

8.4 "How" Aspect Categories

Applying Marton's (1988) definition of the "how" aspect, which in the context of learning is stated simply as *how is it learned*, the "how" aspect for this present study is *how do CFP® professionals act professional*. The following discussion looks at each of the three "how" aspect categories of the conception of the professionalism of financial planners. These are illustrated in Table 8.3.

8.4.1 CATEGORY 1: ACTING IN THE CLIENT'S BEST INTEREST

Professionalism in the United States is experienced by CFP® professionals as *serving the client* and *listening*. What this means is being motivated by serving the client well and

Table 8.3   "How" aspect categories – United States

Category	Description
1. Acting in the client's best interest.	Showing empathy and caring; listening to clients, being motivated by providing advice and not motivated by selling a financial product which may or may not be appropriate.
2. Acquiring and maintaining education and certification.	Completing prescribed and non-prescribed education courses; having CFP® certification.
3. Following a planning process.	By following the six-step financial planning process (which is espoused by the CFP Board and FPSB).

acting in their best interest; and being a listener, not a talker, to clients and having good communication. They do this by acting in the client's best interest.

Acting in the client's best interest is characterised by covering off or looking out for things which may not be part of the compensation agreement but which are to the long-term benefit of the client.

To act in the client's best interest also covers the need to define the client relationship, maintain the client relationship, and run the business of being a CFP® professional in ways that serve the client as well. For example, a business that is not well run cannot serve the client as well as one that is well run. A client–planner relationship where the client is not totally clear on engagement standards is a relationship that is not going to serve the client as well. To act in the client's best interest to listen and serve the client is about more than just advice, recommendations, strategies and products. There are other aspects where the planner needs to act in the client's best interest. Examples of this "how" conception are provided in the following utterances and are graphically depicted in Figure 8.6.

I could have said it's not in the scope of our engagement – but the reality is that if I am going to act in her best interests which is what we are supposed to be doing as CFP® professionals then

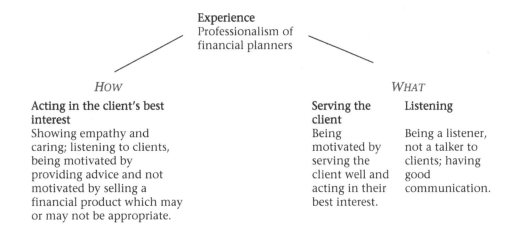

Figure 8.6   "How" category 1 – acting in the client's best interest – with related "what" categories 1 and 2 – serving the client and listening

I need to look out for some of these things that I might not necessarily get compensated for but will benefit her financially long term. [US15:06]

But I can tell when someone is getting concerned and my goal is that this is not supposed to be a bad experience – this is supposed to be a good experience. So that's my concern. [US4:06]

So for my way of thinking – what I do to be professional – is how do I help people accumulate assets, how to help them protect those assets, through insurance or what not – and then how do I them distribute that either in the form of a legacy or some sort of tax efficient fashion they can use in retirement. [US15:16]

Our approach is to make the consequences of client's choices – the trade-offs – explicit as a way of empowering them to make decisions in their lives. But interestingly they often say well my attorney just said – do this – and what's interesting is that one can see the appeal of that because very often clients just want to be told. I think in the end they are more satisfied and the decision is a better decision if we take them through a process that allows them to uncover for themselves through a fuller understanding of consequences and how it relates to their personal history and values. [US16:08]

Thinking in a holistic way – not just – oh well here's someone who walked in today and has $10,000 – I can sell them the product today – no its really understanding more than the client understands what their financial needs are – OK. [US5:22]

And my professionalism was to do everything I could for her and finally have to say this is not working for either of us. [US9:02]

... we had the kids come in and we talked with them about the responsibilities of running the business generating income for their parents and neither one was very comfortable with that. [US10:02]

8.4.2 CATEGORY 2: ACQUIRING AND MAINTAINING EDUCATION AND CERTIFICATION

The "what" conceptions of *having technical competence* and *having standards* are both represented by the "how" conception of *acquiring and maintaining education and certification*. This is depicted in Figure 8.7.

CFP® professionals in the United States have *technical competence* and *standards* by getting *educated* and *certified*. The education means the initial education programme delivered by a CFP Board of Standards registered education provider, and certification means the CFP® certification given to individuals who satisfy all the requirements by the CFP Board of Standards.

To be regarded as being professional, CFP® professionals need to be learning what is on the leading edge, not just what received CFP® continuing education (CE) credit, because some of the most leading edge ideas and science will not actually qualify for CE until they have been around long enough to officially be considered part of the body of knowledge tested for by the CFP® exam.

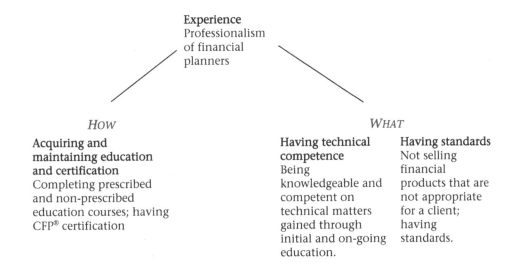

Figure 8.7 "How" category 2 – acquiring and maintaining education and certification – and related "what" categories 3 and 4 – having technical competence and having standards

The following utterances of American CFP® professionals are provided as examples of this conception.

> *… I was developing a business plan and it would involve me renting some office space, I need some stationery and I need a couple of computers and I need some desks and chairs and I guess I need some sort of professional certification to put on my business card – looks like CFP® is probably the one to do and I then embarked on a two-year course of study and over the course of acquiring the CFP® mark, my conception of what it meant to practice as a CFP® changed dramatically. [US15:18]*

> *… and I think I believe there are a lot of CFP® professionals even who have not educated themselves well enough to be giving the type of advice they give. As an example if you don't have any background in economics you shouldn't be designing portfolios and doing tactical allocation and deciding that modern portfolio theory is dead … [US17:10]*

> *Well I think one of the things that I do is I'm involved in client education because really that is most of our job and we have an economics club in Indianapolis and if there is a very good speaker coming through – maybe the – I think we had the head of the world bank that came through hand I brought a prospect to that and then at one point. [US13:02]*

> *… continuing education, I think is another key thing – it keeps people on their toes – keeps them involved in the field. [US12:24]*

> *So I'm meeting them for the first time, so I have to be able to project an image of knowledge and experience and trust right off the bat. So my dress does matter. Being up to date and listening*

to what they say and trying to project to them which is true, that I really do care about their situation. I really do want to help. [US10:08]

8.4.3 CATEGORY 3: FOLLOWING THE FINANCIAL PLANNING PROCESS

The "what" conception of *using the planning process* is acted as *following a planning process*. The "what" and "how" aspects are closely related in this conception. Professionalism means *using the planning process* and CFP® professionals act professionally by *following a planning process*.

Following a planning process is seen as using a powerful process which is applied in helping people achieve better lives. The financial planning process is not just seen as a six-step process, but it also encapsulates a broader context of not simply providing advice as a one-off action. Rather it means continuing through with providing advice, solutions and recommendations to see a client through a complete and thorough process of achieving their goals. While it is important to follow a process, it is also important to allow for the flexibility needed to meet individual client needs. The client is of utmost importance, even over a process. And again, there is even greater need for financial planning theory.

The following utterances of American CFP® professionals provide examples of this "how" conception which is graphically depicted in Figure 8.8.

... what it means to me to be a CFP® professional is to operate in a realm where I am mindful of the fact that I am yielding great and powerful forces – that I am using this incredibly powerful process to help people achieve better lives. [US15:18]

... but they saved the overall estate of a few million and now I am working with the son still fighting because most of the estate was worth like $40m at the date of death and we have paid in about $11m in estate tax – but really that's all we should pay because it was bank stock, and real estate. So it's an ongoing process but to be honoured to help somebody like that at that level with that problem – that's the professional part. [US5:04]

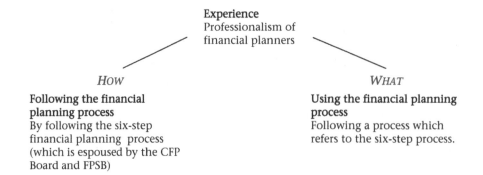

Figure 8.8 **"How" category 3 – following the financial planning process – and related "what" category 5 – using the financial planning process**

I kind of have an unique situation that just occurred – had a client I've had for about three or four years now and part of the regular process is kind of looking at – it's mostly investment management – my specialty is, but we kind of take a look at the complete picture and we were reviewing – she is the trustee for her mum's trust and the trust owns a life insurance policy on her mum for wealth replacement, estate tax, liquidity – and doing a regular review. [US6:04]

You know what I would perceive is that CFP® professionals act in a professional manner. I would not want them to be product pushers. That would be really terrible. What we do is – we don't make any recommendations until we do a financial plan with the client as well as we can with the spouse – hopefully and know their, risk tolerance, their goals, their ambitions where they want to be at what point in time financially – and their concerns – we always ask whether they have an estate plan that they've done – does it need to be updated. We really want to cover the whole ball – the whole spectrum so that there's no – there's nothing that might surprise in a negative way them or their heirs later on. [US13:08]

Financial planning I believe is an incredibly powerful process that can be used to transform people's lives for the better, but only if its allowed to unfold properly as a process – unfold fully over time. Financial planning is incredibly time consuming to do it right. I've seen in some instances CFP® professionals who have promised financial planning – it's a very compelling promise – and then not follow through and then take short cuts that serve their business – collect revenue from client's assets and never return to the financial planning process for example. [US16:10]

8.5   Analysing the Conceptions

How CFP® professionals in the United States experience *professionalism* largely reflects the relatively mature stage of the profession. *Professionalism* means *serving the client* well and *listening*. This demonstrates a deeper understanding of what it is to act in the client's best interest. Financial planning professionals in the United States tend to value serving their clients over their own personal reward (Ioannides 2005). An extension of these two conceptions is another way CFP® professionals in the United States experience *professionalism*, which is by *having standards*. Although intangible, putting clients first and serving the client's best interests over one's own are the essence of financial planning (Ioannides 2005, p. 55). This is about not selling or recommending products to clients which are not appropriate for them. American CFP® professionals think about doing this by showing empathy and caring; listening to clients; being motivated by providing advice and not motivated by selling a financial product which may or may not be appropriate.

Professionalism is experienced as *having technical competence* which means being knowledgeable and competent on technical matters gained through initial and ongoing education. The CFP® certification education programme is delivered by more than 300 academic programmes at colleges and universities across the country as a "registered" programme by the CFP Board of Standards. Completion of one of these programmes is the normal requirement before a candidate takes the 10-hour CFP® certification exam. This is regarded as a stringent requirement and highly regarded by those individuals who have achieved it and those who aspire to achieving it. Professionalism in this regard also encompasses the completion of non-prescribed education courses comprising continuing education (CE) requirements. The CFP Board is very prescriptive about what qualifies as continuing education and how CFP® professionals can maintain their CFP® certification by completing CE hours (CFP Board of Standards 2012a). These requirements influence what and how CFP® professionals experience professionalism in the United States.

The six-step financial planning process was conceived by the CFP Board. Financial planning is defined by the CFP Board as a six-step process CFP® professionals go through when counselling clients (CFP Board of Standards 2012b). This process is reinforced by the CFP Board and is reflected in its list of CFP® certification curriculum topics (CFP Board of Standards 2010) and on its webpage (CFP Board of Standards 2012c) and various other online publications.

Professionalism in the United States with respect to financial planning can be viewed as a normative value system where a group of individuals share common values and beliefs about a particular occupation (Parsons 1951; Evetts 2003). The ways CFP® professionals in the United States experience *professionalism* in much the same way as in Australia and Hong Kong conform to Weber's (1968) distinguishing characteristics of a *profession* to include notions of *rational training, vocational qualifications* and *specialisation*. This is particularly evident by CFP® professionals experiencing *professionalism* as *being knowledgeable* and *competent on technical matters* gained through initial and ongoing education, and having standards by not selling financial products that are not appropriate for a client. CFP® professionals act professionally by completing prescribed and non-prescribed education courses; having CFP® certification. The notion of skills based on theoretical knowledge and being educated and trained in these skills resonates with Millerson's (1964) notion of what defines a profession as well as such notions as *a duty to prepare as fully as possible before practising, a duty to continually improve skills and to freely communicate the knowledge gained from these skills*, and *a duty to set high standards of entry to the profession and to upgrade peers solely on merit and to protect society from substandard or unethical practice* (Roddenberry 1953).

Analysis of the ways CFP® professionals in the United States experience professionalism reveals a close alignment of conceptions against the list of attributes of *profession* and *professionalism* derived from the literature. The "what" conception of *having technical competence* and the related "how" conception of *education and certification* matches the attributes of *vocational qualifications, a specialised (and common) body of knowledge* and *membership of a professional association* derived from the literature. The attribute of professionalism of *having clientele* matches the conception of *serving the client* and the attribute of *a relationship with clients based on trust (fiduciary)* match the conceptions of *listening* and *having standards*. American CFP® professionals think about acting on these "what" conceptions by acting in the client's best interest and adherence to a code of ethical behaviour.

The link to the attribute of *professional responsibilities (acting in the public interest)* is tenuous. The utterances of the research participants shows this conception relates to showing empathy and caring; listening to clients; being motivated by providing advice as opposed to being motivated by selling financial products. While this clearly suggests a link to *a relationship with clients based on trust*, it doesn't go beyond to suggest a broader professional responsibility of acting in the public interest.

An analysis of the conceptions also reveal *following the six-step financial planning process* is specific to the context of financial planning and therefore not presented in the more generic list of attributes of *profession* and *professionalism* derived from the literature.

Table 8.4   Conceptions of professionalism compared to theories of professionalism – United States

Attributes of profession and professionalism (derived from the literature)	What professionalism means	How professionalism is acted upon
• Vocational qualifications.	Having technical competence	Education and certification
• A specialised (and common) body of knowledge.	Having technical competence	Education and certification
• Having clientele.	Serving the client	Acting in the client's best interest
• A relationship with clients based on trust (fiduciary).	Listening Having standards	Acting in the client's best interest
• Professional responsibilities (acting in the public interest).		
• Membership of a professional association.	Having technical competence	Education and certification
• Adherence to a code of ethical behaviour.	Having standards	Acting in the client's best interest

8.6   Validity and Reliability of the Outcomes

The importance and challenges of validating phenomenographic research methods and ensuring the reliability of outcomes was discussed in Chapter 5. The following section discusses issues of validity and member checking as they relate specifically to the data collection (interviews) and analysis in identifying the collective way CFP® professionals in the United States experience professionalism.

8.6.1   VALIDITY

The validity of research refers to the internal consistency of the object of the study, the data and the findings (Sin 2010). In Chapter 5 the issues of validating phenomenographic research were discussed. For this research study, validity strategies proposed by Cope (2004) have been applied. The following section discusses how these strategies have been applied for this current research study as they relate to the conceptions of professionalism of CFP® professionals in the United States.

8.6.2   MEMBER CHECKING

The researcher selected four of the initial 17 interview participants and presented them with a draft list of the categories and outcome space with examples of quotes from the interviews. The prime test applied was did the categories accurately label the descriptions attached to them, and did the outcome space make sense to the interview participant? Secondly, did the quotations used as examples support the labelling of the categories? This process resulted in an exchange of (mostly) email communication between the researcher and interview participant to clarify certain issues and descriptions. The outcome of this process led to some minor revision to the descriptions applied to the conceptions which indicated the communicability and hence reliability of the results to an acceptable level. An example of how members' feedback resulted in revisions to the categories is now discussed.

The initial label given to "what" category 2 was *Having two ears and one mouth*, which is described as *being a listener, not a talker, to clients; having good communication*. The researcher took the label directly from how one of the initial research participants described this conception. Being a listener was a collective experience of the group of CFP® professionals. One of the members provided feedback that described this label as "trite". This member commented that, "I think being a good collaborator, being an effective discussion leader, and walking in the client's shoes is a better representation of communication skills. Emotional intelligence is the new listening skills". Another member's feedback was, "The one thing I would change if I was doing this research, is I would simply call this section Listening". As a result of this feedback, the researcher revised the label to *Listening*, but retained the description.

Another example of a conception which attracted feedback from research participants was "what" category 3 – NOT *being a snake-oil salesman (having standards)*. The researcher adopted this label particularly to provide emphasis to the term "snake-oil salesman". Applying the approach proposed by Sjöström and Dahlgren (2002) of looking at *frequency*, *position* and *pregnancy* of ideas expressed in the participant utterances, the term "snake-oil salesman" satisfied the pregnancy of the idea where participants explicitly emphasised this aspect as more important than other aspects. However this label attracted comment from members. For example, one member provided this feedback:

> I think the comment about snake oil salesmen is cute. But to put it as the title of this category feels creepy to me. There's a bit of a 'well, of course!' to it. I like the 'having standards' terminology much better.

The researcher revised the label for this category to *having standards* but retained the original description of the conception.

9 *Discussion: Similarities and Differences in Conceptions between Australia, Hong Kong and the United States*

9.1   What this Chapter is About

The aim of this chapter is to discuss the similarities and differences in the conceptions of the professionalism of financial planners from CFP® professionals in Australia, Hong Kong and the United States. The Magub study (2006) analysed a phenomenon through the conceptions of participants from Australia, the United Kingdom and the United States. The participants were sourced from project teams from IT projects in each of these countries and comprised different types of employment roles. However this is not the intent of the present study. The present study has been carried out as three separate phenomenographic studies. The researcher took care to ensure that each study was analysed and considered independently. One of the ways this was achieved was to use labels for the categories that were offered from the interview participants themselves. However given the profile of the interview participants and the fact that the same structured six interview questions were asked and the interviewer (as researcher) was the same for each of the separate studies, there were similarities and differences in conceptions. It is also reasonable to expect that there would be a strong correlation between the conceptions from each of the three countries and that any differences would be explained by cultural influences and differences in the regulatory environment.

9.2   Outcome Space

Table 9.1 shows the outcome space for each of the three countries. The table is divided into the "what" aspect and "how" aspect conceptions with a description of their meaning.

Australian CFP® professionals conceive of professionalism as meaning: *client first mantra, integrity, financial doctor, being a project manager* and *holding to a higher standard than government regulation.* CFP® professionals from Hong Kong experience professionalism as meaning: *feeling finding, professional salesman, being credentialed, being knowledgeable* and

Table 9.1   Outcome space – Australia, Hong Kong and the United States

	What aspect		
Category	**Australia**	**Hong Kong**	**United States**
1	**Client first mantra** Putting the client's interests first or acting in the client's best interest.	**"Feeling finding"** This denotes finding out what the client wants, showing empathy and caring to the client; and putting the client's interest first.	**Serving the client** Being motivated by serving the client well, showing the client respect and acting in their best interest.
	Integrity Integrity is used here as a catch-all term to cover acting ethically, honestly, fairly and consistently.	**Professional salesman** This acknowledges that financial planning in Hong Kong ultimately involves selling a product but this can still be done ethically by managing conflicts of interest.	**Listening** Being a listener, not a talker, to clients. Showing empathy.
			Having standards Not selling financial products that are not appropriate for a client; having standards.
2	**Financial "doctor"** The analogy here is to a medical doctor, but also relates to the more general usage of being an expert (or knowledgeable) and being thorough.	**Being credentialed** Being qualified (education) and credentialed (CFP®) as signs of professionalism and ethics to clients.	**Having technical competence** Being knowledgeable and competent on technical matters gained through initial and ongoing education.
		Being knowledgeable Being knowledgeable on technical matters, products and the current economic and regulatory environment.	
3	**Being a project manager** Being a project manager by managing a client's financial affairs which also incorporates the notion of following a process.	**Requiring a process** Requiring a process which refers to the CFP Board of Standards' six-step process.	**Using the financial planning process** Following a process which refers to the six-step process.
4	**Holding to a higher standard than government regulation** Regulations set minimum standards which are built on by dealer group compliance systems and FPA standards.		

	How aspect		
Category	Australia	Hong Kong	United States
1	**Acting in the client's best interest** Providing advice and recommendations on strategies and products that are in the client's best interests; and doing so with integrity.	**Balance client benefit with self/organisation benefit** Act with empathy and caring towards the client and find out what the client needs; acting in a professional way by managing the inherent conflict in client benefit and advisor/organisation benefit.	**Acting in the client's best interest** Showing empathy and caring; being motivated by providing advice and not motivated by selling a financial product which may or may not be appropriate.
2	**Expert** Acting as a financial expert in much the same way as a medical doctor would act as an expert.	**Education and credentials** Acquiring education and professional credentials.	**Education and certification** Completing prescribed and non-prescribed education courses, having CFP® certification.
3	**Managing** Managing the financial affairs of clients in an organised and planned way by following a process.	**Following the financial planning process** By following the six-step financial planning process (which is espoused by the CFP Board and FPSB).	**Following a planning process** By following the six-step financial planning process (which is espoused by the CFP Board and FPSB.
4	**Complying with government regulations and FPA standards** Comply with regulation (ASIC), standards set by FPA Australia and those set by dealers (AFSL holders).		

a process. American CFP® professionals experience professionalism as: *serving the client, listening, having standards, having technical competence* and *a planning process.*

CFP® professionals in Australia conceive acting professionally by: *acting in the client's best interest, acting as a financial expert, managing* and *compliance.* CFP® professionals in Hong Kong act professionally by: *balancing the client benefit with the self/organisation benefit,* by *acquiring education and credentials* and by *following the financial planning process.* American CFP® professionals act professionally by *acting in the client's best interest,* by *acquiring and maintaining education and certification* and by *following a planning process.*

The next section will discuss the "what" and "how" aspects for each country to identify similarities and differences in these conceptions. The relational parts of these "what" and "how" aspects will also be discussed. This discussion will provide an explanation of the similarities and differences and how these can be explained by cultural differences and differences in the regulatory environments.

9.3   "What" Aspect Categories

This section will discuss the "what" aspect categories and the relationship (correlation) between them from each of the three countries.

9.3.1   RELATIONSHIP OF "WHAT" ASPECTS FOR EACH COUNTRY (CATEGORY 1)

There is a high degree of correlation between the "what" conceptions of the three countries. The categories have been grouped to reflect their association with the corresponding "how" conceptions. These are detailed in Figure 9.1.

These conceptions are related closely. The *client first mantra* (Australia), *feeling finding* (Hong Kong) and *serving the client* (United States) all share as their primary characteristic putting the client's interest first.

The conceptions have been labelled differently to reflect the way interview participants' language is used in describing their conception. American CFP® professionals described this conception more in terms of being motivated by serving the client well, showing the client respect and acting in the client's best interest. Australian CFP® professionals' description of this conception was more directly about putting the client's interests first or acting in the client's best interest. This could reflect the more stringent regulatory environment for financial planners. The *feeling finding* (Hong Kong) conception also relates to putting the client's interest first but is expressed as caring for the client; showing empathy, finding out what the client wants and putting the client's interest first. The label given to the conception reflects the cultural influence on language as used in Hong Kong. That is to say, the way people in Hong Kong interpret and use the English language. They may express themselves using different words – such as "feeling finding" – to convey the meaning that a native English speaker may articulate as caring for the client and showing empathy to the client.

Listening as experienced by American CFP® professionals is aligned closely to the *feeling finding* conception of Hong Kong CFP® professionals. These conceptions are about listening rather than talking to the clients. This brings into play notions of empathy,

Experience
Professionalism of financial planners

How ────── *What*

Australia		Hong Kong		USA	
Client First Mantra	**Integrity**	**'Feeling Finding'**	**'Professional Salesman'**	**Listening**	**Serving the client**	**Having standards**
Putting the client's interests first or acting in the client's best interest.	Integrity is used here as a catch-all term to cover acting ethically, honestly, fairly and consistently	This denotes finding out what the client wants, showing empathy and caring to the client; and putting the clients interest first	This acknowledges that financial planning in Hong Kong ultimately involves selling a product but this can still be done ethically by managing conflicts of interest.	Being a listener, not a talker to clients. Showing empathy.	Being motivated by serving the client well, showing the client respect and acting in their best interest	Not selling financial products that are not appropriate for a client; having standards.

Figure 9.1   Related "what" aspect category 1 for each country

finding out what the client wants and implementing recommendations and strategies which serve the client well.

The conceptions of *integrity* (Australia), *professional salesman* (Hong Kong) and *having standards* (United States) are closely related. They share as their primary characteristic the sense of having standards, integrity, not simply selling any product to a client, and if a product has to be sold then this is done in a professional manner. This latter aspect reflects the challenge of CFP® professionals in Hong Kong who more so than in Australia and the United States have to constantly manage and reconcile the inherent conflict of interest they face with client interests and organisational/self-interests.

9.3.2   RELATIONSHIP OF "WHAT" ASPECTS FOR EACH COUNTRY (CATEGORY 2)

The second category of conceptions have been grouped together to reflect the high degree of correlation between these "what" conceptions of the three countries. The categories have been grouped to reflect their association with the corresponding "how" conceptions. These are detailed in Figure 9.2.

These conceptions each share as their common characteristic the notion of being an expert, having knowledge and competence. The labels given to these conceptions are representative of the way the CFP® groups in each country articulated their experience. The descriptions given in Figure 9.2 highlight the differences in how these conceptions are experienced. Australian CFP® professionals see professionalism in the sense of being a *financial doctor* and equate their role to the role played by a medical doctor. In Hong Kong the conceptions of *being knowledgeable* and *being credentialed* reflect generally held views by the community that these attributes equate to being professional.

American CFP® professionals have an experience of professionalism which reflects a more pragmatic awareness of *having knowledge and technical competence* gained through initial and ongoing education programmes. The emphasis on initial and ongoing education clearly represents the requirements for CFP® certification by the CFP Board of Standards.

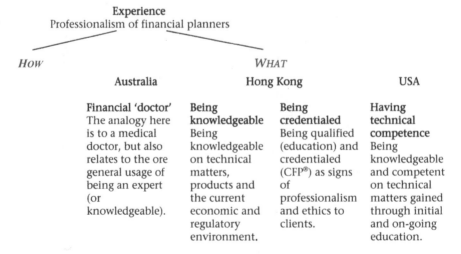

Figure 9.2   Related "what" aspect category 2 for each country

Figure 9.3 Related "what" aspect category 3 for each country

9.3.3 RELATIONSHIP OF "WHAT" ASPECTS FOR EACH COUNTRY (CATEGORY 3)

There is a high degree of correlation between the "what" conceptions of the three countries. The categories have been grouped to reflect their association with the corresponding "how" conceptions. These are detailed in Figure 9.3.

This third category groups related conceptions from each of three countries because of their similarity. The Hong Kong and American CFP® professionals' experience of professionalism as a (planning) process is clearly identical. This describes the six-step financial planning process which is more or less a mantra of the CFP Board of Standards in the United States, and taken up by the other countries that were licensed by the CFP Board to issue the CFP® marks in their countries and today by the Financial Planning Standards Board. Australian CFP® professionals experience professionalism as being a project manager in the sense that they project-manage clients through the process.

The managing is done in the context of a process, although this is not experienced as explicitly as the six-step financial planning process. Financial planning in Australia is much more highly regulated than in Hong Kong and the United States (see Chapter 4) and it could be that Australian CFP® professionals are more guided by regulation than the FPA (United States) and its CFP® standards, than those of the other two countries who are guided principally by CFP® standards as espoused by the CFP Board and IFPHK respectively.

9.3.4 "WHAT" ASPECT: (CATEGORY 4, AUSTRALIA ONLY)

The fourth "what" category of the three countries exclusively relates to what professionalism means to Australian CFP® professionals. The label for this conception, *holding to a higher standard than government regulation*, describes the role played by regulation supported by

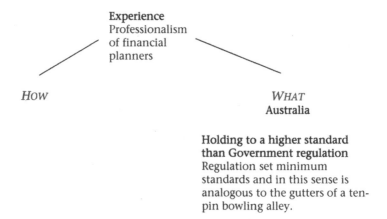

Experience
Professionalism
of financial
planners

HOW

WHAT
Australia

Holding to a higher standard
than Government regulation
Regulation set minimum
standards and in this sense is
analogous to the gutters of a ten-
pin bowling alley.

Figure 9.4   "What" aspect category 4 – holding to a higher standard than government regulation

the analogy of the gutters of the 10-pin bowling alley setting the boundary of acceptable behaviour and keeping financial planners in check. The conception wasn't experienced in Hong Kong and the United States and this clearly illustrates the different regulatory regimes of the three countries. This conception is detailed in Figure 9.4.

9.4   "How" Aspect Categories

This section will discuss the "how" aspect categories and the relationship (correlation) between them from each of the three countries. The "how" aspects have been grouped together as they relate to the corresponding "what" aspects for each country.

9.4.1   RELATIONSHIP OF "HOW" ASPECTS FOR EACH COUNTRY (CATEGORY 1)

The section discusses how CFP® professionals from each of the three countries think about acting professionally for the corresponding "what" aspect categories as shown in Figure 9.2. The "how" aspects of the experience are detailed in Figure 9.5.

The *client first mantra* and *integrity* as "what" aspects of Australian CFP® professionals and *serving the client, listening* and *having standards* as "what" aspects of American CFP® professionals are experienced as *acting in the client's best interest*. This means that this is how CFP® professionals think about acting in a professional manner. The corresponding "how" conception for Hong Kong CFP® professionals is experienced as balancing the client benefit with their own benefit and that of the organisation.

9.4.2   RELATIONSHIP OF "HOW" ASPECTS FOR EACH COUNTRY (CATEGORY 2)

The groupings making up "what" category 2 of the three countries as shown in Figure 9.2 have been related to the corresponding "how" aspects as in Figure 9.6.

The labels given to Hong Kong (*education and credentials*) and to the United States (*acquiring and maintaining education and certification*) have a high level of correlation.

Experience
Professionalism of financial planners

HOW					WHAT				
Australia	Hong Kong	USA	Australia	Australia	Hong Kong	Hong Kong	USA	USA	USA
Acting in the client's best interest.	Balance client benefit with self/organisation benefit	Acting in the client's best interest	Client First Mantra	Integrity	'Feeling Finding'	'Professional Salesman'	Serving the client	Listening	Having standards
Providing advice and recommendations on strategies and products that are in the client's best interests	Act with empathy and caring towards the client and find out what they client needs; Acting in a professional way by managing the inherent conflict in client benefit and advisor / organisation benefit	Providing advice and recommendations on strategies and products that are in the client's best interests.	Putting the client's interests first or acting in the client's best interest.	Integrity is used here as a catch-all term to cover acting ethically, honestly, fairly and consistently	This denotes finding out what the client wants, showing empathy and caring to the client; and putting the clients interest first	This acknowledges that financial planning in Hong Kong ultimately involves selling a product but this can still be done professionally by managing conflicts of interest.	Being motivated by serving the client well, showing the client respect and acting in their best interest	Being a listener, not a talker to clients. Showing empathy.	Not selling financial products that are not appropriate for a client; having standards.

Figure 9.5 "How" aspect category 1 for each country with related "what" aspect categories

Experience
Professionalism of
financial planners

How

Australia	Hong Kong	USA
Expert	**Education and credentials**	**Acquiring and maintaining education and certification**
Acting as a financial expert in much the same way as a medical doctor would act as an expert	Acquiring education and professional credentials.	Completing prescribed and non-prescribed education courses, having CFP® certification.

What

Australia	Hong Kong	USA
Financial 'Doctor'	**Being credentialed**	**Being knowledgeable**	**Having technical competence**
The analogy here is to a medical doctor, but also relates to the more general usage of being an expert (or knowledgeable) and being thorough.	Being qualified (education) and credentialed (CFP®) as signs of professionalism and ethics to clients.	This acknowledges that financial planning in Hong Kong ultimately involves selling a product but this can still be done professionally by managing conflicts of interest.	Being knowledgeable and competent on technical matters gained through initial and on-going education.

Figure 9.6 "How" aspect category 2 for each country with related "what" aspect categories

The way CFP® professionals in these countries think about acting professionally in this conception is essentially the same. The difference in the descriptors – *credentials* and *certification* reflect the different experience of the phenomenon as explained by cultural differences. In Hong Kong professionalism in the general community is associated with having credentials. Hong Kong has a culture where credentials as represented by the number of letters on a business or name card are highly regarded. These letters do not necessarily have to spell out "CFP®" to be highly regarded, as in Hong Kong society the number of "letters" after one's name are as important as what the actual letters stand for. American CFP® professionals act professionally in this regard by getting certified and maintaining that certification. Certification in this aspect clearly refers to the CFP® certification process which is highly valued and distinguishable from many other certifications that exist in the American professional body landscape.

Australian CFP® professionals in this related "what" aspect envision acting professionally in a different way to Hong Kong and American CFP® professionals. Australian CFP® professionals envision acting as an *expert*; in much the same way as a medical doctor would act as an expert. Hence, Australian CFP® professionals as *financial "doctors"* think about acting as an *expert* in their field. This reflects the mature nature of financial planning in Australia as detailed in Chapter 4 where CFP® professionals see themselves very much as professionals to be respected by the community in the same way as medical doctors are.

9.4.3 RELATIONSHIP OF "HOW" ASPECTS FOR EACH COUNTRY (CATEGORY 3)

This third "how" category relates to the corresponding "what" categories as detailed in Figure 9.7.

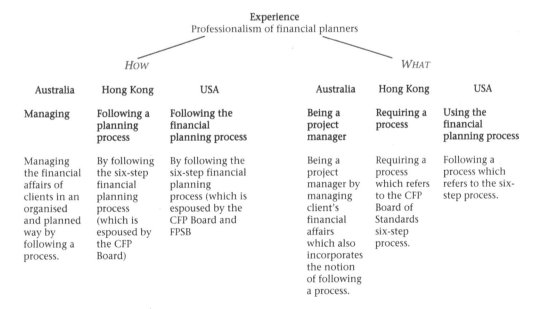

Figure 9.7 "How" aspect category 3 for each country with related "what" aspect categories

CFP® professionals in Hong Kong and the United States experience professionalism as a *planning process* and they think about acting professionally by *following a planning process*. The way of acting professionally refers to the CFP Board of Standards, FPSB and IFPHK's six-step financial planning process which is covered in the introductory education courses required for CFP® certification.

Australian CFP® professionals experience professionalism as *being a project manager*. They think about acting professionally in this aspect by *managing* the financial affairs of their clients. This act of managing also embraces the notion of following a process, but for Australian CFP® professionals this is not necessarily defined as meaning the six-step financial planning process. It certainly embraces this six-step process but this is not the way Australian CFP® professionals envision acting professionally. They are guided more so by regulation under the corporations law and the regulator's (ASIC) administration of this law.

9.4.4 "HOW" ASPECT FOR AUSTRALIA ONLY (CATEGORY 4)

This final "how" category of *complying with government regulations and FPA standards* relates to "what" category 4 and is detailed in Figure 9.8.

Australian CFP® professionals' experience of professionalism is influenced by government regulation. Regulation is an important part of the Australian financial planning operating environment. As discussed in Chapter 4, regulation is principally through corporations law and administered by the Australian Securities and Investments Commission. This experience of compliance relates to both to external regulation and internal company compliance systems. Dealer groups play a role in filtering the compliance requirements for financial planners in Australia. Compliance is an important conception of professionalism which relates to the corporations law requirements of financial planners such as providing an FSG (Financial Services Guide) to clients.

CFP® professionals conceive regulation as setting minimum standards or a professional framework for financial planners. In this sense it is analogous to the role played by regulators and professional bodies as the go-guards of a 10-pin bowling alley. Regulators

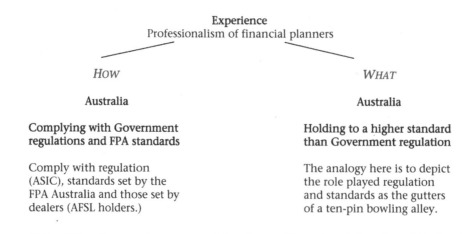

Figure 9.8 **"How" aspect category 4 for Australia only with related "what" aspect for Australia**

and professional bodies provide the rules and standards of the game – by setting the boundaries which should not be broken. These boundaries in 10-pin bowling are the go-guards that keep the ball in check, from going out of bounds.

CFP® professionals however understand that they are held out to a higher standard than minimum standards set by regulation. Regulation provides a framework on which CFP® professionals build their professionalism. The FPA provides higher standards through its professional and practice standards than those prescribed by government regulations.

9.5 Analysing the Differences in the Conceptions

It is important for the reader to understand that this present study carried out three independent phenomenographic studies. The studies examined conceptions of *professionalism* of CFP® professionals in Australia, Hong Kong and the United States. This current research study seeks to understand how CFP® professionals from these three countries experience the phenomenon of *professionalism*. CFP® professionals from Australia and Hong Kong are certified to standards prescribed by FPSB, and CFP® professionals from the United States are certified to standards prescribed by the CFP Board of Standards. The requirements for CFP® certification are common for both FPSB and the CFP Board. FPSB has had more of a challenge because it has licensed organisations from 24 countries or territories to certify individuals against the CFP® certification standards. As a consequence FPSB has had to contend with the challenge of ensuring consistency among its 24 affiliate organisations.

The prescription for CFP® certification in Australia, Hong Kong and the United States is applied consistently against the fundamental requirements of the four Es – *education, examination, experience* and *ethics*. These requirements have been detailed in Chapter 4. The bodies in each country responsible for the applying the CFP® certification process in Australia (FPA Australia) and Hong Kong (IFPHK) are professional bodies as well as certifying bodies. In the United States, the CFP Board is a certifying body, but the majority of CFP® professionals are members of a professional body such as the FPA.

It would be valid for the researcher to treat the three separate studies as one study as all the research participants were certified against standards set by the professional bodies authorised to certify individuals against these standards. Therefore the group in this sense is homogeneous. However the results of the study have the potential to inform the professional bodies, CFP® professionals and the financial planning profession and industry by highlighting the differences in how CFP® professionals experience professionalism.

This study did not seek to explore directly the influence of the research participants' membership to a professional body towards their conceptions of professionalism compared with the influence of CFP® certification. However the reader should acknowledge that for most of the research participants as CFP® professionals, their professionalism exists in the context of professional association. Similarly CFP® professionals also operate or practise in the context of a professional organisation. This study did not seek to directly explore the influence of a research participant's organisation in determining their understanding or awareness of professionalism. Organisations can enhance or detract from a CFP® professional's sense of being professional. An organisation supportive of CFP® certification in ways such as sponsoring employers through the CFP® certification

Table 9.2 Conceptions of professionalism compared to theories of professionalism – Australia, Hong Kong and the United States

Attributes of profession and professionalism (derived from the literature)	What professionalism means			How professionalism is acted upon		
	Australia	Hong Kong	United States	Australia	Hong Kong	United States
• Vocational qualifications.						
• A specialised (and common) body of knowledge.	Financial "doctor"	Being knowledgeable	Having technical competence	Expert	Education and credentials	Education and certification
• Having clientele.	Client first mantra	"Feeling finding"	Serving the client	Acting in the client's best interest	Balance client benefit with self/organisation benefit	Acting in the client's best interest
• A relationship with clients based on trust (fiduciary).			Listening Having standards			
• Professional responsibilities (acting in the public interest).						
• Membership of a professional association.		Being credentialed	Having technical competence		Education and credentials	Education and certification
• Adherence to a code of ethical behaviour.	Integrity	Being credentialed	Having standards	Acting in the client's best interest		Acting in the client's best interest

education programmes and examinations is likely to enhance the experience of being professional compared to an organisation which isn't supportive of CFP® certification.

For this current study, where research participants are all certified against the CFP® certification standards and process, they clearly experience *professionalism* in very similar ways. That is, the qualitatively limited number of ways CFP® professionals experience professionalism are very similar. Conceptions of what professionalism means and how CFP® professionals think about acting professionally are very similar across Australia, Hong Kong and the United States. For example CFP® professionals from the three countries experience professionalism as putting the client's interest first. For Australia and the United States this is essentially the same conception. Given the structure of the financial planning advice model in Hong Kong, putting the client's interests first is balanced with the organisation's interest and the CFP® professional's own interest.

Analysis against the list of attributes of *profession* and *professionalism* derived from the literature was carried out for each of the three countries and discussed in Chapters 6, 7 and 8. This matched similarities in the conceptions of professionalism held by CFP® professionals and also highlighted gaps in conceptions and conceptions which were not represented in the literature. Table 9.2 consolidates this analysis carried out for each country.

Conceptions of CFP® professionals from Australia, Hong Kong and the United States are generally aligned to each other against the attributes of professionalism from the literature. Having *vocational qualifications* and *membership to a professional association* were not evident in the conceptions of Australian CFP® professionals. The attribute identified from the literature of *a relationship with clients based on trust (fiduciary)* is not evident in the conceptions of Hong Kong CFP® professionals. This is supported by the "how" conception of *balance client benefits with self/organisation benefit* experienced by this group, which may act as a tension or block to building a relationship with a client based on trust.

Professionalism experienced as *professional responsibilities (acting in the public interest)* identified as an attribute of profession and professionalism from the literature is not evident in the conceptions of all three countries. This might suggest the notion of acting in the client's interest should be developed and promoted further to embrace a broader responsibility of acting in the public interest by financial planning professional bodies.

Whereas American CFP® professionals' experience of *professionalism* is distinguished by the relative maturity of the profession in that there are more notions of *professionalism* that can be classed as altruistic in nature.

The next chapter provides a summary of the research, conclusions reached, and discusses potential contributions to the financial planning profession. Limitations of the study and opportunities for future research are also examined.

10 *Conclusions, Contributions and Policy Implications*

10.1   What this Chapter is About

The aim of this chapter is to provide a summary of this research study, conclusions reached from the research findings, and contributions to the financial planning body of knowledge. Potential implications that the research findings have on policy in the area of financial planning professionalism are also proposed.

The chapter will begin by providing a summary of the intent of this research project. This study is unique in that it combines a relatively new qualitative research methodology – *phenomenography* – with a relatively new profession – *financial planning*. The outcomes of the research are summarised before the presentation of a reflection on the potential contributions this research project has made to CFP® professionals, professional bodies entrusted with the responsibility of developing the profession of financial planning, and regulators, including any policy implications around professionalism. Several recommendations are also proposed for financial planners, professional bodies and regulators. The contribution of this study to the field of phenomenography will also be discussed. Finally, limitations of the study will be considered followed by a discussion of suggestions for future research.

10.2   Summary of Research

The objective of this research project was to gain an understanding of how financial planners who hold the CFP® professional designation experience *professionalism*. This primary research question was asked in the context of financial planning being a relatively new profession which is making the transition from an industry based activity motivated by selling financial products to a professional activity where the emphasis is on the quality of advice and prioritising the interests of the client.

The interest of the researcher was to attempt to understand what was in the minds of CFP® professionals; to try and understand how they experience the phenomenon of *professionalism*; and to give voice to CFP® professionals. A qualitative inquiry using phenomenography was considered the most appropriate methodology to answer the primary research question.

The approach that was followed was to delimit the study to financial planners who hold the CFP® designation issued by the CFP Board of Standards in the United States and by the Financial Planning Standards Board (FPSB) outside of the United States. The researcher decided to carry out three independent phenomenographic studies by choosing to understand how CFP® professionals from Australia, Hong Kong and the United States experience the phenomenon of *professionalism*. This would enable a discussion around the similarities and differences in conceptions from a transnational perspective, adding depth to the study.

Australia was chosen because this is the country of residence of the researcher and is regarded as having a well regulated and mature financial services industry. Hong Kong was chosen as one of many relatively new countries which have set up financial planning professional bodies and embraced CFP® professional standards. The United States was an obvious choice because it is the birthplace of the concept of financial planning and CFP® certification. Financial planning in each of the three countries was presented by way of case studies to investigate how the activities of financial planners are regulated, how financial planning is delivered and what constitutes the standards and requirements for CFP® certification in each country.

Research participants were selected from each country and were interviewed with digital interview transcripts forming the only evidence of the phenomenon for analysis. The analysis sought to understand the experience of *professionalism* applying the "what"/"how" framework. The "what"/"how" framework has been used in several studies (Pramling 1983; Trigwell and Prosser 1997; Fyrenius et al. 2007) as opposed to the "referential"/"structural" framework, or a combination of both frameworks. The analysis in this present study sought to answer the questions of what professionalism means to CFP® professionals and how they conceive of professionalism.

The validity and reliability of qualitative research is an important consideration to the researcher as the techniques of testing the validity and reliability of qualitative research are much different to quantitative research. Cope's (2004) validity strategies were applied so that a full and open account of the study's method was provided to demonstrate the use of these strategies. The reliability of the research outcomes was tested by applying the reliability method of *member checking*. This involved presenting a summary of the findings of the research to a selection of the research participants from each country. The purpose of this was to see whether the categories of description as "what" and "how" aspects and their descriptions supported by sample participants' utterances made sense to them. This was a useful feedback process as it confirmed that in the main the researcher had captured how CFP® professionals from Australia, Hong Kong and the United States experience the phenomenon of *professionalism*. The member checking feedback resulted in some changes to the labels given to the categories of description.

10.3   Key Findings

The motivation behind this research study was to capture how CFP® professionals think about, experience or become aware of professionalism. Of particular interest was capturing what professionalism means to CFP® professionals and how they think about acting professionally. This was done by applying the "what"/"how" framework to the analysis of digital audio transcripts of the interviews of CFP® professionals. The transnational perspective of this research, by sourcing CFP® professionals from Australia, Hong Kong and the United States, added to the richness of the findings. The questions posed by this study are as follows:

1. What are the variations in the ways CFP® professionals experience *professionalism* from each of Australia, Hong Kong and the United States independently?
2. What are the differences in the variations in the ways CFP® professionals experience *professionalism* from Australia, Hong Kong and the United States?
3. How can the aspects of *professionalism* from the revealed conceptions be used to inform financial planners, professional bodies and regulators of what is required to be a CFP® professional?

The conclusions reached from answering the first two research questions have been answered through the phenomenographic analysis which has formed the major research component of this research project. The third research question is answered by the researcher and discussed later in this chapter. Readers of the phenomenographic outcomes will also make their own discoveries and draw their own conclusions about what the research outcomes mean to them.

The outcome of the phenomenographic analysis for each country produced the "what" aspects as categories of description as shown in Table 10.1. This shows the labels given to the conceptions of what professionalism means to CFP® professionals in each of the three countries. The labels given to what Australian CFP® professionals think of professionalism as meaning are *client first mantra, integrity, financial "doctor", being a project manager, holding to a higher standard than government regulation.* Hong Kong CFP® professionals experience professionalism as meaning *"feeling finding", professional salesman, being credentialed, being knowledgeable* and *requiring a process.* American CFP® professionals experience professionalism as meaning *serving the client, listening, having standards, having technical competence* and *using the financial planning process.*

The outcome of the phenomenographic analysis for each country produced the "how" aspects as categories of description as shown in Table 10.2. This demonstrates the labels given to the conceptions of how CFP® professionals think about the act of professionalism. The labels ascribed to how Australian CFP® professionals think about

Table 10.1   "What" aspects for each country

What aspect		
Australia	**Hong Kong**	**United States**
Client first mantra Integrity	"Feeling finding" Professional salesman	Serving the client Listening Having standards
Financial "doctor"	Being credentialed Being knowledgeable	Having technical competence
Being a project manager	Requiring a process	Using the financial planning process
Holding to a higher standard than government regulation		

Table 10.2 "How" aspects for each country

How aspect		
Australia	**Hong Kong**	**United States**
Acting in the client's best interest	Balance client benefit with self/organisation benefit	Acting in the client's best interest
Expert	Education and credentials	Education and certification
Managing	Following a planning process	Following the financial planning process
Complying with government regulations and FPA standards		

acting professionally are *acting in the client's best interest, expert, managing, and complying with government regulations and FPA standards.* Hong Kong CFP® professionals think about acting professionally as *balancing client benefit with self/organisation benefit, education and credentials*, and *following a planning process.* American CFP® professionals think about acting professionally by *acting in the client's best interest, education and certification*, and *following the financial planning process.*

The relationships between the "what" and "how" aspects were examined in the outcome space for each country. This analysis related "what" aspects, that is, what *professionalism* meant to a CFP® professional, with a corresponding "how" aspect; that is, how CFP® professionals conceive of acting professionally. Simply stated, the outcome space highlighted how *professionalism* was experienced in terms of what it means and how it is conceived as performed or acted. This was followed by an analysis and discussion on the similarities and differences in conceptions of CFP® professionals from each of the three countries.

An analysis was carried out to identify the similarities and differences in the categories of description and outcome space between the three countries. This is highlighted in Table 10.3 which shows the "what" and "how" aspects representing the conceptions of *professionalism* of CFP® professionals from each of the three countries. These have been grouped to represent those categories which have been deemed by the researcher to demonstrate a strong correlation. The groupings have been colour-coded to highlight the relationship. Conceptions of *professionalism* are highly correlated between the three countries. Differences can be explained mainly through an examination of the cultural influences particularly around the use of language. For example, the first "what" aspect categories for each country were given labels of *client first mantra* (Australia), *"feeling finding"* (Hong Kong) and *serving the client* (United States). The descriptions given to these labels were *putting the client's interests first or acting in the client's best interest* (Australia), *this denotes finding out what the client wants, showing empathy and caring to the client, and putting the client's interest first* (Hong Kong), and *being motivated by serving the client well, showing respect and acting in their best interest* (United States). The similarities in these ways of experiencing are obvious and the differences are subtle. Differences can be explained by cultural diversity as reflected by language as the research participants' utterances were the only evidence collected during the research. A conception which didn't appear to have any obvious correlation between the three cohorts of CFP® professionals was

Table 10.3 **Correlation of conceptions of professionalism from CFP®
professionalism in Australia, Hong Kong and the United States**

What aspect		
Australia	**Hong Kong**	**United States**
Client first mantra	"Feeling finding"	Serving the client
Integrity	Professional salesman	Listening
		Having standards
Financial "doctor"	Being credentialed	Having technical competence
	Being knowledgeable	
Being a project manager	Requiring a process	Using the financial planning process
Holding to a higher standard than government regulation		
How aspect		
Australia	**Hong Kong**	**United States**
Acting in the client's best interest	Balance client benefit with self/organisation benefit	Acting in the client's best interest
Expert	Education and credentials	Education and certification
Managing	Following a planning process	Following the financial planning process
Complying with government regulations and FPA standards		

that as experienced by Australian CFP® professionals as *holding to a higher standard than government regulation* ("what" aspect) and *complying with government regulations and FPA standards* ("how" aspect). This can be explained by the relatively stronger influence of government regulation on the activities of financial planners in Australia compared to Hong Kong and the United States. In Australia, CFP® professionals experience the phenomenon of professionalism as government regulation but in the context that it provides a benchmark for a higher standard.

10.4   Contributions

This section examines the potential contributions this research project makes to how financial planners and professional associations understand what it means to CFP® professionals to be professional.

10.4.1   FINANCIAL PLANNERS

This research project was delimited to CFP® professionals, but financial planners who hold other credentials or are simply licensed by the relevant regulator, can also apply the findings. The findings represent how CFP® professionals as a collective experience the phenomenon of *professionalism*. The collective experience is broken into what *professionalism* means and how CFP® professionals think about acting professionally.

These findings are of particular interest to new entrants to the profession and those aspiring towards CFP® certification.

Research into the professional enlightenment of financial planning in Australia (Sanders 2010) found that financial planning in Australia is unable to be confirmed as having achieved enlightenment as a profession. There is no evidence in the literature of similar research or findings in either Hong Kong or the United States. All of the CFP® professionals interviewed for this present study accepted the premise that they do, in fact, experience *professionalism*. This at least is consistent with Sanders' (2010) finding that CFP® professionals (in Australia) are confident in their own professional competence and trustworthiness.

The findings of this present study are relevant to the broader financial planning cohort. The findings allow individual financial planners to benchmark their own experience of professionalism, both in what professionalism means and how it is acted upon. This acts as a way of reinforcing some of the mantras of professionalism, such as the "client first mantra" as experienced by CFP® professionals in Australia, "feeling finding" as experienced by CFP® professionals in Hong Kong and "serving the client" as experienced by CFP® professionals in the United States. The "what" aspect of professionalism clearly provides identifying characteristics of what professionalism means, or ought to mean to the broader cohort of financial planners and aspiring CFP® professionals. There is a high degree of correlation between the three countries in relation to what professionalism means or how it is experienced by CFP® professionals.

Financial planners in Australia do not come from a tradition of being considered as belonging to a profession or being classified as professionals. CFP® professionals in Australia have been encouraged through their membership of the FPA – both by the FPA and by their employer ("dealer" or AFSL holder) to take the CFP® examinations. This presents as a different scenario to other professions, such as the accounting profession. Accounting professionals have been recruited traditionally from the universities and commence on a path of at least an undergraduate bachelor degree, followed by practical experience in the accounting field (often in audit) and then pursuing professional education and examinations offered by the professional bodies. In Australia, this situation is now changing with many universities offering financial planning programmes enabling young people to consciously choose financial planning as a career. This mirrors the experience in the United States. FPA (Australia) has developed a framework to recognise university qualifications as entry to their CFP® certification programmes in very much the same way as the accounting profession. There are fewer options in Hong Kong for individuals to pursue university qualifications in financial planning.

Financial planners, particularly CFP® professionals in the United States, represent a more eclectic group. The United States has a much longer history than Australia and Hong Kong in training professionals for a career in financial planning. The situation is also different in that the relevant membership body, the FPA (USA) does not certify individuals against CFP® standards (as is the case in Australia and Hong Kong). The FPA (USA) recognises a cohort of "allied professionals" such as accountants (as CPA's) as members. Many CFP® professionals who may not be members of FPA (USA) hold other professional designations other than the CFP® designation. This appears to be more prevalent in the United States than in Australia and Hong Kong. One would anticipate that, as the Australian and Hong Kong financial planning profession develops, we will see the same trend in these countries as well.

10.4.2   PROFESSIONAL BODIES

The findings of this research study will be of potential interest to the professional bodies that have responsibility for guiding the profession through CFP® certification requirements and standards, setting ethical codes of conduct and practice standards.

Professional bodies (or associations) exist in a different environment today characterised by a lack of exclusivity to a particular field of knowledge due to many reasons including the increased knowledge of the general population spawned by the Internet. However Karseth and Nerland (2007) argue that, paradoxically, current trends towards disintegration and de-hierarchisation lead to increased demand for academisation, authoritative knowledge and for renewal of a collective knowledge base. This research presented here has confirmed that being knowledgeable, having technical knowledge, having standards and being credentialed would appear to support these demands. New groups arise that serve to regulate professional work in conjunction with international standards.

According to Rusaw (1995) professional associations shape the process of learning by providing formal and informal matrices for developing knowledge, attitudes, values and effective techniques for practice, new frames of thinking, feeling, reflecting and experiencing. They also act as an authority, facilitator and arbitrator of knowledge for change. This notion of developing knowledge is consistent with how CFP® professionals experience *professionalism*. Professional associations can help new members of the profession connect with more experienced professionals in a mentoring relationship. Mentors can find it rewarding and rejuvenating to work with mentees who bring a fresh perspective to professional issues (Zabel 2008). The conceptions of CFP® professionals in this study did not consider mentoring as a "how" aspect in how professionalism might be enacted. Deeper questioning during the interview stage may have uncovered more layers of experience which could have brought mentoring to the surface of how professionalism is experienced.

As posited by Greenwood et al. (2002) professional associations are important because they provide arenas through which organisations interact and provide a collective representation; and they also allow organisations within the same community to interact. It is through these interactions that members develop understandings of reasonable conduct and where the behavioural duties of membership emerge. Professional associations enable the construction of activities and services over which members claim jurisdictional exclusivity determining who can practice authoritatively within that jurisdiction (Greenwood et al. 2002). Membership of a professional association was evident in the utterances of the CFP® professionals with respect to the importance of acquiring knowledge and certification. The acquisition of knowledge and certification comes from a professional association such as the Institute of Financial Planners of Hong Kong, the FPA (Australia), FPA (USA), or from a certification body such as the CFP Board of Standards in the United States.

Sanders (2010) in his study on the "Professional enlightenment of financial planning in Australia" presented a number of recommendations as they relate to professional organisations. This included that the FPA (Financial Planning Association of Australia) dedicate itself to maintaining its leadership position, responding to the ethical and professional challenges within its community; build a public education campaign, and consumer support service, identifying how it is distinct from the professionally lower, regulated concept of financial advice; clarify and ensure resource capacity for its professional structures, so it can dedicatedly demonstrate the role it plays in assuring professionalism and trustworthiness of FPA members. "It should do this by responding to community and member concerns about failures of professional expectation; investigating, prosecuting and sanctioning those members whose actions threaten to undermine the professional community's, and the wider public community's, confidence" (Sanders 2010, p. 202).

This may be seen as a self-serving statement about FPA Australia's reason for existence, which ignores the real reason for professional bodies which is the provision of an association of like-minded individuals. Professional bodies may have become too focussed on their own existence rather than the importance of their members through professional association. Although not the focus of this current study, it would appear that CFP® professionals can consider themselves as "professional" without being a member of a professional association such as the FPA. Having said that, certification through a certification body such the CFP Board of Standards may act as a surrogate. Similarly, it would seem that it is possible for a financial planner without CFP® certification to experience *professionalism* in the same way as CFP® professionals. This was not the focus of this study, but is touched on in the Sanders (2010) and Smith (2009) studies.

Professional bodies should take an interest in understanding how their members experience being professional, rather than simply prescribing professional standards and expectations in the absence of this understanding. A phenomenographic study such as this present study would be useful in informing professional bodies about the standards and expectations they have of their members. Studies of this type might help identify any gaps in how members experience being professional, against how their professional body expects them to act and behave.

A major Australian study by Smith (2009) investigated professionalism and ethics in financial planning and focused many of the recommendations on statutory and regulatory solutions. However Smith (2009) did identify a role for professional bodies in recommending that competency and eligibility criteria for financial planners should include the achievement of an undergraduate degree or other recognised qualification or training in a related field of endeavour. Smith (2009) also recommended that financial planners should hold a professional designation and membership of a recognised professional association with a Code of Ethics and Conduct. Smith (2009) recommended that this Code of Ethics and Conduct be accredited under the Act (corporations law). Knowing how to be a professional and knowing how to act professionally are arguably intrinsic values, yet this present study would seem to suggest that these intrinsic values are reinforced through professional association. In this sense, professional bodies are important vehicles in providing forums for professional association to take place.

Continuing professional development (CPD) requirements of financial planning professional bodies are often criticised as being too prescriptive, and being too easy to acquire the minimum number of hours or points to maintain membership status for CFP® certification. However, it would seem clear that, despite this criticism, CPD does perform a very important role. That role may not purely be restricted to what is measured and recorded, but what is not so measureable, and this relates to the benefits of the association of like-minded individuals, the sense of purpose and belonging and the networking among peers.

Professional bodies or professional associations operate as either membership bodies (e.g. FPA, IFPHK) or as certification bodies (such as the CFP Board of Standards and FPSB).

Some of these bodies perform both roles such as the FPA (Australia) and IFPHK. These bodies exist in an era of post-professionalism and as such face different challenges than professional bodies in earlier times. Professions no longer have exclusivity over a body of knowledge in an era characterised by ease of access to seemingly endless information available on the Internet. It is possible for people these days to self-diagnose – whether that be in relation to physical health, mental health or financial health. In many of the professions, post-professionalism also signals an increase in government regulation, such as in financial services with a motive of consumer protection. Professional bodies are therefore faced with questions about their own relevance and, although many of these bodies are not-for-profit organisations, they have to actively develop alternative income streams other than simply through membership dues.

10.4.3 REGULATORS

The focus of this study has been how CFP® professionals conceive of professionalism. The context for selecting research participants, carrying out phenomenographic interviews on participants and analysing those interviews has been CFP® certification standards as defined by the CFP Board of Standards in the United States and FPSB outside the United States. These were discussed in detail in Chapter 4. Regulation of the activities of financial planning and by implication the activities of CFP® professionals was also discussed in Chapter 4, but regulation per se was not the benchmark for capturing how CFP® professionals think about professionalism.

However, regulators will find this study of potential interest. Regulators generally set licensing requirements and regulate by providing prescription of many of the activities of financial planners. Regulators may be heartened that CFP® professionals in the three countries that are the focus of this study all think about professionalism as meaning putting the client's interest first and think about acting professionally by acting in the client's best interest.

Only Australian CFP® professionals think of professionalism in the context of regulation as evidenced by "what" category 5 – holding to a higher standard than government regulation – and "how" category 4 – complying with government regulation and FPA standards. Specifically, Australian CFP® professionals think about acting professionally not only by complying with regulation but also complying with FPA standards which they think of as holding themselves to a higher standard.

Regulators may take from this study confirmation that professional bodies such as the CFP Board and FPA in the United States, IFPHK in Hong Kong and FPA in Australia have the capacity to build on standards set by regulation and make a significant contribution to improving the professionalism of financial planners.

10.4.4 PHENOMENOGRAPHIC RESEARCH

This study has applied the qualitative research methodology of phenomenography to an investigation of the *professionalism* of financial planners. The study is unique in the sense that it combines a relatively new research methodology with a relatively new profession. It is the first time there has been any investigation that attempted to understand how CFP® professionals experience *professionalism*.

Most phenomenographic studies have been conducted on the content of learning and students' conceptions of the various content domains (Pang 2003). However, phenomenographic research has also been applied to the study of phenomena outside of the educational context such as conceptions of political power, conceptions of death and a study of Nobel laureate views of scientific intuition (Pang 2003). Phenomenography has also been applied to recent research studies to areas which have a relationship to education such as looking at the understanding of competence (Ramritu and Barnard 2001; Huntly 2003), understandings of ethics (Stoodley 2009) and applying phenomenography to nursing research (Sjöström and Dahlgren 2002). Phenomenography has also been applied as research method in management research (Osteraker 2002).

This present study has applied the "what"/"how" framework to understanding what *professionalism* means to CFP® professionals and how CFP® professionals think about acting professionally. The approach taken in this study not only provides a methodology and framework for similar phenomenographic investigations of conceptions of professionalism in other affiliate members of FPSB, it also provides a methodology and framework for investigating conceptions of professionalism among the professions generally.

10.5   Recommendations

This study was designed to discover the qualitatively limited number of ways CFP® professionals conceive of *professionalism*. For the purposes of this study the results of the analysis have been presented as an outcome space of conceptions. The results have added depth by the transnational scope of the study across three countries which enabled a discussion on the similarities and differences in conceptions across regulatory and cultural borders.

As a phenomenographic study, the outcome space constitutes the results, and readers of the study will attach meaning and practical application to the outcome space. In the following discussion, the researcher offers the recommendations for financial planners, professional bodies and regulators.

As a fundamental characteristic of professionalism, it is recommended that individuals who hold themselves out as "financial planners" or who aspire to do so irrespective of whether they hold the CFP® professional designation or not, should place the client's interest above their own interest and the interest of the organisation by which they are engaged or employed. In addition it is recommended that individuals who hold themselves out as "financial planners" or who aspire to do so should attain professional credentials over and above that required by government regulation or licensing. Credentials are highly regarded by the community and respected by other professionals, and in the case of the CFP® credential, demand a rigorous commitment to professionalism.

It is further recommended that individuals who hold themselves up as "financial planners" or who aspire to do so irrespective of whether they hold the CFP® professional designation or not, should always follow the financial planning process to ensure rigour in acting in the client's best interest and to avoid the convenience of expediency.

It is recommended that professional bodies such as the FPA (Australia), IFPHK, and FPA (USA) acknowledge that their fundamental reason for existence is to provide professional "association" for their members. This need for professional "association" should take precedence over the need for the professional body to exist in its own right (that is, to have an existence separate from its members). Professional bodies must therefore remain relevant and this will be achieved by providing a forum for professional "association" of its members to continually define and develop the profession of financial planning and the professionalism of individual members.

It is further recommended that FPSB and IFPHK acknowledge that CFP® professionals in Hong Kong are constantly reconciling their own self-interest and the interest of their employer against the client's interest and that this experience is more pronounced than in Australia or the United States. FPSB should work closely with the IFPHK to identify if the CFP® certification requirements are capturing those individuals who can truly call themselves professionals.[1]

Further, it is recommended that FPSB, as the global financial planning standards setting body outside of the United States, and as part of its efforts to establish global credibility of the CFP® credential and a common CFP® certification framework, should do more research into the similarities and differences in the level of professionalism of its members across 24 countries. Identification of differences will inform future prescription and enforcement of CFP® certification standards.

It is recommended that the CFP Board and FPA (USA) work closely with FPSB and its 24 member organisations to ensure consistency of CFP® certification standards and to ensure global engagement and association of CFP® professionals.

It is recommended that regulators acknowledge that regulation provides at best a minimum or compulsory standard, but professional bodies (including membership and certification bodies), through their role of providing a forum for professional "association", will deliver a more rigorous and altruistic application of "professionalism". Regulators should therefore, where appropriate and reasonable, incorporate or reference the CFP® professional mark in financial planning regulation. Further, regulators should work closely with professional bodies who certify individuals against CFP® certification standards to identify those individuals who fail to act to these higher standards of conduct expected of a CFP® professional and apply appropriate sanctions.

10.6 Limitations of this Study

The participants in this study were selected on the basis of holding the CERTIFIED FINANCIAL PLANNER (CFP®) mark in their respective country. In Australia, participants were selected by the researcher primarily referencing the Financial Planning Association of Australia's (FPA) *find a planner* section of their website. Some participants were personally known by the researcher due to his previous employment with the FPA. Participants from Hong Kong were selected by the IFPHK with due regard to their command of the English language. American participants were sourced from delegates to the FPA (USA) Annual Conference in San Diego in September 2011. Some of these participants were pre-arranged while others were selected at random from the conference delegates. Therefore the selection of participants largely represented a convenience sample. As a convenience sample, a full and open account of the application of the research methodology was

---

1   This recommendation also applies to both Australia and the United States, but based on this research study there is more immediacy in Hong Kong.

provided to address any concerns around the validity of the research. Every attempt was made by the researcher to ensure a good gender balance as well as a mix of different experience levels and different work contexts ranging from fee-only planners to salaried planners in big financial institutions to commission-based planners. Although the study was delimited to CFP® professionals, the findings also have relevance to the broader financial planning profession.

Another area of limitation of this study as a phenomenographic study was the opening up of layers of understanding through follow-up questions seeking clarification of experience. Many of the interviews were held with a limitation of time, such as in the United States during the FPA Annual Conference and in Hong Kong, where there was a variation in the participant's proficiency of the English language. In Australia where most of the interviews were held in the participant's workplace, there were generally time constraints through work commitments. This was addressed by applying the "what"/"how" framework instead of the alternative framework which distinguishes between structural and referential aspects of the experience and which are further broken down into the internal and external horizons. This latter framework requires more in-depth interviews to uncover the various layers of understanding. The "what"/"how" framework does not require the same level of in-depth interview to uncover the deeper layers of understanding as required in the "referential"/"structural" framework. Given the nature of the study being transnational in scope, with the primary research questions focused on the variations in the ways CFP® professionals experience *professionalism* in each of Australia, Hong Kong and the United States independently, the "what"/"how" framework was considered by the researcher an appropriate phenomenographic approach for the study.

10.7 Future Research

More research is required into understanding further how CFP® professionals experience professionalism. The methodology applied in this research project could be applied to other affiliate member organisations of FPSB. This would identify those aspects of professionalism which are experienced similarly across regions and countries and where there are regulatory or cultural influences which may act as a barrier for achieving an objective standard of professionalism. The CFP Board and FPSB have a vested interest in ensuring that all CFP® professionals irrespective of their region or country adhere to a common standard of professionalism notwithstanding cultural influences. FPSB's standards are designed to be consistent across territories with the proviso that these standards may be adapted to fit local regulations, laws and products. However, overlaying regulations, laws and products is culture, and culture determines how those regulations and laws are administered and how products are presented and explained to clients. Culture therefore can act as an impediment to FPSB achieving its desire to have consistent CFP® certification standards across borders.

This present research study has shown a high level of correlation between how professionalism is experienced, and any differences are explained predominately by differences in culture, especially as it relates to use of the English language (as is the case with Hong Kong CFP® professionals). Further research into how CFP® professionals experience professionalism across all of FPSB affiliate organisations can determine the degree of correlation of how professionalism is experienced by CFP® professionals and highlight regulatory, cultural and differences in CFP® certification standards applied.

Future research could take on a longitudinal aspect by undertaking phenomenographic studies on conceptions of professionalism over time. This would be of particular interest to track the development of the financial planning profession to see whether aspects of professionalism as experienced by CFP® professionals change over time. In addition, future research would be useful in understanding whether the differences in conceptions of professionalism between regions and countries become less or more pronounced.

Regulators also have an interest in aspects of the professionalism of financial planners. The activities of financial planners are increasingly being regulated globally against the backdrop of the global financial crisis (2007–9) and several high-profile corporate collapses. The interest of regulators in this area is driven by a need to protect consumers of financial services. Regulators should work closely with professional bodies in ensuring that standards are increased and the quality of advice delivered to consumers improves. Regulation is important, but regulation should exist in a context of encouraging and supporting self-regulation through appropriate and relevant professional bodies.

The methodology of this present study could be replicated with clients of CFP® professionals being the subjects. This could be referred to as a "third-order perspective" on professionalism. The study could be designed to understand professionalism conceived by clients with distinction between what is expected and what is not expected in professionalism provided by CFP® professionals. The results of this study could be compared with the results of this present study to identify and discuss the expectation gap (if any).

References

Åkerlind, G. (2005a). "Academic growth and development: How do university academics experience it?" *Higher Education* 50(1): pp. 1–32.

Åkerlind, G. (2005b). "Learning about phenomenography: Interviewing, data analysis and the qualitative research paradigm", in J. Bowden and P. Green (eds), *Doing Developmental Phenomenography*, Melbourne: RMIT University Press, pp. 63–78.

Aldrige, A. (1998). "Habitus and cultural capital in the field of personal finance", *The Sociological Review* 48(1): pp. 58–79.

Ashworth, P. and Lucas, U. (1998). "What is the 'world' of phenomenography?" *Scandinavian Journal of Educational Research* 42(4): p. 415.

ASIC. (2008). "Regulatory guide 146, licensing: Training of financial product advisors". Available at: from www.asic.gov.au/asic/pdflib.nsf/LookupByFileName/rg146v1.pdf/$file/rg146v1.pdf [accessed 8 October 2009].

ASIC. (2010). "Our role". Available at: from http://asic.gov.au [accessed 18 June 2010].

ASIC. (2011). "Consultation paper 153: Licensing: Assessment and professional development framework for financial advisers". Available at: www.asic.gov.au/asic/pdflib.nsf/LookupByFile Name/cp153.pdf/$file/cp153.pdf [accessed 10 May 2012].

Atieno, O.P. (2009). "An analysis of the strengths and limitations of qualitative and quantitative research paradigms". *Problems of Education in the 21st Century* 13: pp. 13–18.

Australian Government. (2011). "Future of financial advice". Available at: http://futureofadvice.treasury.gov.au/content/Content.aspx?doc=reforms.htm [accessed 8 June 2011].

Barnard, A., McCosker, H. and Gerber, R. (1999). "Phenomenography: A qualitative research approach for exploring understanding in health care". *Qualitative Health Research* 9(2): pp. 212–26.

Barth, M.E. (2008). "Global financial reporting: Implications for U.S. academics". *Accounting Review* 83(5): pp. 1159–79.

Bell, D. (1973). *The Coming of the Post-Industrial Society: A Venture in Social Forecasting*, New York: Basic Books.

Berglund, A. (2002). *On the Understanding of Computer Network Protocols*, Vol. 2002-002, Uppsala: Uppsala University, Department of Computer Systems, Information Technology.

Birkett, W.P. (1996). "Competency standards for financial planning in Australia and New Zealand". Financial Planning Association of Australia Ltd.

Blankinship, J.J.T. (1996) "Milestones and challenges for the financial planning profession", *Journal of Financial Planning* December 1996: pp. 97–8.

Booth, S.A. (1992). *Learning to Program: A Phenomenographic Perspective*, Göteborg: Acta Universtatis Gothoburgensis.

Botzem, S. and Quack, S. (2009). "(No) limits to Anglo-American accounting? Reconstructing the history of the International Accounting Standards Committee: A review article", *Accounting, Organizations and Society* 34(8): pp. 988–98.

Bowden, J. (2005). "Reflections on the phenomenographic team research process", in J. Bowden and P. Green (eds), *Doing Developmental Phenomenography*, Melbourne: RMIT University Press, pp. 11–33.

Boyd, D.T., Boyd, Sanithia C. and Berry, Priscilla (2009). "A primer for accounting certification: Complete analysis of the process with listing of sources", *American Journal of Business Education* 2(7): pp. 83–96.

Brandon Jr., E.D. and Welch, H.O. (2009). *The History of Financial Planning: The Transformation of Financial Services*, Hoboken, NJ: John Wiley & Sons Inc.

Brante, T. (1988). "Sociological approaches to the professions", *Acta Sociologica* 31(2): pp. 119–42.

Brown Jr, J.F. and Balke, T.E. (1983). "Accounting curriculum comparison by degree program of schools intending to seek AACSB accreditation", *Issues in Accounting Education* 1: p. 50.

Brown, R. (1905). "Scottish chartered accountants", in R. Brown (ed.), *A History of Accounting and Accountants*, Edinburgh: T.C. and E.C. Jack.

Bruce, C. (1997). *The Seven Faces of Information Literacy*, Adelaide: Auslib Press.

Bruce, C., Buckingham, L., Hynd, J., McMahon, C., Roggenkamp, M., Stoodley, I. and Knight, L. (2004). "Ways of experiencing the act of learning to program: A phenomenographic study of introductory programming students at university", *Journal of Information Technology Education* 3: pp. 143–60.

Bruce, K. (2007a). *Towards a Global Financial Planning Body of Knowledge*, Financial Planning Standards Board.

Bruce, K. (2007b). "When 40 per cent isn't enough", *Asset*. Sydney: Fairfax Business Media.

Bruce, K. (2008). "Building the financial planning body of knowledge", *Financial Planning Magazine*, Financial Planning Association of Australia Limited.

Bruce, K. and Gupta, R. (2011). "The financial planning education and training agenda in Australia", *Financial Services Review* 20: pp. 61–74.

Burnaby, P., Hass, S. and Abdolmohammadi, M.J. (2006). "A survey of internal auditors to establish the scope of the common body of knowledge study in 2006", *Managerial Auditing Journal* 21(8): pp. 854–68.

Burns, E. (2007). "Positioning a post-professional approach to studying professions", *New Zealand Sociology* 22(1): pp. 69–98.

Camfferman, K. and Zeff, S.A. (2007). *Financial Reporting and Global Capital Markets: A History of the International Accounting Standards Committee 1973–2000*", Oxford: Oxford University Press.

Carey, J.L. (1969). *The Rise of the Accountancy Profession: From Technician to Professional 1896–1936*, New York: American Institute of Certified Public Accountants.

Carlson, J.A. (2010). "Avoiding traps in member checking", *The Qualitative Report* 15(5): pp. 1102–13.

Carlsson, M.A., Fülüp, M. and Marton, F. (2001). "Peeling the onion: Student teachers' of literary understanding", *Scandinavian Journal of Educational Research* 45(1): pp. 5–18.

Carr, W. (1995). *For Education: Towards Critical Educational Inquiry*, Philadelphia, PA: Open University Press.

Carr, W. and Kemmis, S. (1986). *Becoming Critical: Education, Knowledge and Action Research*, London and Philadelphia, PA: The Falmer Press.

Carr-Saunders, A.M. and Wilson, P.A. (1933). *The Professions*, Oxford: The Clarendon Press.

CFP Board of Standards. (2010). "Topic list for CFP® Certification Examination". Available at: http://www.cfp.net/downloads/Financial%20Planning%20Topics%202006.pdf [accessed 11 January 2011].

CFP Board of Standards. (2011). "CFP board mission and history". Available at: http://www.cfp.net/ [accessed 9 June 2011].

CFP Board of Standards. (2012a). "Continuing education standards". Available at: http://www.cfp.net/certificants/ce.asp#1 [accessed 30 March 2012].

CFP Board of Standards. (2012b). "Your career as a Certifed Financial Planner Practitioner". Available at: http://www.cfp.net/upload/publications/165.pdf [accessed 30 March 2012].

CFP Board of Standards. (2012c). "Financial planning process". Available at: http://www.cfp.net/learn/knowledgebase.asp?id=2 [accessed 30 March 2012].

Chang, P.-L. and Hsieh, P.-N. (1997). "A qualitative review of doctoral dissertations on management in Taiwan", *Higher Education* 33(2): pp. 115–36.

Cheetham, G. and Chivers, G. (2005). *Professions, Competence and Informal Learning*, Northampton, MA: Edward Elgar Publishing, Inc.

Chieffe, N. and Rakes, G.K. (1999). "An integrated model for financial planning", *Financial Services Review* 8: pp. 261–8.

Clarke, M. (2000). "The professionalisation of financial advice in Britain", *Sociological Review* 48(1): pp. 58–79.

Clayton, B., Lynch, B. and Kerry, M. (2007). "Financial planners in Australia: An examination of loyalty", *The International Journal of Knowledge, Culture and Change Management* 7(3): pp. 13–24.

Collier-Reed, B.I., Ingerman, A. and Berglund, A, (2009). "Reflections on trustworthiness in phenomenographic research: Recognising purpose, context and change in the process of research", *Education as Change* 13(2): pp. 339–55.

Cooper, D.J. and Robson, K. (2006). "Accounting, professions and regulation: Locating the sites of professionalization", *Accounting, Organizations and Society* 31(4–5): pp. 415–44.

Cope, C. (2004). "Ensuring validity and reliability in phenomenographic research using the analytical framework of a structure of awareness", *Qualitative Research Journal* 4(2): pp. 5–18.

Cowen, J.E., Blair, W.T. and Taylor, S. (2006). "Personal financial planning education in Australian universities", *Financial Services Review* 15(1): pp. 43–57.

CPA Australia. (2009). "CPA Australia 2009 annual report". Available at: http://www.cpaaustralia.com.au/cps/rde/xbcr/cpa-site/annual_report_2009.pdf [accessed 28 June 2010].

Creswell, J.W. and Miller, D.L. (2000). "Determining validity in qualitative inquiry", *Theory into Practice* 39(3): pp. 123–30.

Creswell, J.W. and Miller, G.A. (1997). "Research methodologies and the doctoral process", *New Directions for Higher Education* 99: pp. 33–46.

Dator, J. (2005). "Universities without 'quality' and quality without 'universities'", *On the Horizon* 13(4): pp. 199–215.

Downie, R.S. (1990). "Professions and professionalism", *Journal of Philosophy of Education* 24(2): pp. 147–59.

Edwards, S. (2005). *Panning for Gold: Influencing the Experience of Web-based Information Searching*. PhD thesis, School of Information Systems, Faculty of Information Technology, Queensland University of Technology.

Entwistle, N. (1997). "Introduction: Phenomenography in higher education", *Higher Education Research & Development* 16(2): 127–34.

European Financial Planning Association. (2010). "What is the €uropean Financial Planning Association (€FPA)?" Available at: http://www.efpa-europe.org/ [accessed 2 September 2010].

Evetts, J. (2003). "The sociological analysis of professionalism", *El análisis sociológico del profesionalismo: cambio ocupacional en el mundo moderno* 18(2): pp. 395–415.

Eyssell, T.H. (1999). "Learning by doing: Offering a university practicum in personal financial planning", *Financial Services Review* 8: pp. 293–303.

Fajardo, C.L. (2007). "The move towards convergence of accounting standards world wide", *Journal of American Academy of Business* 12(1): pp. 57–61.

Fetisov, G. (2009). "Measures to overcome the global crisis and establish a stable financial and economic system", *Problems of Economic Transition* 52(5): pp. 20–33.

Financial Planning Association (USA). (2011). "Who we are". Available at: http://www.fpanet.org/AboutFPA/WhoWeAre/ [accessed 9 June 2011].

Financial Planning Institute. (2010). "Certification". Available at: http://www.fpi.co.za/Certification/tabid/2580/Default.aspx [accessed 21 July 2010].

Financial Services Regulator of Hong Kong. (2011a). "What we do". Available at: http://fsrhk-gov.org/about/what/index.html [accessed 9 June 2011].

Financial Services Regulator of Hong Kong. (2011b). "Licensing". Available at: http://fsrhk-gov.org/licensing/index.html [accessed 9 June 2011].

Firestone, W.A. (1987). "Meaning in method: The rhetoric of quantitative and qualitative research", *Education Researcher* 16(7): pp. 16–21.

FPA Australia (2001). "Celebrating 10 Years", *Financial Planning*, p. 38.

FPA Australia. (2007). "A framework for financial planning professionalism". Available at: http://www.fpa.asn.au/media/FPA/Website%20files/Prof_/Prof_ProfessionalismFramework.pdf [accessed 11 January 2011].

FPA Australia. (2010a). "CFP® Certification Assessment". Available at: http://www.fpa.asn.au/FPA_Content.aspx?Doc_id=5003 [accessed 18 June 2010].

FPA Australia. (2010b). "Becoming a CFP® professional". Available at: http://www.fpa.asn.au/FPA_Content.aspx?Doc_id=5002 [accessed 21 July 2010].

FPA Australia. (2011). "The pillars of our profession". Available at: www.fpa.asn.au [accessed 23 March June 2012].

FPA Australia. (2012). "Consultation paper: Higher education standardising the curriculum and accreditation framework for financial planning in Australia".

FPA Malaysia. (2010). "Education providers". Available at: http://www.fpam.org.my/fpam/certification-and-standards/education/education-providers/ [accessed 28 June 2010].

FPA Singapore. (2010). "Education providers". Available at: http://www.fpas.org.sg/Prog.asp#Edu [accessed 28 June 2010].

FPSB. (2008–9). "FPSB's financial planning practice standards". Available at: http://www.fpsb.org/site_docs/090800-FPSB-082_PracticeStandards.pdf [accessed 11 January 2011].

FPSB. (2010a). "FPSB's standards and certification". Available at: http://www.fpsb.org/certificationandstandards.html [accessed 11 January 2011].

FPSB. (2010b). "FPSB facts & figures – CFP professional growth [1995–2009]". Available at: http://www.fpsb.org/resources/factsandfigures.html [accessed 17 June 2010].

FPSB. (2010c). "FPSB's financial planner competency profile". Available at: http://www.fpsb.org/certificationandstandards/competencyprofile.html [accessed 18 June 2010].

FPSB. (2010d). "Education requirement for CFP certification". Available at: http://www.fpsb.org/certificationandstandards/education.html [accessed 18 June 2010].

FPSB. (2010e). "FPSB members". Available at: http://www.fpsb.org/members.html [accessed 24 June 2010].

FPSB. (2010f). "Body of knowledge and career path". Available at: http://www.fpsb.org/ [accessed 28 June 2010].

FPSB. (2010g). "Brazil, India, Indonesia and China lead global growth of CFP professionals". Available at: http://www.fpsb.org/news/pressreleases/410-biic-growth-2010q1.html [accessed 16 July 2010].

FPSB. (2010h). "FPSB's financial planning curriculum framework". Available at: http://www.fpsb.org/certificationandstandards/curriculum-framework.html [accessed 26 October 2010].

FPSB. (2010i). "FPSB standards under development & 2010 activities". Available at: http://www.fpsb. org/certificationandstandards/standards-under-development.html [accessed 7 January 2011].

FPSB. (2013). "FPSB facts & figures – CFP professional growth". Available at: http://www.fpsb.org/ resources/factsandfigures.html [accessed 14 June 2013].

FPSB of India. (2010). "Authorized education providers". Available at: http://www.fpsbindia.org/ [accessed 28 June 2010].

Freidson, E. (1986). *Professional Powers: A Study of the Institutionalization of Formal Knowledge*, Chicago, IL: University of Chicago Press.

Freidson, E. (1999). "Theory of professionalism: Method and substance", *International Review of Sociology* 9(1): p. 117.

Freidson, E. (2001). *Professionalism, the Third Logic: On the Practice of Knowledge*, Chicago, IL: University of Chicago Press.

Frowe, I. (2005). "Professional trust", *British Journal of Educational Studies* 53(1): pp. 34–53.

Funnell, W. (1996). "Preserving history in accounting: Seeking common ground between 'new' and 'old' accounting history", *Accounting, Audit & Accountability Journal* 9(4): pp. 38–64.

Fyrenius, A., Silen, C. and Wirell, S. (2007). "Students' conceptions of underlying principles in medical physiology: An interview study of medical students' understanding in a PBL curriculum", *Advances in Physiology Education* 31: pp. 364–9.

Garrett, A.A. (1961). *History of The Society of Incorporated Accountants 1885–1957*, Oxford: Oxford University Press.

Garrick, J., Chan, A. and Lai, J. (2004). "University-industry partnerships: Implications for industrial training, opportunities for new knowledge", *Journal of European Industrial Training* 28(2/3/4): pp. 329–38.

Garrison, L. (2004) "Financial planning history made in Malaysia", *Journal of Financial Planning*: pp. 1–4.

Gaskell, J. and Ashton, J. (2008). "Developing a financial services planning profession in the UK", *Journal of Financial Regulation and Compliance* 16(2): pp. 159–72.

Gaytan, J. (2007). "Qualitative research: Emerging opportunity in business education", *Delta Pi Epsilon Journal* 49(2): pp. 109–27.

Goddard, R. (2002). "Development of the accounting profession and practices in the public sector: A hegemonic analysis", *Accounting, Audit and Accountability Journal* 15(5): pp. 655–88.

Godfrey, J., Hodgson, A., Holmes, Scott and Tarca, A. (2006). *Accounting Theory*, New York: John Wiley & Sons.

Goetz, J.W., Tombs, J.W. and Hampton, V.L. (2005). "Easing college students' transition into the financial planning profession", *Financial Services Review* 14: pp. 231–51.

Goss, R.P. (1991). "Path to profession", *Journal of Financial Planning*: 8.

Government Accountability Office. (2011). "Regulatory coverage exists for financial planners, but consumer protection issues remain". Available at: http://www.gao.gov/ [accessed 28 November 2011].

Gower, J. (1984). "Review of investor protection", HMSO, London, Cmnd 912.

Greasley, K. and Ashworth, P. (2007). "The phenomenology of 'approach to studying': The university student's studies within the lifeworld", *British Educational Research Journal* 33(6): pp. 819–43.

Greenwood, R., Suddaby, R. and Hinings, C.R. (2002). "Theorizing change: The role of professional associations in the transformation of institutionalized fields", *Academy of Management Journal* 45(1): pp. 58–80.

Guba, E.G. and Lincoln, Y.S. (1994). "Competing paradigms in qualitative research", in N.K. Denzin and Y.S. Lincoln (eds), *Handbook of Qualitative Research*, Thousand Oaks, CA: Sage, pp. 105–17.

Gurwitsch, A. (1964). *The Field of Consciousness*, Pittsburgh, PA: Duquesne University Press.

Hara, K. (1995). "Quantitative and qualitative research approaches in education", *Education* 115(3): p. 351.

Harris, L.R. (2008). "A phenomenographic investigation of teacher conceptions of student engagement in learning", *The Australian Educational Researcher* 35(1): pp. 57–79.

Harris, L.R. (2011a). "Phenomenographic perspectives on the structure of conceptions: The origins, purposes, strengths, and limitations of the what/how and referential/structural frameworks", *Educational Research Review* 6(2): pp. 109–24.

Harris, L.R. (2011b). "Secondary teachers' conceptions of student engagement: Engagement in learning or in schooling?" *Teaching and Teacher Education* 27: pp. 376–86.

Higley, W.M. and Baker, R.E. (1987). "A comparative analysis of professional education and licensure preparation", *Issues in Accounting Education* 2(2): p. 220.

Hong Kong Monetary Authority. (2011). "The HKMA". Retrieved 9 June 2011, from http://www.info.gov.hk/hkma/eng/hkma/index.htm.

Hong Kong Special Administrative Region Government. (2010). "Hong Kong: The facts – financial services". Available at: http://www.gov.hk/en/about/abouthk/factsheets/docs/financial_services.pdf [accessed 9 June 2011].

Hor, J. and Juchau, R. (2005/2006). "International accounting education: An Australian perspective", *International Journal of Learning* 12(5): pp. 355–70.

Horsley, M. and Thomas, D. (2003). "Professional regulation and professional autonomy: Benchmarks from across the professions: The New South Wales experience", *Change: Transformations in Education* 6(1): pp. 34–47.

Howitt, H. (1966). *The History of The Institute of Chartered Accountants in England and Wales 1880–1965 and of its Founder Accountancy Bodies 1870–1880*, London: Heinemann.

Huntly, H. (2003). *Beginning Teachers' Conceptions of Competence*. Unpublished PhD thesis, Central Queensland University, Rockhampton, Australia.

Institute of Financial Planning. (2010a). "CFP certification". Available at: http://www.financialplanning.org.uk/planners/cfp.cfm [accessed 21 July 2010].

Institute of Financial Planning. (2010b). "The IFP". Available at: http://www.financialplanning.org.uk/consumers/the_ifp.cfm [accessed 17 June 2010].

Institute of Internal Auditors. (2010a). Available at: http://www.theiia.org/theiia [accessed 18 June 2010].

Institute of Internal Auditors. (2010b). "About the Common Body of Knowledge (CBOK)". Available at: http://www.theiia.org//research/common-body-of-knowledge/about-cbok/?search=CBOK [accessed 18 June 2010].

International Organization for Standardization. (2005). ISO 22222:2005 Personal Financial Planning – Requirements for Personal Financial Planners.

International Organization for Standardization. (2010). Available at: http://www.iso.org/iso/home.htm [accessed 18 June 2010].

Ioannides, K.K. (2005). "Financial planning: Bright times ahead, 2005–2015", *Journal of Financial Service Professionals* 59(1): pp. 49–55.

Jackling, B. and Sullivan, C. (2007). "Financial planners in Australia: An evaluation of gaps in technical and behavioral skills", *Financial Services Review* 16: pp. 211–28.

Karseth, B. and Nerland, M. (2007). "Building professionalism in a knowledge society: Examining discourses of knowledge in four professional associations", *Journal of Education & Work* 20(4): pp. 335–55.

Kedslie, M.J.M. (1990). *Firm Foundations: The Development of Professional Accounting in Scotland 1850–1900*, Hull: University of Hull Press.

Kramer, B.K.P., Johnson, C.W., Crain, G.W. and Miller, S.J. (2005). "The practitioner-professor link", *Journal of Accountancy* 199(6): pp. 77–80.

Kritzer, H.M. (1999). "The professions are dead, long live the professions: Legal practice in a postprofessional world", *Law & Society Review* 33(3): p. 713.

Lander, G.H. and Reinstein, A. (1987). "Identifying a common body of knowledge for management accounting", *Issues in Accounting Education* 2(2): p. 264.

Lankshear, C. and Knobel, M. (2004). *A Handbook for Teacher Research*, Berkshire: Open University Press.

Larsson, J. and Holmström, I. (2007). "Phenomenographic or phenomenological analysis: Does it matter? Examples from a study on anaesthesiologists' work", *International Journal of Qualitative Studies on Health & Well-Being* 2(1): pp. 55–64.

Lee, T.A. (1995). "The professionalization of accountancy: A history of protecting the public interest in a self-interested way", *Accounting, Auditing & Accountability Journal* 8(4): pp. 48–69.

Lee, T.A. (1996). "Identifying the founding fathers of public accountancy: The formation of The Society of Accountants in Edinburgh", *Accounting, Business & Financial History* 6(3): pp. 315–35.

Lee, T.A. (1997). "The editorial gatekeepers of the accounting academy", *Accounting, Auditing & Accountability Journal* 10(1): pp. 11–30.

Leveson, L. (2004). "Encouraging better learning through better teaching: A study of approaches to teaching in accounting", *Accounting Education* 13(4): pp. 529–48.

Levy, R.B.-B. and Ben-Ari, M. (2009). "Adapting and merging methodologies in doctoral research", *Computer Science Education* 19(2): pp. 51–67.

Linder, C. and Marshall, D. (2003). "Reflection and phenomenography: Towards theoretical and educational development possibilities", *Learning and Instruction* 13(3): pp. 271–84.

Lock, A. (1999). "Accreditation in business education", *Quality Assurance in Education* 7(2): pp. 68–76.

Magub, A. (2006). *Experiences of the Phenomenon of Internet Use for Information Sharing on Construction Projects and Skills Set Identification for Effective Project Participation*. Doctor of Philosophy thesis, Queensland University of Technology.

Marshall, T.H. (1950). *Citizenship and Social Class and Other Essays*, Cambridge: Cambridge University Press.

Marton, F. (1981). "Phenomenography: Describing conceptions of the world around us", *Instructional Science* 10: pp. 177–200.

Marton, F. (1986). "Phenomenography: A research approach to investigating understandings of reality", *Journal of Thought* 21(3): pp. 28–49.

Marton, F. (1988). "Describing and improving learning", in R. Schmech (ed.), *Learning Strategies and Learning Style*, New York: Plenum.

Marton, F. (1994). "Phenomenography", in *The International Encyclopedia of Education* 2(8): pp. 4424–9.

Marton, F. and Booth, S. (1997). *Learning and Awareness*, New Jersey: Lawrence Erlbaum.

Marton, F. and Pong, W.Y. (2005). "On the unit of description in phenomenography", *Higher Education Research & Development* 24(4): pp. 335–48.

McMillan, K.P. (2004). "Trust and the virtues: A solution to the accounting scandals?" *Critical Perspectives on Accounting* 15(6/7): pp. 943–53.

Meyer, J.H.F., Shanahan, M.P. and Laugksch, R.C. (2005). "Students' conceptions of research. I: A qualitative and quantitative analysis", *Scandinavian Journal of Educational Research* 49(3): pp. 225–44.

Millerson, G. (1964). *The Qualifying Association*, London: Routledge & Kegan Paul.

Moehrle, S.R., Anderson, K.L., Ayres, F.L., Bolt-Lee, C.E., Debreceny, R.S., Dugan, M.T., Hogan, C.E., Maher, M.W. and Plummer, E. (2009). "The impact of academic accounting research on professional practice: An analysis by the AAA research impact task force", *Accounting Horizons* 23(4): pp. 411–56.

Morse, J. (2006). "Insight, inference, evidence, and verification: Creating a legitimate discipline", *International Journal for Qualitative Methods* 5(1): pp. 1–7.

Morse, J.M., Barrett, M., Mayan, M., Olson, K. and Spiers, J. (2002). "Verification strategies for establishing reliability and validity in qualitative research", *International Journal of Qualitative Methods* 1(2): pp. 1–19.

Most, B.W. (1999). "One profession, one designation", *Journal of Financial Planning*.

Munter, P. and Reckers, P.M.J. (2009). "IFRS and collegiate accounting curricula in the United States: 2008 a survey of the current state of education conducted by KPMG and the Education Committee of the American Accounting Association", *Issues in Accounting Education* 24(2): pp. 131–9.

Murphy, B. and Watts, T. (2009). "Financial planning in Australia: Industry or profession?" *14th Finsia-MCFS Banking & Finance Conference*, Melbourne, Melbourne Centre for Financial Studies, pp. 1–24.

Napier, C.J. (2006). "Accounts of change: 30 years of historical accounting research", *Accounting, Organizations and Society* 31(4–5): pp. 445–507.

Needles, J.B.E. and Powers, M. (1990). "A comparative study of models for accounting education", *Issues in Accounting Education* 5(2): pp. 250–67.

Needles Jnr, B.E. (2005). "Implementing international education standards: The global challenges", *Accounting Education: An International Journal* 14(1): pp. 123–9.

Nicholls, D. (2009). "Qualitative research: Part two – methodologies", *International Journal of Therapy & Rehabilitation* 16(11): 586–92.

Oakeshott, M. (ed.) (1989). "Teaching and learning", in T. Fuller (ed.), *The Voice of Liberal Learning*, New Haven, CT: Yale University Press.

Onwuegbuzie, A. and Leech, N.L. (2005). "On becoming a pragmatic researcher: The importance of combining quantitative and qualitative research methodologies", *International Journal of Social Research Methodology* 8(5): pp. 375–87.

Onwuegbuzie, A.J., Johnson, R.B. and Collins, K.M.T. (2009). "Call for mixed analysis: A philosophical framework for combining qualitative and quantitative approaches", *International Journal of Multiple Research Approaches* 3(2): pp. 114–39.

Osteraker, M. (2002). "Phenomenography as a research method in management research". Available at: http://ecsocman.edu.ru/data/972/650/1219/phenomenography.pdf [accessed 4 October 2010].

Overton, R.H. (2008). "Theories of the financial planning profession", *Journal of Personal Finance* 7(1): pp. 13–41.

Pahl, D. (1996). "An emerging partnership: AFS and the CFP board", *Financial Services Review* 5(1): pp. 7 1–81.

Palmer, K.N., Ziegenfuss, D.E. and Pinsker, R.E. (2004). "International knowledge, skills, and abilities of auditors/accountants: Evidence from recent competency studies", *Managerial Auditing Journal* 19(7): pp. 889–96.

Pang, M.F. (2003). "Two faces of variation: On continuity in the phenomenographic movement [1]", *Scandinavian Journal of Educational Research* 47(2): p. 145.

Parsons, T. (1951). *The Social System*, New York: Free Press.

Peck, M. (2004). "Expanding the body of knowledge", *Journal of Financial Planning* 17(3): p. 12.

Perkin, H. (1989). *The Rise of Professional Society: England since 1880*, London: Routledge.

Perl, E.J. and Noldon, D.F. (2000). "Overview of student affairs research methods: Qualitative and quantitative", *New Directions for Institutional Research* 2000(108): p. 37.

Pole, K. (2007). "Mixed method designs: A review of strategies for blending quantitative and qualitative methodologies", *Mid-Western Educational Researcher* 20(4): pp. 35–8.

Pramling, I. (1983). *The Child's Conception of Learning*, Goteborg: Acta Universitatis Gothoburgensis.

Professions Australia. (2010). "Definition of a profession". Available at: http://www.professions.com.au/defineprofession.html [accessed 7 June 2010].

Ramritu, P.L. and Barnard, A. (2001). "New nurse graduates' understanding of competence", *International Nursing Review* 48: pp. 47–57.

Reckers, P.M.J. (2006). "Perspectives on the proposal for a generally accepted accounting curriculum: A wake-up call for academics", *Issues in Accounting Education* 21(1): 31–43.

Renström, L., Andersson, B. and Marton, F. (1990). "Students' conceptions of matter", *Journal of Educational Psychology* 82: pp. 555–69.

Richardson, J.T.E. (1999). "The concepts and methods of phenomenographic research", *Review of Educational Research* 69(1): pp. 53–82.

Ritzer, G. (1975). "Professionalization, bureaucratization and rationalization: The views of Max Weber", *Social Forces* 53(4): pp. 627–34.

Roddenberry, E.W. (1953). "Achieving professionalism", *Journal of Criminal Law, Criminology & Police Science* 44(1): pp. 109–15.

Roy, R.H. and MacNeill, J.H. (1966). "Horizons for a profession: The common body of knowledge for CPAs", *Journal of Accountancy* 122(3): pp. 38–50.

Rueschemeyer, D. (1964). "Doctors and lawyers: A comment on the theory of the professions", *Canadian Review of Sociology & Anthropology* 1(1): pp. 17–30.

Rusaw, A.C. (1995). "Learning by association: Professional associations as learning agents", *Human Resource Development Quarterly* 6(2): pp. 215–26.

Salierno, D. (2007). "In search of greater knowledge", *Internal Auditor* 64(6): pp. 35–7.

Sandberg, J. (1991). "Competence as intentional achievement: A phenomenographic study", paper presented at the meeting of the International Human Science Research Association, Göteberg, Sweden.

Sandberg, J. (1994). *Human Competence at Work: An Interpretive Approach*. PhD thesis, University of Gothenburg, Sweden.

Sandberg, J. (1997). "Are phenomenographic results reliable?" *Higher Education Research and Development* 16(2): pp. 203–12.

Sanders, D. (2010). *Professional Enlightenment of Financial Planning in Australia*, DProfSt thesis, CQUniversity Australia.

Saville, H. (2007). "International education standards for professional accountants (IESs)", *Accounting Education* 16(1): pp. 107–13.

Schaefer, T.E. (1984). "Professionalism: Foundation for business ethics", *Journal of Business Ethics* 3(4): pp. 269–77.

Shafer, W.E. and Owsen, D. (2003). "Policy issues raised by for-profit spinoffs from professional associations: An evaluation of a recent AICPA initiative", *Journal of Business Ethics* 42(2): pp. 181–95.

Sin, S. (2010). "Considerations of quality in phenomenographic research", *International Journal of Qualitative Methods* 9(4): pp. 305–19.

Sjöström, B. and Dahlgren, L.O. (2002). "Applying phenomenography in nursing research", *Journal of Advanced Nursing* 40(3): pp. 339–45.

Smith, J. (2009). *Professionalism and Ethics in Financial Planning*, PhD thesis, Victoria University, Australia.

Sonnemann, U. (1954). *Existence and Therapy*, New York: Grune & Stratton.

Stone, D. (2004). "Transfer agents and global networks in the 'transnationalization' of policy", *Journal of European Public Policy* 11(3): pp. 545–66.

Stoodley, I. (2009). *IT Professionals' Experience of Ethics and its Implications for IT Education*, unpublished PhD thesis, Queensland University of Technology, Brisbane, Australia.

Subrahmanyam, G. (2009). "Global financial crisis of 2008–09: Triggers, trails, travails, and treatments", *IUP Journal of Applied Economics* 8(5/6): pp. 32–47.

Suhonen, J., Thompson, E., Davies, J. and Kinshuk (2008). "Applications of variation theory in computing education", in Raymond Lister and Simon (eds), *Conferences in Research and Practice in Information Technology*, Vol. 88.

Svensson, L. (1994). "Theoretical foundations of phenomenography", *Phenomenography: Philosophy and Practice Conference*, Queensland University of Technology, Brisbane, Australia.

Svensson, L. (1997). "Theoretical foundations of phenomenography", *Higher Education Research and Development* 16(2): pp. 159–71.

Svensson, L. and Theman, J. (1983) "The relation between categories of description and an interview protocol in a case of phenomenographic research", paper presented at the Second Annual Human Science Research Conference, Duquesne University, Pittsburgh, United States, 18–20 May 1983 [Report from the Institute of Education, Göteborg University, No. 1983:02].

Tan, K. (2009). "Variation theory and the different ways of experiencing educational policy", *Educational Research for Policy & Practice* 8(2): pp. 95–109.

Taylor, S., Juchau, R. and Houterman, B. (2010). *Financial Planning in Australia*, 4th edition, Chatswood: LexisNexis Butterworths.

Theman, J. (1979). "The interview as a research instrument", paper presented at the NFPF (Nordic Society for Educational Research) annual conference, 25–28 October 1979, Lillehammer, Norway [Report from the Institute of Education, Göteborg University, No. 86, 1979].

Thompson, D.R. (2002). "Financial planner DNA", *Journal of Financial Planning*: pp. 27–9.

Trigwell, K. (2000). "A phenomenographic interview on phenomenography", in J. Bowden and E. Walsh (eds), *Phenomenography*, Melbourne: RMIT University Press, pp. 47–61.

Trigwell, K. (2006). "Phenomenography: An approach to research into geography education", *Journal of Geography in Higher Education* 30(2): pp. 367–72.

Trigwell, K. and Prosser, M. (1997). "Towards an understanding of individual acts of teaching and learning", *Higher Education Research and Development* 16(2): pp. 241–52.

Trump, G.W. and Ball, J.T. (1968). "An evaluation of the common body of knowledge study and its probable impact upon the accounting profession", *Journal of Accountancy* 125(2): pp. 86–9.

Uljens, M. (1996). "On the philosophical foundation of phenomenography", in Gloria Dall'Alba and Biörn Hasselgren (eds), *Reflections on Phenomenography: Toward a Methodology?* Göteborg: Acta Universitatis Gothoburgensis, pp. 105–30.

VanZandt, C.E. (1990). "Professionalism: A matter of personal initiative", *Journal of Counseling & Development* 68(3): p. 243.

Wagner, P., Hendrich, J., Moseley, G. and Hudson, V. (2007). "Defining medical professionalism: A qualitative study", *Medical Education* 41(3): pp. 288–94.

Wagner, R.B. (2004). "To think … like a CFP", *Journal of Financial Planning* 17(2): pp. 64–70.

Wagner-Moore, L.E. (2004). "Gestalt therapy: Past, present, theory, and research", *Psychotherapy: Theory, Research, Practice, Training* 41(2): pp. 180–89.

Walker, L.J. (1990). "Future trends: Thirty something", *Journal of Financial Planning*: p. 55.

Warschauer, T. (2002). "The role of universities in the development of the personal financial planning profession", *Financial Services Review* 11(3): p. 201.

Webb, G. (1997). "Deconstructing deep and surface: Towards a critique of phenomenography", *Higher Education* 33(2): pp. 195–212.

Weber, M. (1968). *Economy and Society*, Totowa: Bedminster.

Wilkerson Jr, J.E. (2010). "Accounting educators as the accounting profession's trustees: Lessons from a study of peer professions", *Issues in Accounting Education* 25(1): pp. 1–13.

Ying, L.I.U. and Dong, L.-w. (2009). "Major historical events affecting the accounting profession: An overview", *Journal of Modern Accounting & Auditing* 5(9): pp. 40–46.

Zabel, D. (2008). "The mentoring role of professional associations", *Journal of Business & Finance Librarianship* 13(3): pp. 349–61.

Zald, M.N. (1968). "The common body of knowledge for CPAs: Some problems in analysis", *Journal of Accounting Research* 6(1): pp. 130–40.

Index